To Deprave
and Corrupt

ALSO BY CATHERINE SCOTT

*Thinking Kink: The Collision of BDSM,
Feminism and Popular Culture*
(McFarland, 2015)

To Deprave and Corrupt

Obscenity Battles in British Law and Culture

CATHERINE SCOTT

McFarland & Company, Inc., Publishers
Jefferson, North Carolina

Publisher's note: Catherine Scott died in May 2018, after completing and delivering the manuscript for this book.

LIBRARY OF CONGRESS CATALOGUING-IN-PUBLICATION DATA

Names: Scott, Catherine, 1983–2018 author.
Title: To deprave and corrupt : obscenity battles in British law and culture / Catherine Scott.
Description: Jefferson, North Carolina : McFarland & Company, Inc., Publishers, 2019. | Includes bibliographical references and index.
Identifiers: LCCN 2018037644 | ISBN 9781476672830 (softcover : acid free paper) ∞
Subjects: LCSH: Obscenity (Law)—England. | Censorship—England. | Pornography—Law and legislation—England. | Obscenity (Aesthetics)
Classification: LCC KD8075 .S33 2019 | DDC 344.4205/47—dc23
LC record available at https://lccn.loc.gov/2018037644

BRITISH LIBRARY CATALOGUING DATA ARE AVAILABLE

ISBN (print) 978-1-4766-7283-0
ISBN (ebook) 978-1-4766-3310-7

© 2019 The Estate of Catherine Scott. All rights reserved

No part of this book may be reproduced or transmitted in any form or by any means, electronic or mechanical, including photocopying or recording, or by any information storage and retrieval system, without permission in writing from the publisher.

Front cover: Photo illustration of Queen Victoria from an 1882 photograph by Alexander Bassano

Printed in the United States of America

McFarland & Company, Inc., Publishers
  Box 611, Jefferson, North Carolina 28640
  www.mcfarlandpub.com

For Guy

Acknowledgments

The author would like to thank the following for their help and support during the creation of this book: Jerry Barnett, Beatrice Behn, Anna Berry, Paul Bernal, Cathryn Bishop, Sean Maddison Brown, Blake, Neil Brown, Emily Brady, Claire Calman, Ellen Creighton, Jill Creighton, Hannah Crosby, Brian Dillingham, Megara Furie, Lidija Haas, Kazuki James, Carrie Kania, Zak Jane Keir, Grace Lau, Sita Mae, Emilia McKenzie, Layla Milholen and the team at McFarland, Kathy Navin, Sam Poulton, Andy Phippen, Joanna Morris Seymour, Suraya Sidhu Singh, Jonathan J Scott, Richard Scott, Rosslyn Scott, Laura Scott, Guy Silberrad, Sez Thomasin, Phil Turner, Philippa Willitts, Jessica Wakeman and Lowery Woodall.

Table of Contents

Introduction   1

1. The Current Situation   17
2. Then and Now   37
3. Won't Somebody Please Think of the Children?!   54
4. A Very Great Mischief   74
5. 20th-Century Smut   90
6. Women Don't Want That Sort of Thing   106
7. That Special Relationship   124
8. Shoving It Down Our Throats   142
9. Privilege and Platforms: Obscenity in the Modern World   153

Afterword   171

Chapter Notes   177

Bibliography   183

Index   185

Introduction

Obscenity is a relative concept.

Definitions of this controversial term have varied wildly across time periods, cultures, religions, genders, races, class systems and communities. It is not a term that has ever been defined democratically, even in self-declaredly progressive Western countries. The 21st-century British idea of obscenity is, at best, a confused one. At worst, it enables an outdated legal machine and a prurient media to savage anyone whose lifestyle falls outside narrow norms.

While the rest of the world was relaxing its obscenity laws in the mid-20th century, Britain's authorities reinforced a century-old piece of legislation to ensure no such liberalization could take place here. Despite hardcore pornography's becoming more acceptable in mainland Europe during the 1960s and '70s, the UK clung to its ban on depicting sex until the year 2000. By 2008, our leaders had trained their sights on digital erotica via a law against possessing "extreme pornographic images." Even more recently, British sexual expression was further hemmed in by the 2014 revision of the Audiovisual Media Services (AVMS) regulations, followed shortly by the invasive Digital Economy Act of 2017.

Whatever our opinions regarding representations of sexuality, the internet and freedom of speech, we cannot deny that the British government has passed an astonishing amount of anti-obscenity legislation in less than a decade. Relaxation of social standards in this country has been accompanied by increasingly repressive attempts to regulate what adults view online, on television and in print media. Some view this as a stealthy form of state control, especially now that digital surveillance of the individual is possible on a massive and sinister scale. Some call it censorship; of which, much more later.

I was born in Britain in 1983 and have been a published writer since

2009, when *Bitch* magazine first printed the work of this fledgling journalist. Between then and now, I've researched and written articles on a myriad of sex- and gender-related topics; some lighthearted, such as my piece about clones of Justin Bieber's genitalia, and others much more serious, such as an account of anti-gay laws in Kenya. I've always enjoyed threading together the issues thrown up by law, sociology and pop culture in my writing, and I endeavor to inject both humor and a feminist perspective into everything I write.

In 2015 I was thrilled to publish my first nonfiction book, *Thinking Kink: The Collision of BDSM, Feminism and Popular Culture*. The response I received from those who bought, read and studied *Thinking Kink* showed me how great an appetite there is for work that deals with sexuality in a fun, frank and clear manner. Several readers confided their kinks in me and told me they felt unable to tell anyone else because they feared ostracism and shaming. Others thanked me for bringing an often-lacking feminist perspective to the BDSM community, where sexism and misogynist abuse is still far too often unreported and unpunished. The feedback from *Thinking Kink* confirmed for me that Britain (plus its good friend across the Atlantic) is still tainted by a cultural belief that sexuality is dangerous, corrupting and in need of legal suppression. Following the publication of my first book, I've done my utmost to speak out against this in blog posts, articles and speaking engagements; it took me until January 2016 to realize that the (mis)uses of British obscenity law merited a book of their own.

At that time I was a freelance reporter for the *Daily Dot* and my beat was stories with a sex, gender or relationships angle. I had recently pitched an idea to my editor, Jessica Wakeman, who deserves a great deal of credit for encouraging me along the path to creating this book. I wanted to write an article on the theme "AVMS: One Year On," which would look at how the tightening of British obscenity regulations had affected creators of adult material. Having written about the initial protests against AVMS back in December 2014, I knew that several independent porn producers had fallen foul of the new rules during the intervening year. I also knew that the victims had much in common: for one thing, their work invariably depicted BDSM, female dominance and male submission. The three creators I interviewed were all articulate, independent women who had lost work, money and peace of mind thanks to the repressive actions of the shadowy Authority for Television on Demand (ATVOD). I wanted to tell these stories, which were getting little to no attention in the press, and which were only briefly discussed in the kink or porn communities.

Introduction

In my research, I learned that Britain's Obscene Publications Act (OPA) has been in force for over 160 years and states that a piece of media must "tend to deprave and corrupt" in order to qualify as obscene. However, when I tried to establish how British legislation had moved from an 1857 law to the 2014 tightening of the AVMS rules, I hit a brick wall. All I needed was one up-to-date book explaining how Britain's stance on obscenity had started with the original 1857 OPA and ended with today's lengthy list of banned acts, most of them sexual.

I could not find it.

I soon realized that there was no book on this convoluted legal journey, and believe me when I say I looked for such a book *everywhere*. I trawled libraries and secondhand bookstores, looked in the British Library archives and raked over the World Wide Web for a single tome that would clearly summarize Britain's various dances with obscenity. One thing I definitely established was that neither depravity nor corruption has ever been satisfactorily defined, but as a journalist on a deadline, I didn't have time to worry about that particular debate. Instead, I had to piece together my answer from a mishmash of blog posts, articles and interviews and a lot of time spent going square-eyed at my laptop screen. I found that the current British position on obscenity sits at the end of an unwieldy legal chain riddled with acronyms and that attempting to unpick these tangled threads is an excellent cure for insomnia. This was a source of great frustration to a writer whose gargantuan desire to write is only outstripped by her lifelong thirst for reading. All I wanted was a clear, engaging book on this issue, written in a manner that was accessible to the average person. And what does a good writer do when she finds the book she wants to read doesn't exist?

She writes it herself.

I filed my article in January 2016 and quickly started planning this book, not just to fill a gaping chasm in the market, but because I was now experiencing a strong sense of unfinished business. In my research for one 1,200-word article, I had uncovered so much material on legal, social and cultural tussles over obscenity that I knew creating five or even ten articles on the subject wouldn't leave me satisfied. If I wanted to do this bizarre tale justice, I would have to write a book.

Geoffrey Robertson QC published his book *Obscenity* in 1979, and it has proved an excellent research text for the historical aspects of this book, but it is more of a law textbook and was also obviously written before that great game-changer and convenient scapegoat, the World Wide Web. Attitudes, laws, the media and the cultural landscape of Britain have altered beyond all recognition in the four decades since Robertson was writing. The advent of the internet isn't solely or even, I would argue, largely to blame for this, but its current ubiquity does raise many questions about how we define obscenity.

As I began trawling through dusty old textbooks and legal archives, as well as taking on the more enjoyable task of interviewing sex educators, lawyers, academics, technologists and porn producers, I quickly discovered that Britain's historical tussles over obscenity divide into two halves: the filthy, risqué, sex-smeared half, and the really, really boring half.

As an experienced fact-checker who enjoys a well-written history book, I started off trying to write about the latter, yet it soon became apparent that I had no hope of retaining my own interest, never mind that of my future readers, if I focused only on dates, laws and dry legal jargon. There are already several books which attempt a chronology of obscenity law, and their authors deserve to be credited with this painstaking work. It's also important to state now that I am not a legal expert nor a historian by trade. I'm a feminist writer specializing in gender, sexuality and how those two things translate into the granting or withholding of rights. I'm also an advocate for sexual freedom, and I agree with the view of Martha Nussbaum and others that "disgust and shame should not influence what gets criminalized or how criminals get punished."[1]

Therefore, I turned my attention to the smutty half of this story, and tried to center my book on the argument that the Britain of today and yesteryear is uniquely repressive when it comes to matters sexual. I naively imagined it would be easy to create a book focused on this notion, because there's so much commonly known evidence to support it: the prudishness of Victorian Britain, the 1960 trial against Penguin for publishing the D.H. Lawrence novel *Lady Chatterley's Lover*, the Profumo political scandal of the early '60s, and numerous other examples of British sexual suppression.

Yet that didn't feel quite right either.

Ultimately, this story showed itself to be much more nuanced. I could find no simple, polarized way to tell it, because its unfolding has been anything but straightforward. Instead, I've selected and woven together the most interesting, relevant and sometimes hilarious instances that have brought the UK to its current stance on obscenity. I've taken a wry look at hysteria regarding sexuality, censorship and the law; focused on the voices of real people rather than just celebrities or the already infamous; kept dry legal jargon to a minimum; and noted how pop culture can serve as a better barometer of public opinion than loftier forms of discourse. I've looked at how notions of obscenity are used to target those whose sexuality falls outside of the heterosexual, monogamous, vanilla norm, and compared the UK's stance with that of the United States. Although this book is focused on British law and culture, I feel that the symbiotic relationship with our friends across the Atlantic merits a chapter of its own, not least because cultural and legal shifts in the two countries have often paralleled one another.

Nine years ago, I hit a landmark as an author, when I received my first warning that religious fundamentalists might find my writing offensive. If that sounds wild to you, let me assure you it was anything but. I'll grant that sometimes my writing has taken me to exciting places, but I've never heard of a fatwa being placed on the head of a non-religious, non-criminal 25-year-old from South-East England.

What kicked off the concern was a letter I had sent to the left-leaning UK newspaper *The Independent*, which printed my missive in its daily edition. This was long before my days as a professional journalist, when I was still plugging away at an office job to pay the bills, so I was thrilled to see my name in print for the first time since my high-school magazine printed one of my essays on feminism.

I was writing to agree with a young gay journalist who'd stated he felt no obligation to respect homophobic or misogynistic religions. As a left-leaning, anti-bigotry feminist, I wanted to show my support for the writer, who was about my age at the time. I wrote that I thought certain branches of Christianity, especially Catholicism, had wreaked havoc on the world's population by preaching against condom use and abortion rights. Incidentally, I do still hold the Catholic Church partially responsible for the spread of HIV and AIDS in the developing world, but that's another rant for another book. I also wrote that I felt no obligation to respect a religion that mandated misogyny, be it Christianity, Islam or any other. It's worth mentioning that I've written the bulk of this book surrounded by images and sculptures of Hindu gods, but my love of Indian art and religious culture will never blind me to the major problems of sexual and domestic violence in Hindu communities.

It wasn't Catholicism or Hinduism that caused a relative to tell me I should be careful, though—it was that trigger word, *Islam*. My letter stated that I did not respect any use of Islam to treat women as if they were lesser, shameful or tempting objects that had to be covered. In concerned tones, a close relative told me I should remove my address from anywhere it might appear online, even somewhere as innocent as my Amazon wish list, presumably in case the terrorist organization *du jour*, Al-Qaeda, decided to gift me a bomb.

You can decide for yourself which you find more offensive: the criticism of religion, or the presumption that upholders of said religion are such ridiculous thin-skinned babies that they would try to murder me for dissing it in print. Anyway, I sighed, rolled my eyes and indulged my loved one for the sake of a quiet life. I removed my address from Amazon and thought little else about it. Nearly a decade later, my policy is generally to note that homophobia and religion-based bigotry don't affect me very much on a daily basis, so I try wherever possible to pass the microphone to those who are affected. I am certainly not the most qualified journalist to write on issues such as female-genital mutilation, forced marriage, gender-selective abortion and the spread of HIV, but I am happy to use my platform to boost the voices of those on the front lines.

However, misogyny does affect me on a daily basis, and I make no apology for stating that; anti-feminists should know now that those who misuse the concept of obscenity in order to oppress women do not get an easy ride in this book. In 2011, Ana Barahona (not her real name) wrote a book called *Bearing Witness: Eight Weeks in Palestine* and prefaced it with a statement that I agree with so strongly I reproduce it in full here: "I have been hoping to go to Palestine for quite a while now. Not that I have ever felt attracted to the Palestinian issue or the Arab culture. As a woman, I profoundly disapprove of the social ostracism women seem to be relegated to in most Arabic cultures, and would only travel to one of those countries with … people I could trust."

My online searches as to Barahona's ethnic background came up with nothing, which was disappointing, since I try to preempt complaints that white women have no right to criticize brown women's culture by ceding my platform to the latter group. How could I be sure I wasn't just quoting another ignorant, Islamophobic white woman? I quickly found out that I couldn't. On the book's website, the author notes, "All the names in the text, including the author's, have been changed, to try to avoid repressive actions by the State of Israel."

The paradoxes inherent in trying to define or expand freedom of speech are perfectly exemplified by these bizarre parallel situations. I was told to hide my identity after dissing Islam in case fundamentalist Muslims came after me, whereas Barahona was happy to air her prejudices against the Arab world in print, but did not dare use her real name in case Israeli authorities came after her. You may draw your own conclusions as to which group poses more of a threat to freedom of expression; personally, I consider it utterly obscene when *any* faction tries to intimidate a writer into not speaking his or her truth.

Introduction

It's nearly a decade since I denounced the malign influences of religion in print, in a newspaper that now only exists online. That last fact alone is an indicator of the massive changes that the British media has undergone over the past decade, and in Chapter 9 I address the swirling debates over racism, sexism and online freedom of expression that have mushroomed during that time. This is the chapter that I must most strongly preface with a statement that I offer no conclusions or answers to 21st-century battles over no-platforming, hate speech and cultural appropriation. The best I can offer is my own account of life both as a journalist who has had to evolve in order to follow the move of dominant media from printed page to digital screen and as a feminist who often dislikes the reductionist nature of online debates. This is my way of placing obscenity in its modern context.

When I've told people what this book is about, I have often received a response along the lines of "UK obscenity law is outdated, stuffy and ridiculous, but what can you expect when Brits are so uptight about sex!" I don't disagree with every facet of this statement, but it's important to add that the country of my birth and upbringing has always been a country riddled with paradoxes.

Britain is a tiny island that used to be a world power, and significant chunks of the population still regularly forget that we do not hold dominion over other countries now. Britons have a reputation for politeness and chivalry, yet we're also known for thuggery and hooliganism, often linked to an inability to drink in moderation. We're a mongrel nation with no claim to ethnic purity and we boast a fantastically diverse population, yet our decades of social progress are still tainted by contemporary xenophobia and racism. And when it comes to sex? My *God*; the British are never more self-contradictory than when it comes to *that*. We have a reputation for being prudes, repressed and uptight about all matters carnal, yet our deeds have rarely matched our words. We've made an international name for ourselves as prurient hypocrites who commit all manner of filth with one hand and point the finger with the other.

Between January 2016 and the completion of this book some 21 months later, Britain has celebrated the anniversaries of several landmark laws, reminding us that intolerance of alternative sexual lifestyles went unchecked in this country until very recently. The year 2017 marked 50 years since the British parliament legalized sex acts between men, a watershed moment I explore in much more detail in Chapter 8. There was also the anniversary of the Abortion Act 1967, which, along with the introduction of the Pill, gave British women an unprecedented amount of control over their bodies and sex lives. Unlike in America, where a conservative war on abortion is constantly raging, in the UK this act has never been under any real threat of repeal, and the vast majority of modern Britons support a woman's right to choose.

Yes, 21st-century Britain is a fantastic place to reside in terms of sexual freedom, freedom of speech and freedom of religion. We can be proudly Christian, Muslim, Hindu or atheist and not be persecuted for it. We can blog about our prime minister being an incompetent moron and not be thrown in jail for it. Same-gender couples have equal marriage rights. Our health service offers free birth control and abortion to women, a right our Irish sisters are still denied by their retrogressive, religiously influenced government. In London, Brighton or Manchester, a same-gender couple holding hands or kissing in public is less likely to raise eyebrows or ire than a bus being late. Trans visibility is increasing, albeit at a slower clip than gay visibility. This in turn outstrips lesbian and bi visibility—of which, much more in Chapter 4—and British TV shows are now falling over themselves to include LGBT characters. British women watch, read about and talk about sex with a degree of openness that would have been considered the strict preserve of men only a few decades ago.

This is certainly an invigorating era in which to be a thirtysomething feminist who spent much of her teens and 20s baffled by the failure of her peers to care about sexism, misogyny and gender. Now I only have to open up my web browser to find community (or simply glance toward my bookshelves). The publishing market for feminism/gender/sexuality absolutely exploded in the 2000s, and as a lifelong book addict I am thrilled by this. I do not believe the battle for women's rights is anywhere near won, but I feel the trajectory of my own writing career is testament to an increasing acceptance of the idea that feminism need not entail repressing one's sexuality.

This book aims to walk the middle path between a discourse that mandates nothing less than absolute personal freedom and one that advocates censorship in the name of protecting women or children. It examines how the persistent idea that men need to be saved from their own sexuality, whereas women need to be saved from men, underpins much of obscenity legislation. Teenage girls are regularly invoked by the British media as victims of an overly sexualized society, one that's causing them to suffer body-image worries, be coerced into sending nude selfies and sexts or be pressured into having sex. They are rarely, if ever, portrayed as sexual agents, even though, as someone who was a teenage girl and retains a very clear memory of those years, I can attest to the power of my own sexual curiosity and desire. I fail to believe I was the only female adolescent who never felt like a victim of evil, over-sexed boys, and I hope this book finds its way into the hands of women who feel similarly. Chapter 6 looks at why and how such misperceptions still hold water and how this affects women's access to adult material. Women's undressed bodies are already ubiquitous in UK media, but penises still enjoy protection from public scrutiny. As I discovered, the only reason for this is conservative fears masquerading as law, since there exists no UK legislation banning the depiction of aroused male genitalia. I also found that the vast majority of British publishers, distributors and audiences believe that such a law exists, and so this imaginary rule gets repeated as fact. My interviews with Suraya Sidhu Singh and Zak Jane Keir, both experienced writers and publishers who have battled with male censors to create erotica aimed at straight women, showed me just how difficult it is to go up against a dominant culture that keeps telling us "women don't want that sort of thing." I hope you find their stories as fascinating and revelatory as I did.

As I hope you will already have gathered, this book gives no quarter to excuses for sexism. I have heard multiple justifications for treating women's bodies as decorative and men's as active and powerful, and I remain unmoved by them all. Feminists are regularly accused of being envious of glamour models or porn stars, yet these women make up a significant percentage of my interviewees for the book and have taught me a great deal about how prudery and hypocrisy map on to the definition of obscenity. It's also worth adding here that if I want to see breasts or bottoms or pudenda, I can look down my shirt or stand in front of one of the many mirrors that decorate my home. I'm a white, able-bodied, cisgender woman of average build and I'm familiar with the female body to the point that it is utterly uninteresting to me. I've worked in healthcare on and off for 12 years in order to support the erratically paid pursuit of writing, and believe me when I say that nude bodies get really tedious really quickly. I have zero time for the argument that "women's bodies are just nicer to look at," because that statement prizes a plasticized, airbrushed vision of the female body over its reality—that is, a body that defecates, urinates, menstruates, sags, ages, grows hair and emits odors just as much as the maligned, smelly, hairy male body does.

I won't ever embrace the cultural narrative that tells me I should accept 50 percent of the population's being treated as sexy window dressing, and I'm definitely going to question the Western notion that the sole definition of "sexy" is a naked, slim, young white woman. If this were true, then the human race would have died out a long time ago, because only about 3 percent of the population would ever get laid; not to mention how the modern porn market would have disappeared up its own exhaust pipe within the first few years of its inception.

This is not a book demanding free speech without consequences. I am neither a libertarian nor a provocateur, and I firmly believe that the devil has enough people advocating for him already. I tend to believe that those who deliberately stir the shit should also be obliged to lick the spoon, and I've long grown out of wading into pointless, never-ending arguments online. I do dislike the knee-jerk tendency to pull any author, speaker or activist straight down off his or her pedestal for having said or written something disagreeable years or decades previously, but this isn't the same as saying I endorse the transphobic words of Germaine Greer or Benedict Cumberbatch's habit of referring to "colored people." Rather, I want to encourage open, mature discussions about how concepts like "harmful speech" are defined, plus a critical attitude to those whose voices are most amplified in the debates. Those who believe they are striking a blow for freedom simply because they get to shout the loudest belong in a school playground, not an adult debate.

This is definitely a book that explores who is most regularly afforded the right to speak publicly and why. It examines in detail the question of whose sexuality is approved and represented in the British legal system, and whose bedroom preferences are most likely to be hushed up or denounced. This is a book about which bodies are regularly served up for consumption by the dominant media and which bodies are permitted a degree of privacy. It's about the UK's many and varied laws, how unclear and contradictory they have been and continue to be, who gets to make and change those laws and how such groups obtained their power. It's an examination of centuries of sexism, homophobia, racism and colonialism, and it's also a look at how millions of intelligent, open-minded, creative Britons have fought against those who would police language, minds, hearts and genitalia.

If your palms are already moist with the idea that this book is going to strike a blow against "political correctness," let me stop you right there. I don't wish to waste your time, and I would not dream of wasting mine, so it's important that you know the following. I love Britain; I was born, raised and educated here and have lived in this country for 34 years. However, I'm not so starry-eyed with nationalist sentiment that I don't also see intolerance of feminism, immigration and gay rights still running rampant in my country. If you love to shout down any dissenting voices with the complaint "It's political correctness gone mad," you might want to put this book down and stroll on. I have no time for that hackneyed statement because my mind instantly translates it to: "I used to be able to call people wog, Paki, faggot, poofter, bitch or cunt without any consequences. I am now extremely annoyed to learn that I might face some consequences for these lapses in human decency."

The complainant in question also invariably forgets that if he or she were to move to the right country, he or she could still merrily execute gay people, oppress women and be openly racist with impunity. I suppose a quick relocation to Saudi Arabia or the Sudan sounds like too much hard work to some Brits. This is not to say any oppressed group has the monopoly on squeaky-clean behavior; I've heard women say disparaging things about women, LGBT folk bitch about one another, and mixed-race people refer to themselves as "half-caste" or "Paki." However, I find it incredibly telling that I've only ever heard "It's political correctness gone mad!" from the lips of white, middle-class, usually male, usually straight Westerners, and they're nearly always aged 40 and above. It's often prefaced or suffixed with the complaint "You can't say *anything* any more!" As a writer, I must demand accuracy wherever the English language is used, because it's a fantastic tool deserving of respect, even when we're just using it to graffiti "SEND NUDES" on a parking-lot wall. I'm also a philosophy graduate who suffered through three years of studying logic in mind-numbing detail, so allow me to apply a little semantic logic to this nonsensical statement.

Of course you *can* say anything. Just ask any woman who has ever posted something on the internet what responses she received. I guarantee you her detractors will not have paused before calling her every name under the sun, sending her pictures of penises and propositioning her for sex or threatening her with rape, torture and murder. Or have a chat with Salman Rushdie, if you'd like to go back a little further into Britain's history of free speech being met with death threats. Rushdie could and did say what he liked in his famous book *The Satanic Verses*, but he also paid a high price for doing so. Being threatened with death by religious fundamentalists isn't pleasant, but it's also not the same as Rushdie's work being censored from the get-go, and this is a very important distinction to draw. If you're used to saying what you like without being challenged, it stands to reason that you would dislike the social changes that mean you are now likely to be pulled up on your bigoted blusterings. Hence your loud claims that you're being oppressed or prevented from speaking the ugly contents of your mind. If that were true, though, why hasn't an ax-wielding executioner shown up yet and silenced your ponderings on why gay people have too many rights? All that's changed is you are now being held to account, and we're all apt to get a little defensive when that happens.

Disgust, discomfort and anger are all common responses to material that we find offensive or simply weird, but it is a massive leap from experiencing these emotions to claiming harm has taken place. This idea that words or pictures can harm human beings is at the center of current UK obscenity law, yet as a theory it remains completely unproven. Chapter 3 digs into precisely how this nebulous notion is treated as gospel even when those painted as most vulnerable—children and teenagers—are asking for more open, honest discussions of explicit material. It unpacks studies that deny any link between children's seeing adult content and developing sexually violent or coercive habits, and it encourages readers to question the monolithic portrayal of children and teenagers by an increasingly febrile media.

This book does not align with either the hard-left- or extreme-right-wing views on sex, censorship and state control. It does not endorse the mockery of those who dare to renege on the social (media) contract by use of terms like "special snowflakes," "triggered" or "safe spaces." It also disagrees with the idea that it's only young or left-wing people who are oversensitive to the odd bit of name-calling. After all, the current crop of neo–Nazis are obviously aware of the power of words, because they insist on being called the "alt-right," lest they be revealed as the craven fascists that they so clearly are. I am aware that there exists a whole new generation of teenagers and adults who hide behind keyboards, computer screens and stupid profile pictures and then type or record or film noxious, provocative statements, but I believe that these people originate from all points on the political spectrum. I've also witnessed plenty of calls from within the feminist, anti-racist activist and LGBT communities for increasing tolerance of or critical engagement with unpalatable views. In her recent autobiography, the decidedly left-wing music journalist Sylvia Patterson railed against "the platoons of Twitter trolls on constant trawl for the sackable offence,"[2] and I feel a great deal of sympathy for her. No one with a public internet presence escapes finger-wagging from keyboard warriors, and criticizing these people isn't a pastime restricted to the right wing.

I will certainly discuss free speech in this book, but my basic view is that while one can say anything in modern Britain, no one enjoys absolute freedom to speak without consequence. We are *all* imbued with a fear of saying exactly what we think, whether that's from British politeness, political ambitions, or lack of inclination to deal with internet mobs. Even HRH Queen Elizabeth II, who supposedly reigns over me and my fellow Britons, has to choose her words carefully. Even fantastic role model and author J. K. Rowling, whom I'm thrilled to see regularly talking feminism on

Twitter, does not enjoy consequence-free speech, and I'm not here to debate whether that's right or wrong.

It's worth mentioning here that, as a feminist, I've had my views on obscenity altered wildly during the past two decades. I wasn't even out of my teens before I was tired of a culture where breasts and sex scandals were never far away from our media, yet Brits seemed incapable of educating their children honestly and adequately about sex. By my early 20s I was utterly sick of seeing scantily clad women on the covers of lads' mags every time I walked into a newsagent's. I've run my own blog for nearly a decade now, and the first three years of posts were effectively one long rant against the hypocrisy of British tabloid culture, which condemned pedophiles on one page while holding countdowns to female celebrities' 16th birthdays on the next. In my mid-20s, I happily attended feminist conventions and marches where it was roundly agreed that pornography and sex work were misogynistic, damaging to society and needed to be banned. I subscribed to this condemnation of the sex-work industry as utterly corrosive to decent gender relations, even though, at this stage, my experience of that world was entirely vicarious.

I did have some uneasy moments during that complicated decade, though. Sometimes I felt aroused, not sickened, by anti-porn feminists' descriptions of the supposedly terrible things that went on in the industry. I didn't feel there was anyone to confide in, lest I be labeled a handmaiden of the patriarchy and booted out of the sisterhood. So I started writing. I created blog posts, online articles, reviews and op-eds in which I demanded that women be allowed to live their sexual lives free from judgment by the very women who were supposed to have our backs. In developing this critique, I came to feel a lot more empathy with porn stars, strippers, cam girls, dominatrices and other women condemned by feminists for the crime of not having sex in a preapproved manner. It started to disgust me that feminists were writing their fellow women off as brainwashed if they enjoyed a spanking, liked rough sex or watched porn. I realized how often condemnation of a person's sexual actions simply translates to "I do not think I would enjoy this," usually reinforced by a failure to imagine why other adults might. In 2012, I wrote a 19,000-word blog series expanding on this theme, and three years after that I published *Thinking Kink*, a fullfrontal assault on the idea that you cannot be kinky and a feminist too.

There are hundreds of feminist and sexuality-related texts competing for space on my bookshelf, and the majority of them tell us that obscenity law has never been a friend to women. For centuries, moralistic censorship prevented women from accessing contraception and abortion or receiving any sex education at all. It resulted in the seizing and destroying of LGBT literature, and, in the case of the notorious 1960 *Lady Chatterley's* trial, painted women as fragile, asexual creatures who required a fainting couch at the slightest mention of sex. I've learned a great deal from the excellent writings of Gayle Rubin and Pat/rick Califia regarding how individual sexual preferences get elevated to the social or legal standard for moral cleanliness. More recently, I've been thrilled to see academics such as Meg-John Barker add more British voices to the mix. The funny and informative *Queer: A Graphic History,* Barker's 2016 collaboration with Julia Scheele, has never been far from my fingertips while putting this book together.

No one has ever explained to my satisfaction how to have the "right" kind of sex, not least because every religion, society or activist movement has its own definition of which adult activities are acceptable and which are perverted. To quote Rubin, "Instead of judging sexual tastes according to an arbitrary line, we should emphasize the way partners treat one another, the level of mutual consideration, the presence or absence of coercion, and the qualities of the pleasures they provide."[3] I would never want to be mistaken for a neoliberal, but I agree with Rubin that other adults' sex lives should not be a matter of state concern. I also believe that the world would be a much better place if people were more honest about their sexual desires, fantasies and needs. Not to mention if world leaders got laid or spanked more often.

What started with one law a century and a half ago has long since more than devolved into a cyclone of smut, hate, protest and counterprotest, which as I type continues to eat its own tail. No concept has been more energetically explored, criticized or defended throughout Britain's numerous moral panics and fights for sexual freedom. No term has seen its definition alter so wildly throughout history either: until a few centuries ago, British law treated atheism and criticism of the monarchy as the ultimate obscene practices.

So how did we get here from there?
The answer does not boil down to easy bullet points.
It's not just because of the Victorians.
Britons *aren't* naturally more prudish than people of any other nation; we have an international reputation as being sexually open-minded, successfully multicultural and the producers of fine literature, art, music, theater and movies.

Is it perhaps the cold weather that leaves Brits so scandalized by naked bodies, whereas elsewhere in Europe, breasts, bottoms, pudenda and penises are such common sights on warm, golden beaches that no one bats an eye?

Is it Britain's commitment to politeness and manners that means, although said bodies regularly appear in daily newspapers, online magazines and in our local shops, we're still rather rubbish (British for "to suck at something") at actually discussing sex with children and teenagers?

Is it our shyness, our famous reserve, our need for a cup of tea or some alcohol before tackling strong subjects, that makes our Continental cousins regularly laugh at us for being so hung up on sex?

Come with me now and I will tell you.

1

The Current Situation

"It might not be your cup of tea. But pornography is the canary in the coal mine of free speech. It is the first freedom to die."—Myles Jackman, British obscenity lawyer[1]

It's a breezy British autumn day and I'm standing on a patch of grass opposite London's Houses of Parliament. Tourists meander along the nearby pavements in clumps, open-topped double-decker buses trundle past, but my eyes are on the memorial plinth in front of me. Furious sex workers, porn performers and free-speech advocates have gathered around it to protest proposed restrictions to UK-produced erotic media. They've brought some fantastic homemade placards with them too.

Over 50 years ago, the Greater London Council made the eminently reasonable statement that "it would be wrong and illogical … if the range of things prevented by the censors was greater than the range of things prohibited by law."[2] Yet this is precisely the situation in 21st-century Britain. As laws dictating sexual behavior have been peeled away in the UK, laws dictating how sex can be depicted have sprung up in their place like so many whack-a-moles. Sexual standards have relaxed: cohabiting before marriage and serial monogamy are now accepted as legitimate relationship models, same-gender relationships are becoming less taboo and there is even a growing acceptance of polyamory in some quarters. When I see two men holding hands on the London Underground I smile to myself, pleased at this sign of social progress. Yet were those two men to consensually whip or fist each other and videotape it, current British law would prevent me from either watching or distributing the film. This feels so head-scratchingly backwards that I can't understand why more attention isn't paid to it.

What also disturbs me is how the UK government's crackdown on

The 2016 Kink Olympixx protest included kink-themed games as well as impassioned speeches against the proposed Digital Economy Act (photograph by the author).

obscenity has flown almost entirely under the mainstream media's radar. Sexual freedom comes a very poor second to Donald Trump's determination to start World War III, and most days even a motorway pile-up will rank higher in British news priorities than the increasing censorship of adult sex acts. To be fair, the Brits as a nation probably do spend more time stuck in traffic jams than having sex. We find a stationary M25 easier to talk about too.

Sex blogger Girl on the Net writes, "If it's legal to do but illegal to depict in porn, that's a clear sign that the law is an ass." This is why kinky protesters keep taking to the London streets and, to the delight of many, making entertaining games of their cause. In the last three years I've either read about or witnessed face-sitting protests, fisting volleyball and squirting water fights being staged outside the Houses of Parliament. Have you ever seen two dominatrices play two latex-clad gay men at volleyball outside the ancient seat of British government? This author has, and I can honestly say that it beats working for a living.

However, these shows of playful smut have a serious objective—to fight the ever-growing tide of state control over adult material. More than one person has suggested to me that Britain's infamous 2016 vote to leave the European Union (which I will try to mention as little as possible in this book) was an act of defiance against growing government interference in adult life. I can see the truth in this statement, even if I still want to smack most of my countrywomen and -men who voted in favor of B****t. I will never consider their actions justified, but I can understand the logic of what happened in the summer of 2016. If you give millions of angry, frightened and exhausted people one chance to spit in their government's face, they will happily take it and to hell with the inevitable backsplash.

Back to the far more fun topic of risqué protests. I watched these kink-themed publicity stunts both as a believer in sexual freedom and as someone who—to no one's greater surprise than my own—found myself pushed to write a book on BDSM (bondage and discipline, domination and submission, and sadism and masochism, or S&M as it used to be known) precisely because I was tired of Western media hijacking sexual preferences in order to shame ordinary people. I watched with increasing fascination and dismay as my fellow countrymen and -women lost their sexual liberty and didn't seem to notice or care. I also hungered to truly unpick and understand the arbitrary targets of Britain's laws.

The Restrictions on UK Porn: A Quick Primer!

It's easy to get swept away on a sea of acronyms and jargon when trying to trace British obscenity law back to its roots. It's also much more simply expressed in diagram form.

The issues most recently protested divide roughly into three camps:

—the AVMS regulations themselves, in force since 2009;
—the 2014 tightening of the AVMS regulations; and
—the Digital Economy Bill, which became law in 2017.

The latter demands that all UK websites showing adult content have age-verification software in place, an unwieldy, costly burden on porn producers. Opponents of the bill claim that smaller businesses will simply go bust under the financial strain, which can mean spending 50 pence per website visitor in order to ask them to provide credit-card details. This obligation also creates massive potential for data harvesting, hacking and

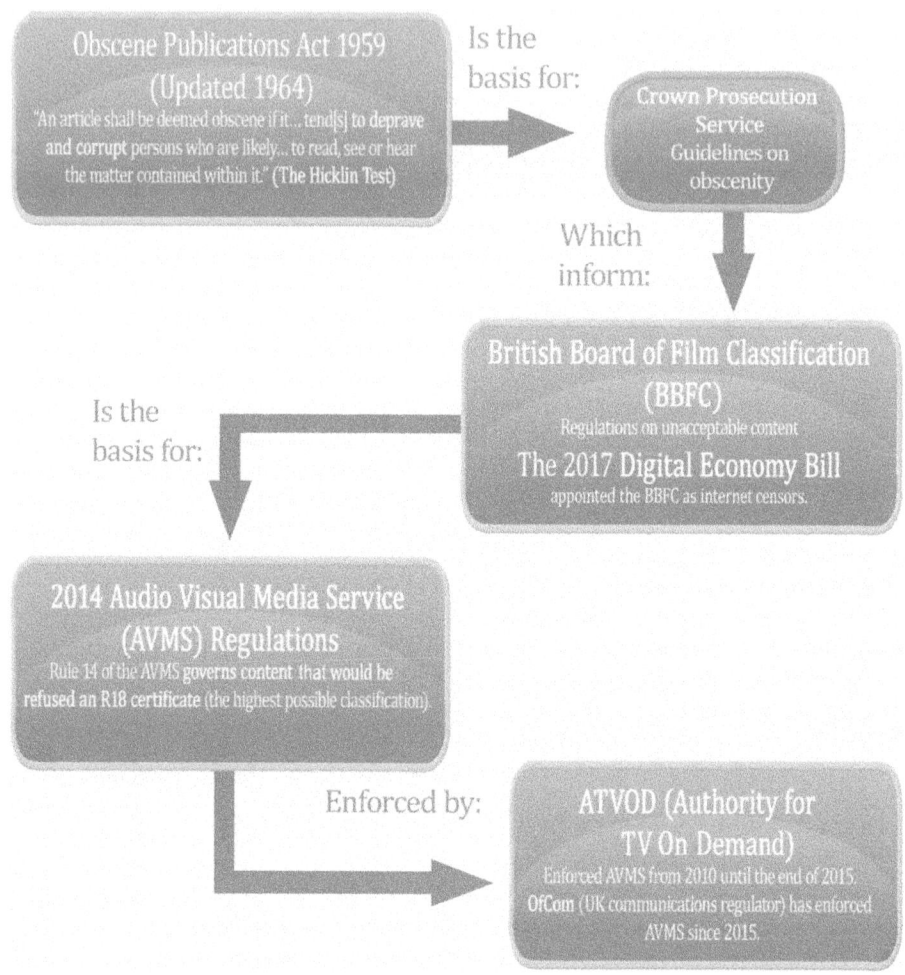

How UK obscenity law works (diagram by Emily Brady).

fraud. We only need look at what happened when the "have an affair discreetly" website Ashley Madison had its user base hacked in 2015. Millions of people were outed, and they weren't just middle-aged white men looking to cheat on their wives; some were gay men from homophobic cultures looking for discreet encounters with men. Several suicides resulted from this needless exposure. As we'll see later in this book, it was not the first time people had taken their own lives as a result of sexual shame, and I hate to say that it won't be the last, either.

Regardless, the Digital Economy Bill was pushed through British parliament just before the summer of 2016, a deliberate ploy to ensure it received minimal media attention (the British government shuts down for a month during the summertime). June 2016 saw such relentless reporting on B****t that few other stories made it into the UK's mainstream media channels. Meanwhile, the government was quietly encroaching on adult privacy to very little objection. Had it not been for the likes of Blake, Jerry Barnett and Myles Jackman, I would not have heard about this sleight of hand myself, and I owe a big hat tip to the writers, activists, lawyers and porn performers who opened my eyes to these insidious regulations. The rest of the British public missed a treat by being deprived of this news, not least because those campaigning provided such colorful viewing. And so much for democracy in action—only 13 members of Parliament (MPs) even bothered to attend the actual vote that passed the Digital Economy Act in April 2017.

This cloak-and-dagger encroachment on freedom of speech isn't new: the AVMS regulation changes were pushed through at the end of 2014 with no public consultation and hardly any media attention. The decision to ban face-sitting, female ejaculation and certain BDSM acts from all UK-produced porn would not have gained any coverage at all were it not for the persistent blogging and social-media protests of a few grassroots activists.

The Obscene Publications Act (OPA) was introduced by Lord Campbell and passed by Parliament in 1857, revised in 1959 and last updated in 1964. The OPA has never, in any of its forms, defined particular acts, words or pictures as obscene. In fact, it wasn't until 1868, when Campbell's act was first put to the test in the case *Regina v. Hicklin,* that the British judiciary actually bothered to offer a definition of the term. That was when the presiding judge, Lord Chief Justice Alexander Cockburn, famously stated the following: "I think the test of obscenity is this, whether the tendency of the matter charged as obscenity is to deprave and corrupt those whose minds are open to such immoral influences, and into whose hands a publication of this sort may fall."[3]

This definition, now referred to as the Hicklin Test, is still the UK standard for obscenity, and it's not difficult to see why the debate over what actually possesses the power to deprave and corrupt the average British adult is still raging today. However, there do exist advisory lists of which acts are most likely to be banned from UK media, and these lists all ultimately derive from the OPA. First, there's the Crown Prosecution Service (CPS) guidelines on material "most commonly prosecuted as obscene." Here is a non-exhaustive sample of the CPS guidelines, with my own emphasis added:

—fisting;
—sadomasochistic material which goes beyond trifling and transient infliction of injury; "thus reddening of the skin is acceptable but raised welts, blood and bruising are not" (clarification from obscenity lawyer Myles Jackman[4]);
—bondage where all four limbs are tied, especially where gags are used with no apparent means of withdrawing consent; and
—activities involving perversion or degradation such as drinking urine, urination or vomiting on to the body, or excretion or use of excreta. This also includes female ejaculation if done on another person's body or consumed.

The 2014 revision of the AVMS regulations means none of these acts can be shown through video-on-demand (VOD) services, i.e., via online streaming. This means UK porn producers wanting to depict kinky sex or simply female pleasure are hamstrung by the threat of fines, website shutdowns and prosecution. This news was received with dismay in December 2014; hence dozens of dominatrices turning up outside the Houses of Parliament on a winter morning to sit on their delighted male subs' faces.

Regardless of how one feels about any of these acts—and most are not my personal cup of tea—performing any of them is not illegal under UK law. As for how safe they are, well! Take it from someone who plays a contact sport that has concussed me and has broken my friends' thumbs, collarbones and ankles (not all the same friend, I hasten to add): you can do a lot of very extreme and violent things to other human beings while remaining completely within the law. I've also been in the BDSM scene for half a decade, and I know that all the highlighted acts can be practiced safely and legally among consenting adults. If I haven't seen it with my own eyes, I can easily find you an intelligent, safety-conscious adult who has. I also fail to understand why current law permits me to read about golden showers and scat play in Belle de Jour's popular memoir *Secret Diary of a Call Girl*, yet deems me a criminal should I wish to watch the same acts on video.

The lists of rules don't stop here, either. The CPS guidelines inform the rules of the British Board of Film Classification (BBFC), which decides age ratings for all movies released in the UK. The ratings available are U, PG, 12, 12A, 15, 18 and R18. If the BBFC deems a work too obscene for even an R18 certificate, it cannot legally be released. Instead, the maker must make the BBFC's required cuts and resubmit the work. The BBFC has also recently been given the power to rate or withhold ratings for VOD online. I don't have to spell out how much clout the BBFC now wields in defining obscenity, and the concerning implications this has for both artistic and sexual freedom in the UK.

Furthermore, while few are likely to complain about the BBFC's promise to "refuse material which is in conflict with criminal law, or has been created through the commission of a criminal offence," several of its other guidelines are up for debate.

The BBFC will deny an R18 certificate to a video including any of the following (emphases and parenthetical explanations my own):

—acts likely to encourage an interest in sexually abusive activity, **which may include adults role-playing as non-adults**;
—portrayals of sexual activity which involves real **or apparent lack of consent.** Any form of physical restraint which prevents participants from indicating a withdrawal of consent;
—depictions of the **infliction of pain** or acts which may cause lasting physical harm, **whether real or (in a sexual context) simulated**. Some allowance may be made for moderate, non-abusive consensual activity. (This includes face-sitting as breathing restriction. Obscenity lawyer Myles Jackman clarifies on his blog, "The airways must remain open ... the rationale for this distinction is that men trying this at home might die"[5]);
—penetration by any object associated with violence or likely to cause physical harm. (Given the possibility of dishing out a fair beating with a dildo, and the intimidating size of some anal plugs, it's unclear how we define an "object associated with violence"!); and
—sexual threats, humiliation or abuse which do not form part of a clearly consenting role-playing game. Strong physical or verbal abuse, **even if consensual**, is unlikely to be acceptable.

The phrases in bold are all problematic as soon as BDSM enters the equation. Age play, consensual non-consent, threats and simulated violence are all part of BDSM play. How can the BBFC pass movies such as *The War Zone*, which graphically depicts a father sexually abusing his daughter, yet refuse to rate videos depicting two adults consensually role-playing a schoolgirl fantasy?

It should be noted here that there is no evidence to support the BBFC's statement that viewing adults engaging in, say, an age-play scenario is "likely to encourage an interest in sexually abusive activity." The idea that a grown person dressing as a schoolchild or a baby is a gateway drug to pedophilia has no basis in psychiatry, criminology or any other credible area of research. It also demonstrates willful misunderstanding of the psychology underpinning sexual role play, an issue I wrote about extensively in my first book, *Thinking Kink*. The clue is in the word *play*. As seasoned BDSM practitioner Mollena Williams-Haas writes in her book *The Toybag Guide to Playing with Taboo*, "The abuse of vulnerable youth, or the exploitation of a sacred trust, is never ever acceptable. However, between consenting adults, that scenario has the frisson of a profound transgression."[6]

The transgression is exactly where the thrill originates; human beings will always get a kick out of playing with the forbidden. Williams-Haas's fascinating *Toybag Guide* takes on society's deepest taboos by examining fetishes for necrophilia, bestiality, incest, Nazism/white supremacy and scat play. Williams-Haas herself is a black American who has written and spoken publicly about her enjoyment of racialized kink play; she describes being voluntarily tied up and threatened by white men who hold knives to her throat and call her "nigger." She emphasizes that regardless of others' discomfort, adults must feel free to explore any of these dark fantasies with consenting partners, and that it is cathartic, exhilarating and erotic to do so. Yet the BBFC would have us believe that depicting these scenarios on film is somehow more dangerous than carrying them out.

The BBFC rules are also inconsistent, both in their formulation and in their application. They claim to ban media depicting "the infliction of pain or acts which may cause lasting physical harm," but I've watched enough fights, rapes and murders depicted on British television to know that the ratings body doesn't much care about sex and violence provided they're portrayed negatively. There's plenty of strong, bloody violence and verbal abuse in *Goodfellas*, *Casino* and the "Stuck in the Middle with You" scene in *Pulp Fiction*, yet these movies made it through UK cinemas and still show up on British TV with regularity.

I have long concluded that, for whatever reason, portrayals of adults enjoying sex are more likely to be deemed obscene than those of violence. However you slice it, and whichever list you are looking at, the CPS and BBFC guidelines blatantly target any sexual practices that land outside the straight, vanilla mainstream. This may be news to the majority of Britons, but it's not a new phenomenon: the CPS guidelines have been in place since the year 2000. The rules may only have received publicity in recent years, thanks to protests, online campaigns and social media activism, and because they continue to be altered so that more producers come under their repressive remit. But it's clear that sexism, homophobia and kinkphobia have been at work in the UK legal system for much longer than anyone realizes.

Extremism

Since 2008, UK-produced porn has also been bound (ha!) by the Criminal Justice and Immigration Act, which contains a section on "Possession of Extreme Pornographic Images." This criminalizes possession of "pornographic images that depict acts which threaten a person's life; acts which result in or are likely to result in serious injury to a person's anus, breasts or genitals; bestiality; or necrophilia."[7]

For possession of an image to count as an offense, it must meet the following three criteria:

1. That the image is pornographic; and
2. that the image is extreme, namely grossly offensive, disgusting, or otherwise of an obscene character; and
3. that the image portrays in an explicit and realistic way any of the extreme acts set out [above].

This law was brought in following the 2003 murder of Jane Longhurst, a Brighton schoolteacher. The murderer, Graham Coutts, allegedly had a fetish for extreme and violent sexual acts including strangulation, and Longhurst's bereaved mother campaigned for a law that would protect women against the horrific fate her daughter had suffered.[8] This was a deeply emotive premise and almost impossible to argue against without seeming like a hard-hearted monster, or indeed an apologist for murder. Unfortunately, the 2008 act did nothing to protect women from dark desires. As Nick Cowen notes in his report "Nothing to Hide: The Case Against the Ban on Extreme Pornography," plenty of UK citizens, both male and female, watch pornography.[9] Plenty of women and men also have aggressive sexual fantasies, and fantasize about playing dominant or submissive roles. Yet, Cowen adds, "there is no powerful evidence base to suggest that any of these individuals pose a specific risk of committing sexual offences." Nonetheless, thousands of Britons are being charged with possessing extreme porn every year, and the vast majority plead guilty. They are afraid to challenge the accusations against them, because they know that even if they are vindicated, the damage to their reputations will already have been done.

It's not hard to see why when we look at the example of Andrew Holland, one of the first to be charged under Extreme Pornography legislation, in 2009, for allegedly possessing an image of a woman having sex with a tiger. It turned out to be a cartoon image, emailed in jest by one of Holland's friends, and the case was thrown out of court. Unfortunately, by the time common sense prevailed Holland had spent six months on police bail, lost custody of his children (temporarily) and been assaulted and abused by people in his hometown. All his neighbors knew was that he had been accused of a "serious sexual offence." To their minds, this could easily have been child rape, and they weren't interested in fact-checking their misapprehensions before heading out to beat Holland up.

Another example of how an accusation can be nearly as damaging as a conviction is the story of Simon Walsh, a young aide to the mayor of London who was charged under the law in 2012. Walsh was sacked from his job after he was accused of receiving an email (to his personal, not work, inbox) that contained five images depicting consensual fisting and urethral sounding between adult men. After a protracted and well-publicized trial, Walsh was acquitted, but not before his privacy had been destroyed and his employability shattered. The bias against gay sexual activity is a consistent aspect of British obscenity law that I explore in Chapters 4 and 8. For now, let's consider the absurdity of a law that doesn't criminalize going to a party and watching fisting and urethral sounding, but does prosecute those in possession of images from said party. Let's also remember how such laws ignore any possibility that women might be the viewers and consumers of porn, rather than just its victims.

Unfortunately, proponents of legal changes that are linked to a horrific case of rape, child abuse or murder know they have an unassailable case, at least in the British media. Forget the pesky facts that anecdotes don't equal patterns, correlation doesn't equal causation, and emotive stories about individual instances of sexual violence don't actually amount to a watertight case against anyone except the people committing such crimes. In a media culture prone to hysteria about sex and/or sexual violence, it's a brave person, and an even braver feminist, who will stand up and point that out. If I sound flippant, chalk it up to over three decades of watching how the UK media works.

Of course, a grieving parent who has lost their child in the most vile way imaginable is going to want to see every possible step taken to prevent what happened to their child ever happening to someone else. But the ordeals of rape or murder victims cannot be expiated by denying justice to adults who like to look at extreme erotica. Adults make their own choices, and it is especially important to remember this when individuals guilty of heinous crimes try to blame porn or violent films for their actions. Brooke Magnanti has reported on how American serial murderer Ted Bundy claims that pornography drove him to assault, rape, murder and dismember multiple women "were repeated and reported as gospel truth."[10] What's that you say, a charming, manipulative psychopath blames something other than himself for his vile actions? Well, that certainly sounds credible!

Magnanti rightly scolds a media too eager to find easy explanations for Bundy's actions, despite the more tedious truth that they will always remain inexplicable to any sane individual: "Why give his porn claims any weight? Of course, he wanted to reduce his own responsibility in these crimes… He was facing death row." She concludes with her knock-out punch: "And by the way; Bundy's crimes were committed decades before the web even existed."[11]

Saving Face(-Sitting)

Back to December 2014, when a group of female porn performers, dominatrices and sex-positive feminists appeared outside Parliament and sat on the faces of some extremely happy-looking men. This protest highlighted how the AVMS changes rendered face-sitting obscene, yet "gagging on cock and deep throat are acceptable if not for the whole scene" (as long as the words "choke on my cock" aren't used).[12] If you're choking on your cup of tea while reading this, I do apologize, but it's important to get to the bottom of this double standard. Both face-sitting and deep-throating are forms of oral sex that could compromise a person's ability to breathe, so why is one banned? The prejudice against face-sitting is also not borne out by the facts: The most common pornographic scenes that require the BBFC to step in and make cuts are of women performing oral sex on men, precisely because the women in the shot are choking or gagging.[13]

The utter absence of logic and consistency has led many to conclude that UK censors have a serious problem with sex scenes that depict female pleasure and/or female dominance. Why else would female ejaculation be automatically considered obscene, while male ejaculation on another's body and the consumption of ejaculate remains legal to depict? If British lawmakers really wanted an easy political victory, they would have deemed male ejaculation obscene a long time ago because of its frankly tedious ubiquity in modern porn. The BBFC claims: "We will apply these Guidelines in relation to sex to the same standard regardless of sexual orientation of the activity portrayed." Yet, if kink is viewed as a sexual orientation, the rules and their application demonstrate no such consistency.

Not all my interviewees agreed with this idea, though. The British technologist, writer and sexual-freedom activist Jerry Barnett first became aware of how porn sites were targeted by censors when he worked as a web developer in the '90s. In his 2016 book *Porn Panic! Sex and Censorship in the UK*, Barnett states that whether they originate with the OPA, the BBFC or the CPS, rules on what adults can view are simply an easy method of eroding civil liberties. "Often, sexual expression is the first form of expression to come under attack by a repressive state machine, simply because it represents the softest target; it is easier to convince a frightened public that pornography [is] somehow harmful than it is to openly attack free speech."[14]

I agree that it's a very brave individual who publicly announces their love of flogging or fisting, so it stands to reason that these are the first acts to be quietly censored, usually with no public knowledge and therefore no public opposition. However, I also agree with the dominatrices and feminist porn producers who told me British law contains a strong anti-female-dominance, anti–BDSM bias. Here is why.

A New Agenda: The 2014 AVMS Regulations

The kerfuffle at the end of 2014 came about because online video-on-demand services now came under the remit of AVMS, whereas before they had not been subject to any regulations. At the time, enforcement fell to the Authority for Television on Demand (ATVOD), whose workings and members were both shadowy and deeply suspect. ATVOD was dissolved and folded into the Office of Communications (Ofcom) at the end of 2015, for reasons that have never been publicly stated.

Rule 14 of the newly expanded AVMS regulations restated all of the BBFC's criteria for denying an R18 certificate. British porn producers predicted that they were going to be targeted by ATVOD under this rule, and they were correct. During 2015, their annus horribilis, four small, independent porn producers, Blake,[15] Mistress R'eal, Mistress Megara Furie and the Bondage Mistress Club, were all forced to shut down their websites for violating Rule 14. All four showed BDSM-themed content, and the latter three were dominatrix-themed.

British dominatrix and porn creator Mistress R'eal was targeted for two of the videos on her website. ATVOD said the first video, "Bullwhipping in the Woods Part 2," showed a "man whipped with consequent red marks on his back, includes sight of infliction of injury. This constitutes material which 'Involves the infliction of pain or acts which may cause lasting physical harm, whether real or (in a sexual context) simulated,' which is prohibited by the BBFC in a pornographic work. This appears to go beyond the allowance made by the BBFC for 'moderate, non-abusive consensual activity.'"[16]

The clip was also in violation of the "degradation and perversion" aspect of the CPS guidelines, because the same man was whipped for "not eating shit off the shoe of Mistress R'eal." ATVOD stated that "the implied eating of faeces would not be passed by the BBFC in a pornographic work, as it may constitute 'material judged to be obscene under the current interpretation of the Obscene Publications Act 1959.'"

It's crucial to note the wording here: an act that isn't even shown, but is merely implied, can still be deemed obscene. This opens up a massive loophole, whereby any references to, simulations of or hints at obscene acts can be found in violation of the rules. Yet in John Waters's *Pink Flamingos*, drag queen Divine is *seen* eating actual dog feces, and the movie received a pass by the BBFC to be released uncut in the UK in 2008.[17]

ATVOD also claimed that Mistress R'eal's second video, "Double Domme CBT and Pegs," was in violation of BBFC guidelines because "the still images and preview video show a man who it is implied is bound by the hands and feet and has a ball-gag in his mouth restricting clear speech. This constitutes 'physical restraint which prevents participants from indicating a withdrawal of consent,' which is prohibited by the BBFC in a pornographic work."[18] Continuing and active consent is certainly an essential part of ethical and safe BDSM, and I suppose Mistress R'eal could have given the man a bouncy ball or heavy piece of metal to drop should he want to stop the scene. However, threatening a small-business owner with fines, jail time and public ruination for this teeny omission is ridiculous when multiple scenes of nonconsensual violence get passed for viewing every hour of the British day. Mainstream porn regularly depicts scenes in which consent is unclear, dubious or presumed; why was ATVOD suddenly interested in championing what feminists and kinksters have been demanding for decades?

Megara Furie was the next British dominatrix to have her website sanctioned by ATVOD. She believes ATVOD behaved in a deliberately intimidating manner, as she received "no warning whatsoever. Just a plain recorded delivery envelope through my door with a bunch of scary looking paperwork inside which told me I had breached four rules." She was terrified, faced with the prospect of "five years of building an ethical reputation for domination completely tarnished. I scoured the paperwork for any indication of penalties or next steps and found nothing. Just contact details and a deadline of ten days. I looked on their site and found that the majority of people found in breach had been mistresses like myself."

The video on Furie's site that breached Rule 14 was titled "Ballbusting." It showed sustained kicks to a man's genitals causing pain and bleeding, ruled by ATVOD to be "beyond the allowance made by the British Board of Film Classification … for moderate, non-abusive consensual activity." I know kicking a man in the family jewels is not an act to be taken lightly, but considering I've watched the same act carried out by multiple women with vigor in the BBC drama *Peaky Blinders*, I'm not sure why we trust actors to know the limits better than dominatrices, who are paid to kick men in the balls without doing permanent damage. Safety and first-aid training are regularly discussed and reinforced in the BDSM community. Players do not carry out any acts of violence without first being certain that they can do so without causing permanent injury. A rule of thumb among dominants is never to use a flogger, whip or other kinky toy on a submissive without testing it on themselves first. This isn't just lip service, it's essential legal practice. Without such an attitude, kinksters would be no better than criminal abusers. Furie adds: "There needs to be clear, specific guidelines on compliance. Right now, the language is woolly and subjective. Someone from the kink scene needs to be involved in these consultations to ensure they are fair for everyone and written clearly."

After speaking to other independent producers who had tangled with ATVOD, Megara Furie concluded that she did not have the energy or money to fight the charges and instead took her website offline. She condemns the list of banned acts as prejudiced and inconsistent: "I personally find watching a woman being tag teamed and covered in ejaculation obscene, as I believe this has a more detrimental effect on men's attitudes towards women in general than face-sitting. [However,] I wouldn't ban or deter anyone from enjoying what they like. Each to their own and in my opinion, it is no one's place to judge or shame anyone's tastes so long as everyone consents." Furie was fortunate enough to find work with a new clips website, and also turned some of the publicity from the case to her advantage, receiving invites from UK universities to lecture on responsible BDSM. However, she lost a significant amount of money from her website's being shut down and no longer has creative control over her videos.

The third domino to fall during ATVOD's 2015 blitz was the Bondage Mistress Club website. The ruling stated that TBMC had violated Rule 14 by hosting a video depicting anal penetration of a man by a dildo and later a woman's fist and breath restriction via face-sitting. I was unable to track down the owners of the Bondage Mistress Club, as they shut down their site in 2015, never to resurface. Fellow porn producer Pandora Blake commented: "It seems as though [ATVOD has] a particular distaste for the sight of a woman dominating and fucking a man, whereas an equivalent film of a man dominating and fucking a woman is seen as perfectly acceptable." Ms. Tytania, a British dominatrix whose website had been targeted by ATVOD in 2014, agreed that the regulatory body was deliberately "decimating Femdom-themed websites. Apparently, women's sexual agency is especially dangerous, or abhorrent, to them."[19]

Blake was the fourth and most publicly active victim of ATVOD when their website Dreams of Spanking was shut down in July 2015 for hosting a video that "showed a male being caned by a female, with consequent red marks to the buttocks ... a female bent over a bed whilst another female gave her 25 cane strokes ... a man being whipped with consequent red marks to his back."[20] Blake wrote to me that "I was contacted by ATVOD very soon after appearing on *Newsnight* and BBC *Woman's Hour* talking about the ways in which the [2014 AVMS] regulations are needlessly oppressive and sexist ... it seems [that] my public criticism of the new regulations brought me to ATVOD's attention." There was also more than a whiff of religious prudery about this shadowy regulatory body. Blake told me over the phone what happened when she met six ATVOD members, including CEO Pete Johnson, to discuss her website. The only female member in the room gave "a talk about what was banned and what wasn't. She could barely say the word 'vagina,' she was blushing so hard."

For reasons still unspecified, Ofcom absorbed ATVOD at the end of 2015 and has not initiated Rule 14 proceedings against any producers since it took over. Blake adds that "there's a general sense that ATVOD were quite embarrassing and were a PR blunder." Blake appealed against the shutdown of Dreams of Spanking, arguing that "the primary purpose of the website wasn't video on demand, that the purpose of the site was community of interest for like-minded people," meaning it did not come under ATVOD's remit. Blake won their appeal in April 2016, and the website is now back up, but they had to rebuild it from scratch, meaning thousands of hours of work and content were lost forever. During the ten months it took to get their appeal heard, Blake's site was forced by law to remain offline. Blake had to scramble to find other income and, unsurprisingly, this took its toll on their physical and mental health. Mistress R'eal also appealed against her website shutdown on the same grounds and won. As much as these two instances can be viewed as individual victories for free speech, neither has resulted in a review of UK obscenity guidelines.

Blake is unequivocal in their condemnation of AVMS and ATVOD, stating in an email that the latter was only ever a money-making racket.

Their ire is directed in particular at the CEO, Pete Johnson. Blake alleges that Johnson asked Ofcom for "seed money so that he could set up ATVOD as a new regulatory body, which extorted fees and fines from small business owners, paying himself a handsome salary in the process…. Any business that didn't volunteer their money in exchange for being censored was found to be in breach, and forced to comply or close. In any other context, this bullying behavior would be seen for what it is: a protection racket."

Ms. Tytania agrees: "When I first received ATVOD's initial extortion letter, demanding a fee and suggesting that I was in breach of the OPA … I thought it was a hoax. Their claims and accusations are so ridiculous, I had to double-check with a lawyer … [ATVOD] operates with a mixture of threats that one thought only existed in a Scorsese film."[21]

Although I should emphasize that these are allegations only, the word "extortion" was used by numerous interviewees during my research on ATVOD. Jerry Barnett did stress that ATVOD started life as a genuine trade association, in 2007, and believes that the body only morphed into a sinister censorship machine in 2010. This was when Ofcom delegated regulation of video-on-demand content to it and made Johnson the CEO. Barnett alleges that after "everyone else was kicked out" of ATVOD, Johnson made paid membership mandatory for all British VOD providers, so that ATVOD became "effectively publicly funded." They were certainly getting their money from somewhere. A search of Britain's National Archives found that non-executive board members of ATVOD were paid £10,000 a year plus travel expenses for working two to three days a month. Nice work if you can get it!

ATVOD's dissolution at the end of 2015 may have paused the modern war on obscene content, but it didn't stop it. Ofcom's takeover of VOD regulation simply means that a larger, much more powerful and opaquely funded body now dictates what is obscene for all British broadcast media, including online content. The 2017 passing of the Digital Economy Act cemented the powers of the BBFC to censor internet videos and reaffirmed all the previously mentioned lists of obscene acts. There is clearly much more at work here than our government's simply whispering, "Let's go for the extreme stuff." I do believe that some sexual lifestyles get a pass from the UK government, while others are automatically considered obscene, and I want to know why.

A quick note here for my non–British readers: UK governments serve terms of between four and five years, and unlike in the United States, it's legal for the prime minister to hold three consecutive terms of office. (Tony Blair and Margaret Thatcher are the two most recent examples of this.) It stands

One person's obscenity is another's Saturday night delight. Who should get to draw the line, and why (courtesy Hannah Crosby)?

to reason that no PM or government is going to suggest legal changes that may harm their reputation or scandalize a nation when they have, at best, a decade in which to change this country. To use an American example, Barack Obama did some great things for black, female and low-income people while he was president, but even the charming Barry only started to make headway after eight years of hard slog against racism, misogyny, homophobia and anti-immigrant vitriol. He also saw much of his good work reversed as soon as the current POTUS took office. Any UK politician with good intentions faces a similarly daunting fight, and MPs who go into Parliament with lofty social ideals will soon be brought crashing down to reality.

Jerry Barnett felt it was a simple case of priorities: there are only so many hours in the day, and even the most honest social crusader of an MP will not have the time to examine every piece of legislation thrown in their lap, or at least not in the forensic detail that we authors, journalists and lawyers can manage. I may have little money and only a tiny public profile, but I do have the time and space to sit down and take apart UK obscenity law word by word, and then write a book about it. I can also do so with no cost to my reputation, earnings or privacy. This is clearly not the case when you're a public servant. Barnett suggested that the British home secretary probably will sign any piece of paper if her advisers reassure her that the contents will result in good publicity "because it will make us look tough on pornography/pedophiles/insert other moral threat here." Michael Warner states, "The sexual order overlaps with a wide range of institutions and social ideologies. To challenge the sexual order is sooner or later to encounter those institutions as problems."[22]

Every crusader for free speech has their limits. I know that complaining about dumbing down is a sign that I'm getting old, but since I've always felt at least 92 years old in terms of cynicism and exasperation at human folly, I'm OK with that. I see around me a media landscape devoid of nuance, a terrifying number of women complacent about feminism and convinced its work is already done and an even larger number of men blissfully unaware that there was any work to be done in the first place. I see intense hostility to any changes in the status quo, be that voting to set fire to the UK economy just because you don't like having a Polish family live next door, or aggressively demanding your right to look at an 18-year-old's breasts in your daily newspaper.

This curmudgeon remains troubled by a lot of modern erotica, and I hate the thought of my six-year-old cousin stumbling across some of the images I've encountered. However, I'm old enough to know that proclaiming things obscene is not a solution. Once we buy into the idea that certain images or words can deprave or corrupt us, we start to think it's acceptable to demonize and dehumanize anyone who makes, consumes, enjoys or is aroused by them. That much has been made clear by the fact that acts currently considered obscene under UK law are carried out regularly by sane, intelligent adults, yet this not inconsiderable group of people is still dismissed as a minority of perverts, freaks and deviants.

A Sacred Cow

> "Nothing has ever been censored on the ground that it had a tendency to promote dishonesty or cruelty or cowardice. No significant legislative attempt has ever been made to suppress books except to preserve the political order, the established piety or theoretical standards of sexual behavior."—Charles Rembar, American obscenity lawyer[23]

I've often wondered what it is about sex that makes it the go-to answer when defining obscenity. Why has so much time, money and energy gone into first creating a definition of obscenity that is almost entirely preoccupied with sex, and then enforcing it through prosecutions, fines, imprisonment, persecution and public shaming?

When writing the proposal for this book in the spring of 2016, I reflected that I'd seen some awful things online just that week. A picture of human feces had appeared on my Facebook feed, a clear reminder that I needed to prune my Friends list. I'd also clicked on a story from a major UK newspaper about the murder of Reeva Steenkamp at the hands of Oscar Pistorius, only to see an image of the victim's bruised and bloodied corpse. The image had been released by the Steenkamp family deliberately to impact a public in danger of letting Pistorius's celebrity blind them to the horrific murder he committed. I completely understand the Steenkamp family's reasoning, but I'm not sure I gained anything by seeing the picture. It reminded me of a discussion in school circa 2001, when a classmate admitted they had found and watched the video of Oklahoma bomber Timothy McVeigh being executed. I don't know what my peer had hoped to gain either, but the answer is usually little more than the satisfaction of morbid curiosity.

Sexualized imagery is clearly not the only thing whose popularity and accessibility has mushroomed in the last two decades. Horrific violence is easier than ever to see, and the majority of it does not consist of CGI or special effects; it's real life. I remember watching Colonel Gaddafi's last ride in the back of a van before being executed in 2011. It was not a sleazy website that showed Gaddafi's beaten and bloodied face but the BBC news channel. In 2016, I saw previously unreleased footage of the 1989 Hillsborough football stadium disaster that will probably haunt me forever. No guts or gore were visible, but a bird's-eye view of a tangled heap of unmoving, lifeless bodies crushed at the front of a pen—completely unreachable in the chaos, all beyond help—epitomized the life-ruining horror of that day. None of these things is deemed obscene, and we as viewers understand why. The option to see them, to stare terror in the face, is an important right. It's news. It's our world.

Sex forms an escape from this world and its horrors of war, famine and genocide, not to mention constant footage of leaders in suits attending endless summits while the planet burns. Whether you view sex as for procreation or recreation—most people understand it as a mix of both—chances are you see it as providing a welcome refuge from the helplessness that accompanies watching the news. Sex makes human beings feel alive. It reminds us we have the potential to create life. And even if we don't fancy doing so, we can still use it to create connections, sensations, revelations, releases. Unfortunately for those of us who feel that way about sex, the same state machinery that sanctions the destruction of lives through wars, welfare cuts and an increasingly privatized healthcare system also functions to prevent adults from enjoying such innocuous pleasures.

2

Then and Now

"Terra-cottas depicting vaginal, anal and oral sex as well as sex work and same sex relationships, dating from 3,000 BC, have been excavated in Mesopotamia. The Ancient Greeks had laws for sedition, blasphemy and heretical expression, but none for sexual obscenity. Medieval literature also has a lot of fun with sex, and there were no laws relating to obscene material."—Kate Lister

The modern paranoia about sex and nudity forms a tiny and recent sliver of Britain's battle with obscenity. The 17th-century definition of "pervert" was "an atheist"; a modern application of the old meaning would render Richard Dawkins "one of the world's most recognizable perverts."[1] Before the original OPA passed in 1857, "expression, however lascivious or pornographic, was still deemed outside the purview of the law, so long as it was not seditious, heretical, or blasphemous."[2] Unlicensed works, which mostly consisted of deeply unsexy, dry philosophy, were energetically pursued and punished for much of the 17th, 18th and 19th centuries, while raunchy writing passed through bookshops into upper class libraries and bedrooms without anyone seeming to care. Writing about this legally hazy era, Geoffrey R. Stone makes the perceptive point that "the authorities were not concerned with obscenity.... In some odd way it feels like the UK landscape has become more sexually prudish, not less."[3]

Kate Lister, who teaches literature at Leeds University and specializes in historical representations of sexuality, told me that during the Middle Ages, the most controversial swear words in Britain were blasphemous terms such as "God's teeth" or "God's wounds." From 1557 onwards, the English government empowered the Stationers' Guild to seize and destroy works by unlicensed publishers, as well as anything considered anti-government or subversive. Lister adds that this included "pamphlets wherein any doctrine of opinion [was] asserted ... which is contrary to Christian faith," but that it made no mention of sex or modern forms of profanity.

The Stationers' Guild was a group of bookbinders, booksellers and illustrators who enjoyed a total monopoly on publishing, as you had to be a member in order to publish any written work. The Guild's role as a censor was apparently to protect readers of books, who at the time also comprised a small, educated elite. It's not clear which works were believed to threaten the moral purity of these rich and powerful souls, but a safe guess would be any book that criticized the Church, monarchy or government. In the mid–1600s, John Milton's writings on divorce were met with calls to burn his work and, if I know anything about pitchfork-wielding mobs, probably Milton himself too.

Until 1857, Britain had only a few vaguely worded laws that tangentially referred to obscenity, and no one was sure how to apply them. Just as the current spread of the World Wide Web threatens to render the OPA redundant, the Stationers' Guild saw its stranglehold on the book market disappear when printed erotica exploded across Europe after 1660, mostly "produced in limited editions for aristocratic and affluent audiences."[4] It's tough to argue against the demands of your own peers.

Several of my interviewees told me that Britain's vestigial class system is a major contributor to the current confusion over obscenity. I can certainly see how a ruling body that's almost entirely composed of middle- and upper-class, university-educated individuals would be hostile to the idea of poor and working-class people having access to culture, be that free art, free music, free movies or—yes, you're ahead of me—free pornography. Sex researcher Brooke Magnanti adds: "The history of pornography is littered with such arbitrary divides between who is assumed to be corruptible and who is not. Private galleries of Pompeiian icons of Priapus and his giant penis were once fine for men of a certain class, but not suitable to be seen by the general public."[5]

This reminds me of a passage from Margaret Atwood's dystopian 1985 novel, *The Handmaid's Tale*. This is where the Commander justifies keeping glossy women's magazines, material that has long been forbidden under the rules of the austere, misogynistic dictatorship Gilead:

> What's dangerous in the hands of the multitudes, he said ... is safe enough for those whose motives are...
> Beyond reproach, I said.
> He nodded gravely.[6]

If this comparison seems hyperbolic, remember that British women could not serve on juries until 1920, nearly 60 years after the original OPA passed. Until 1972, one also had to own property or be lead tenant in order to qualify for jury service, which rendered the pool of potential jurors overwhelmingly white, wealthy, and male. Nowadays, Britons may console themselves with the thought that their current government is more representative of the average wo/man in the street than ever before, but that's not saying very much. Parliament is currently only 29 percent female and 6 percent non-white. For a terrifying few weeks during the summer of 2016, the UK faced the prospect of swapping one white, upper-middle-class, privileged male prime minister for another who went to the same private school. That's Eton, by the way, whose alumni include Prince William.

However, classism is not a prejudice that's limited to old, sexist men. I've spent more of my writing career than I ever intended answering back to feminists who deride other women's erotica choices as hindering the movement. For the record, I can attest that there is absolutely no literary value in the book *Fifty Shades of Grey*—the prose, storyline and stunning lack of editing all make for a work of fiction so fist-chewingly bad that it's amazing anyone could have had the patience to be entranced or aroused by it. But there's no denying the numbers: millions of readers, most of them women, lapped up E. L. James's novel, plus the sequels, movies and spin-offs that followed. As I wrote when the first movie was released: "I can't help but feel that some of the outrage over *Fifty Shades* is both selective and elitist. [The book] faces the same kind of criticism that's lobbed at romance in general: 'Oh, look at those uneducated women and their trashy reads! Bless them for not knowing that classier books exist!' I wonder if many critics care less about misrepresentations of kink in the book and more about saving the undiscerning masses from themselves."[7]

The last sentence feels particularly relevant when we consider how class, educational background and social mobility still dictate the ease with which Britons may access erotica. A few months after I wrote the above, I was at a flea market selling off some of my unwanted DVDs when a teenage Irish traveler sidled up to my stall holding a copy of *Cruel Intentions* and sweetly asked my partner, "Do they take their clothes off in this film, mister?" I was touched by how innocent this lad seemed in contrast to the tech-savvy, jaded middle-class teenagers I knew, sleek adolescents who all possessed smartphones and access to a dizzying array of filth at the swipe of a screen. As part of the traveling community, this boy would have lived in a trailer or caravan and had very limited internet access if indeed he ever got online at all, so I appreciated that he had to get his kicks where he could, and smiled as my partner offloaded various '90s DVDs onto him and his friends. What this encounter emphasized to me was that those on the edges of society (and travelers are definitely subject to prejudice from all corners and classes in the UK) have always accessed erotica, had sex and whacked off when they were horny. They may have had to find more creative or underhand ways of doing so, but teenage boys are teenage boys wherever you go, and as a group they tend to like the idea of seeing Sarah Michelle Gellar in the nude. This is unsettling and bothersome to elites who prefer to think that only they are educated, intelligent and discerning enough to really handle looking at porn.

It's a British media pastime to point to any sex lives that fall outside the heterosexual, monogamous, non-kinky norm as a convenient and comforting way to distinguish yourself from the freaks; all you have to do is check the box that says you don't do *that*, therefore you're not like *them*. Even those whose job it is to stay on the right side of the law are being affected by the new conception of obscenity, one in which self-censoring features heavily. Neil Brown, a British solicitor who has provided some fantastically interesting perspectives for this book, told me, "So many lawyers have contacted me online and said, 'Are you sure you want to talk publicly about sex tech?!'" A fine may inconvenience you, a criminal record may damage your employment prospects, but few transgressions are likely to dog you as much as saying something thoughtless online. Not only can your regrettable tweet, questionable Snapchat or obnoxious Facebook post be spread across the globe and back in the time it would take for the police to knock on your door with an obscenity charge, your faux pas is guaranteed to live on in digital infamy forever. There are now whole books on internet-mob shaming, as well as the methods to deal with it. Did you know, for example, that you can pay a company to create numerous fake websites linked to your name so that you can "bury" unflattering online mentions of you on page two of Google search results—because, let's face it, whoever bothers to look there?

In April 2017, the UK government released a report titled "Hate Crime: Abuse, Hate and Extremism Online,"[8] which concludes that social-media platforms aren't doing enough to combat anti–Semitism, Islamophobia, racism and misogyny, including but not limited to violent threats against individuals. The fact that YouTube, Twitter and Facebook have refused to take down such content can be viewed as a victory for free speech or a show of contemptuous apathy, depending whom you ask. In a 2017 *Guardian* article explaining why she quit Twitter,[9] the feminist writer Lindy West says that it wasn't being called a cunt or the men who "inform me, for the thousandth time, that they would gladly rape me if I weren't so fat" that drove her to close her account but rather "the global repercussions of Twitter's refusal to stop them. The white supremacist, anti-feminist, isolationist, transphobic 'alt-right' movement has been beta-testing its propaganda and intimidation machine on marginalized Twitter communities for years now—how much hate speech will bystanders ignore? When will Twitter intervene and start protecting its users?—and discovered, to its leering delight, that the limit did not exist."

In such a digital landscape, it's hard to see what purpose is served by the OPA or any of the legislation tied to it. Adults are already deciding for themselves what they consider foul abuse and what they consider light-hearted teasing, and they're voting with their computers, tablets and smartphones. West, for one, felt that she couldn't win: "I talk back and I am 'feeding the trolls.' I say nothing and the harassment escalates. I report threats and I am a 'censor.' I use mass-blocking tools to curb abuse and I am abused further for blocking 'unfairly.'"

West adds that this normalization of hate speech "greased the wheels" for a Trump presidency, a weighty condemnation indeed. However, it's undeniable that the favored mode of communication for the leader of the free world is Twitter, and that only a few months into his presidency Donald Trump's tweets were the means most likely to escalate the world towards nuclear annihilation. Social-media platforms have limited powers to stop their millions of users from behaving obnoxiously; just as we could never expect the post office to steam open every envelope in case of what it might contain, there's no way on Earth any company can check every one of the millions of new pieces of content uploaded per hour. Also, much of the content West mentions should be caught by the net of other British laws—the 2006 Terrorism Act, for example, forbids the publishing or distribution of any material encouraging or relating to terrorism. The Communications Act 2003—that's three years before Jo/sephine Public could even create a Facebook or Twitter account—made it a crime to send messages of a "grossly offensive or of an indecent, obscene or menacing character over a public electronic communications network."

The 2017 government report claims that online hate speech has exploded, and that platforms are simply stonewalling some of those who report illegal content. It claims that Google failed to remove content from the neo–Nazi group National Action, which is supposedly on the internet giant's banned list: "Despite us making Google aware that videos that promoted National Action were available on their platform, it failed to remove numerous other videos that celebrated the far-right group. One such video featured masked men who shouted 'they fear us because they think we will gas them, and we will.'"

These are unsettling words to say the least; they may be deeply hurtful, frightening and upsetting for a Jewish person or Holocaust survivor to hear. I am not about to downplay that distress rather, I want to consider what law, if any, should apply to such statements. Under the UK's current definition, should threats which elliptically reference concentration-camp gas chambers be considered "obscene"? I've found no consensus, but a lot of dogma, surrounding this question. The rantings of National Action could, after all, simply be dismissed as unspecific threats from men who aren't even brave enough to show their faces, and therefore utterly lacking in the power to deprave or corrupt anyone who isn't already a Nazi sympathizer. Furthermore, we would do well to remember that using the anonymity provided by the internet to bully those whose words we dislike is not a pastime limited to the far right. When one-time darling of feminists and anti-racists Chimamanda Ngozi Adichie was pulled into the debate over whether the category "women" includes transgender women, many of her former supporters dragged her over the internet coals for a few ill-chosen words. Addressing the fallout, feminist writer Vonny Moyes pointed out: "Sometimes someone you love and admire will say something you don't agree with. Sometimes they'll drop an absolute clanger. Sometimes it'll be so tone deaf you wince—but that doesn't mean everything they've ever said until this point is invalid. It also doesn't mean that person loses the capacity to say important and necessary things going forward."[10]

Moyes adds that neither alleged child molester Woody Allen nor spousal abusers Mel Gibson and Casey Affleck have had their films boycotted; so why the increased speech policing among women? Perhaps the draining experience of being feminist in the digital age has left us so tired we're now pursuing any low-hanging fruit we can pluck, even when it's our own allies we're tearing down. Regarding the author of three acclaimed fiction books, plus the much-praised *We Should All Be Feminists*, Moyes goes on to say, "Adichie expressed an opinion—one that has caused controversy and has hurt many—but will her important work now be rejected? Will her books be closed? Will her lectures be protested? Will people enact a coloniality of the present and view her previous work through the prism of these words?"

In the current climate, these don't feel like rhetorical questions. The likelihood of Adichie suffering major career setbacks for expressing one unpalatable opinion is strong in an online culture of "virtue signaling," defined as loudly and publicly condemning a perpetrator in order to highlight your own moral superiority. The funny thing is, Adichie's books are *full* of unpalatable opinions—a quick skim of the Goodreads reviews of my favorite novel of hers, *Americanah*, throws up paragraphs of white outrage regarding the black female protagonists' racial critiques of modern America. Yet Adichie was never in danger of having her views muffled until feminists and the left wing got wind of them.

Sylvia Patterson's experiences as a veteran journalist navigating the shifting standards of acceptable discourse mirror my own discomfort with the one-strike-and-you're-out rule of online feminism. Patterson reported that two female artists had uttered a few less-than-complimentary words about untouchable pop-culture icon Beyoncé Knowles and was rewarded with an online dogpile that accused Patterson of misrepresenting the two women and encouraging "slut-shaming." I'm not going to dig into Patterson's account any further, although you are welcome to do the online legwork should you be hungry for more. For me, it's a story that's too depressingly familiar to doubt its accuracy. I've watched too many feminist idols, many of them British, fall like dominoes as they tweeted or wrote or said something that deviated from the dictates of intersectional feminism, and were then written off entirely as news of their transgressions spread like wildfire through the online space. Elsewhere in this book, I look at how Caitlin Moran went from British feminist icon to being labeled a privileged racist in the space of a few tweets, and I can't say that anyone comes out of that particular shitstorm looking good.

Moral panics need fuel to maintain them; social media provides this in spades. Never before have humans had instant access to so much sexualized, violent or otherwise stomach-turning images and words, and if you're looking to build a case for the suppression of a group or activity, these will provide you with plenty of campaign material. Anti-abortion activists have known this for some time, which is why they love to bring out the placards that (supposedly) show dismembered fetuses; a picture is worth a thousand pro-choice words. Anti-porn feminists love to use graphic descriptions of sexual acts to show how degrading porn is to women and in so doing end up mimicking exactly the tactics of the pornographers. Writing about Andrea Dworkin's book *Mercy*, Harriett Gilbert raised a question that echoes that of how it's possible for censors not to be "depraved and corrupted" by watching obscene material: "Why has [Dworkin] played with the fires of rape, predatory men, woman-as-victim, descriptions of torture—all within what could easily be perceived as a sexually arousing context—when she has spent so much energy trying to shield us from just these things?"[11]

I feel something similar is going on with online factions. Those at both extremes—whether defending trans women or dismissing sex work as exploitative—love nothing better than to screenshot the bad behavior of the other side, blow it up to as many dpi as their screen can take and share the hatred to show how loathsome these people are. In doing so, they are giving more airtime to allegedly harmful words. Much like how anti-porn feminists believe that *they're* allowed to luridly describe potentially arousing sex acts, but that pornographers should be banned from doing the same, it becomes acceptable to share the hateful words of a trans-exclusionary feminist as long as we claim that we're doing so in order to name and shame. That the original speaker or writer might also deserve freedom of speech is rarely, if ever, considered; you may only repeat harmful words as long as you're standing on the correct side of the divide. I don't like to overuse the term *cognitive dissonance*, but its presence is strong here.

This scramble to crucify and dismiss other feminists has much in common with the hysterical reaction to suspected pedophiles that I mention in Chapter 3. The logical extension of this mind-set—where if you say something problematic once, it renders all your other work void of value—was seen in Canada in February 2017, when the Vancouver Women's Library was subject to a protest over its lack of diverse texts. The problem was not the protesters' demand for more books that spoke to the experiences of trans women, sex workers, women of color and indigenous women—it was their request for the *removal* of 21 titles they claimed were "written by non-trans women and non-sex workers that dehumanize, speak over, and advocate harm [towards trans women and sex workers]."[12]

Feminists aligning themselves with censorship advocates is not historically unusual, but it's only recently that the work of *other feminists themselves* has moved into the crosshairs. I find this concerning, although I also recognize that it's not my place to state what is or isn't harmful to trans women or sex workers, because I'm not one. For the record, I don't support or endorse feminism that is anti-sex work, anti-trans, or anti–BDSM. However, the notion that my own writings on sex, gender and women deserve to sit in a feminist library, while the words of older, more radical feminists should be removed from those same shelves, is morally inconsistent. Such feminists may refer to the likes of me as brainwashed dupes of the patriarchy, but that is their right. Their books should be acknowledged as of their time, as outdated, embarrassing, even, but that still does not justify turning history into a propaganda exercise where less-than-flattering examples of second-wave feminism are excised altogether.

In my first book I wrote about the UK social worker—pseudonym Legally Bland—who was both sacked and arrested after a malicious ex-partner told police she had partaken in BDSM.[13] Legally Bland had to undertake and self-fund a lengthy legal battle to get her job back, on the grounds that the European Declaration of Human Rights includes the right to privacy. She won, but not without suffering significant personal and financial havoc, and all because of an allegation vaguely relating to sex. It's also worth mentioning that the police took no further action against Legally Bland after her initial arrest, but I imagine that didn't make it any easier for her to face her friends, family, neighbors and ex-workmates.

On the one hand, I believe that both the British legal system and the wider culture need to do much more to support victims of sex crimes to come forward. As I write this chapter, allegations of sexual harassment against various members of British parliament are exploding across the news; personally, I can't believe anyone who professes surprise that powerful men have got away with it for so long. However, as a writer who has extensively covered the damage that being outed as kinky can do, I'm also aware of the need to tread carefully. It remains far too easy to ruin a person's life with a careless whisper about their sex life, even if it turns out to be untrue, unfounded or simply irrelevant. Furthermore, in the age of social media, the ruination will be done in seconds, will have the potential to reach millions and can never be erased.

Many of the arguments against the Digital Economy Bill highlighted its encroachment on adult privacy, which it achieves by mandating age verification controls on all porn websites. This means adults would be obliged to enter credit-card details and/or other personal information in order to see 18- or R18-rated content. Earl Erroll objected to putting this onus on consumers, pointing out that "if a Cabinet Minister happens to view some pornography or adult material, that is perfectly legal but, if certain newspapers were to find out, the Minister's career would be destroyed overnight."

In an ideal liberal society this would not be the case, but as Richard Davenport-Hines puts it, there remains a belief among the British public and press that "collective respectability [is] maintained by newspaper bullying and abasement of vulnerable individuals."[14] I've just watched BBC News today, and the current secretary of state, Damian Green, is in the headlines over allegations that extreme pornography was found on his computer during a raid in 2008. Green strenuously denies the Metropolitan police's claims that this material was found, and says he is the victim of a smear campaign.[15] The nature of the extreme content is not specified, leaving an intrigued public to imagine videos and images of the most depraved nature possible. I have little time or sympathy for Britain's current government, and I can understand the hunger of a cynical, exhausted public to see a rich, powerful public servant get his comeuppance. However, I find it disgusting that Green's private life is being dangled over the wolves like a juicy steak dripping blood. I'd rather know why these allegations are only coming out nearly a decade later, and what was done about them at the time. I'd like to know if any adults, animals or children were harmed in making the content and if they received justice for their ordeals. If they weren't harmed, what public interest is served by shaming yet another adult who might simply enjoy BDSM-themed erotica? It's depressing that we still live in an era where our leaders are obliged to pretend they are asexual androids in order to be above suspicion. It's possible to masturbate and still be a good politician, after all.

There's a delicious irony in the way our current government censors the very acts—whipping, caning, spanking that leaves marks—that its forerunners practiced on those accused of subversive speech. Five centuries ago, a writer or publisher could be imprisoned, be branded, have their ears sliced off or their nose mutilated for any work that criticized the government, the Church or the monarchy. In 1604, English playwright Ben Jonson had both his nose and ears threatened after he poked fun at King James in the script for *Eastward Ho*; Jonson was fortunate enough to escape having his face rearranged, but he did serve jail time, along with his collaborators John Marston and George Chapman. For our ancestors, criticizing the king in fictional writing was a crime worthy of extreme and violent censure, whereas the attempted-rape scene in Jonson's 1606 work *Volpone* passed into publication without comment. In fact, the moment where the hero, Volpone, is about to force himself on his innocent victim Celia was usually played for humor on a Jacobean stage, a sign of the times that I hope appalls modern readers as much as it does me. Seventeenth-century censors had no problem with sexual violence against women, but the king's fragile ego and the illusion of inviolable royal power had to be protected by any means necessary.

The first recorded use of the word *obscene* in English history was at the 1688 trial of booksellers Joseph Streater and Benjamin Carle. However, there exists no linear nor consistent explanation for how the term went from connoting heresy to the sexual obsessions of 21st-century Britain. The sex-education guide *The Mysteries of Conjugal Love Reveal'd* was published with no outcry in 1703, despite its condoning healthy sexual appetites in both genders and dismissing society's preoccupation with female virginity. In a passage that makes this modern feminist cheer, the book bluntly states that "outmoded notions of honour … thwart Nature's purpose."[16] It's heartening to hear such a confident disavowal of sexist nonsense from over three centuries ago, and it's a statement that today's religious conservatives still badly need to hear. I do wonder how the author and publishers got away with it, though. Weirdly, no one seemed to care that much if books advocated sexual freedom, even for those evil temptresses known as women. When the odd prosecution of raunchy literature did take place, it was anomalous and never involved harsh punishment. In 1709, John Marten's *Gonosologium Novum*, which purported to be a medical sex-education guide, was accused of "intending to corrupt the subjects of the Lady the Queen," but the charges were dismissed.

In 1680, an English printer-bookseller known as John Coxe or John Tartar (I guess it depended who was asking) was accused of "debauching and corrupting young men and others of the said King's lieges and subjects" when he published the French novel *The School of Venus (L'Ecole des Filles)*. Whether it was really young men who were the target of concern or rather the vaguely mentioned "others" is up for debate. Scholar Joan DeJean believes that what the authorities really feared about this inoffensively named book is that it would "carry into [bourgeois] households information directed at their 'womenfolk,' knowledge that can give them control over all aspects of their sexuality."[17]

DeJean's claims are credible: two of the ten passages from *The School of Venus* condemned as obscene were about "contraception and sex aids"; the third dared to suggest that if women took charge of society, sex would no longer be censored or punished. It's a brave writer who challenges the patriarchal status quo, even nowadays. Take it from a feminist writer who in 2012 received a barrage of profane tweets for asking why breast cancer awareness must always be advertised using young, pert, non-malignant breasts.[18] So it doesn't surprise me to learn that over 330 years ago, a wily English publisher was arrested for publishing work that advocated for women's sexual and personal freedom.

Thanks to the totally nebulous legal system operating at the time John Coxe/Tartar was charged, we'll never know for sure what was really being punished: the advocation of unrepressed female sexuality or the questioning of male religious authority. I suspect it was a bit of both, but the censors inconsiderately never specified. The case against *The School of Venus* was brought without reference to religion or to any actual statute, and history does not even tell us how it played out. However, DeJean records that following the *School of Venus* scandal, "common law" was reinforced so that censors could prosecute a publisher without ever "determining the nature of the civil offense committed with the work's publication."[19] If that sounds completely insane and illogical to you, you're not alone.

This innovation of common law would not publicly rear its head until 1727, when Edmund Curll was charged with "disturbing the King's Peace" for publishing the anonymously penned *Venus in the Cloisters*. The book contains the kinds of push-button images that would still scandalize many Britons today—nuns engaging in sex, female masturbation, same-gender sexuality and plenty of flagellation—so it's not surprising that it earned Curll the wrong kind of attention. Scholars like Alexander Pettit believe that the book might have gone unnoticed had the author righted their wrongs by killing off the main sexual agents of the story. However, since these characters failed to die, suffer punishment or otherwise repent, and the author was unknown, it was time to pursue the book's publisher.

Pettit's idea "that the state punished was ... the representation of sex—lesbian sex in particular—that was not punished intratextually"[20] feels particularly accurate in relation to modern media. Depictions of sex or violence seem to be more acceptable to the censors as long as the offending characters come to a gory end, because then we can feel reassured that the deviants got their comeuppance. It strikes me as a plausible explanation for why murdered sex workers are such a staple of modern TV and film crime drama. What better way to avoid confronting collective unease about the way our society, media and legal system view and treat sex workers than to ensure all storylines relating to sex work end up in a police mortuary. It could, of course, just be simple misogyny, program makers getting their kicks by showing beaten and bloodied bodies of young attractive women; I've yet to see the body of a handsome young male sex worker lying on a slab, but then I can't stomach trawling through enough episodes of *CSI* to find one. As I detail much more in Chapter 7, America's Motion Picture Production Code of the early 20th century would make this idea official: you could only show crime in a movie if you emphasized to the viewers that it didn't pay.

As for the *Venus in the Cloisters* prosecution, Edmund Curll was imprisoned for two years and fined, and had to stand for an hour on the pillory at Charing Cross. In the absence of any stone or rotten fruit being hurled at him, Curll merely served his hour in peace and then was lifted down on to his friends' shoulders and carried to the nearest pub for a restorative ale. Not a bad outcome for a convicted smut peddler.

The Original OPA

Although the Victorian era is presumed to be one of continuous sexual repression, the people of 19th-century Britain defy any neat or polarized categories regarding their attitude towards obscenity. The publication of erotic material actually thrived during Queen Victoria's reign: *Lady Bumtickler's Revels, Colonel Spanker's Experimental Lecture,* and the intriguing *Story of a Dildo* are just a few of the hilariously named erotic books one could purchase. Apart from the honorifics pointing to a deeply entrenched class system, these sweetly kinky titles could be mistaken for comical names of modern porn films.

Historians have often preferred to emphasize the flipside to this fun smut: that is, fervent public condemnation of masturbation, prostitution and any act that wasn't procreative sex within marriage. While preachers and MPs spoke out against such immoral sources of pleasure, London's Holywell Street, which functioned as a sort of forerunner to Soho, was a hotbed of smutty publication, and in 1845 a raid on two dealers yielded over 27,000 obscene prints plus 555 books. History does not specify where, or in whose hands, these materials came to rest. Groups such as the Society for the Formation of Manners, set up to target prostitutes and pornographers, had foundered in the 1700s but reemerged with book-burning vigor in Victorian Britain. The Society for the Suppression of Vice was established in 1802 and over the next half-century would bring 159 prosecutions against publishers and booksellers in Holywell Street. The Society was instrumental in passing the Vagrancy Act, which criminalized the public sale of indecent material, and as Geoffrey Robertson puts it, "served as an amateur Obscene Publications squad, their puritan zeal overcoming procedural difficulties which hampered routine police action."[21] Still, the vigilante powers of the Society were limited—by 1857 there were still at least twenty bookshops operating on Holywell Street. This was fortuitous timing, because a new weapon was about to emerge in the fight against printed filth; this was the year that Lord Chief Justice Campbell brought his Obscene Publications Bill to Parliament.

Campbell introduced his bill with a statement of intent to clean up Holywell Street and its beneficiaries. The country badly needed such a law, he added, because "a sale of poison more deadly than ... strychnine or arsenic—the sale of obscene publications and indecent books"[22] was corrupting the populace. Anti-vice groups were delighted, but the bill actually met considerable opposition in both the House of Lords and the House of Commons. The objections from Lords and MPs highlighted exactly the problem we are still arguing about today, namely the bill's total failure to define obscenity. One person's idea of fine literature or art could be another's idea of despicable smut, and as Lord Lyndhurst—himself a former chief justice, and strongly opposed to the bill—pointed out in a statement of striking clairvoyance: "An act of Parliament does not mean what its sponsors intend it to mean, but what later generations of judges want it to mean."[23]

In the 160-plus years since the Obscene Publications Act was first passed, the truth of Lyndhurst's words has been demonstrated so many times that there simply isn't space to list them in this book. Even though Lord Campbell scrambled to reassure Parliament that works of art or literature would not be targeted under the OPA, that is exactly what happened. In 1868, a vaguely erotic anti–Catholic pamphlet, *The Confessional Unmasked*, was found to be obscene, and it's anyone's guess whether that was due to the sexual content or the criticism of religion. Few remember the publication or its contents, since both were quickly eclipsed by Lord Chief Justice Cockburn's famous statement that obscenity required "a tendency to deprave and corrupt."

Finally, the anti-vice crusaders and legislators had what they wanted—a law against obscenity and a wonderfully vague, subjective definition under which they could categorize anything that personally offended them. The OPA meant that parts of a book could be judged out of context; if a section of a work was considered obscene, the whole work would be banned. American obscenity lawyer Charles Rembar adds disgustedly, "Note how thoroughly repressive this is. The Crown need not demonstrate that harm *will* occur, or even that it is likely—all that is needed is a 'tendency.'"[24]

A Little Education

The Victorian war on obscenity now had legal backing, and with terrible predictability, the first heads to go on the chopping block belonged to those trying to educate, rather than arouse. There may still be significant problems with sex education today, but that's nothing compared to what our ancestors had to endure. They were presented with "scientific" books stating that the left testicle spawned male children while the right brought female progeny, and that women were most sexual in spring and autumn due to the balance of the Four Humors, a belief left over from Ancient Greek medicine. A paradoxical situation persisted throughout the 17th, 18th and 19th centuries, whereby sex was out in the open, in the form of rampant street prostitution, and widely written about—from Restoration pornography to smutty cartoons mocking the prince regent—yet the average person was still likely to be hopelessly misinformed about the basics of reproduction, contraception and sexual biology. This, of course, is presuming our foremothers and -fathers could even read, which was by no means a given for the average Briton until well into the latter half of the 20th century.

The Victorian take on the OPA did not consider that books about sex could actually benefit the populace, and in 1874, all copies of *The Fruits of Philosophy,* a book advocating birth control, were seized and destroyed. The book had already been available for forty years, so what possible benefit this U-turn could have had for British society is anyone's guess. The pointlessness of trying to censor a book that has long been distributed has been matched by 21st-century efforts to control what can be seen on the internet. Furthermore, anyone who watches the news will be well aware of what happens to a cultural artifact when it is banned: its stock immediately rises, as our natural fascination with the forbidden comes into play. In *Thinking Kink,* I described what happened in 1984 when the BBC banned Frankie Goes to Hollywood's song "Relax" from both radio and TV: "The British public, perhaps operating on the prurient assumption that if something gets banned, then it must be interesting, rewarded the moralists by sending the song to number one for five weeks."[25]

In a similar manner, the trial regarding *The Fruits of Philosophy* (whose obscenity conviction was quashed on appeal anyway) had only one result: the book's circulation leapt from a few hundred copies sold a year to 120,000.[26] Suffragist and left-wing activist Annie Besant, one of those tried for publishing the book, saw her own pamphlet, *The Law of Population,* sell 175,000 copies over the next decade.

Unfortunately, the misuse of obscenity law to stop ordinary people from learning about contraception continued in Victorian Britain. The Malthusian League, founded in 1877 with the purpose of spreading information about birth control, was "declared illegal, its publications pornographic, in part because they were priced to be affordable to working-class people."[27] Doctor and "political radical" Henry Albutt dared to publish a cheap pamphlet, *The Wife's Handbook,* aimed at educating poor and working-class women about contraception; his reward was to be struck from the Medical Register in 1887, after the Leeds Vigilance Association grassed him up to the General Medical Council. The 1889 Indecent Advertisements Act made posters and handbills advertising contraception illegal, presumably to protect the working classes from information their middle- and upper-class counterparts had long been free to access.

This was in spite of the fact working-class women had long been practicing birth control, often as a means of survival in a time when death in childbirth was not uncommon. As Susie Steinbech records, "Women were more eager to control family size than men, and used many [contraceptive] strategies without consulting or even informing their partners." Since Victorian doctors were too afraid of prosecution to advocate birth control to their female patients, "women often learned about birth control techniques

Sometimes the best publicity a work can receive is to be condemned as obscene; nothing entices an audience more (courtesy Emily Brady)!

from other women, including family members, friends and neighbours."[28] Not to be thwarted by the squeamishness of lawmakers, Victorian people devised their own methods of preventing pregnancy, and many small business owners capitalized on this market. "Something for the weekend, sir?" was the barber's way of asking his male clientele if they required condoms, a fact I learned in chemistry class when I was 15 (thank you, Dr. Legg, for answering my somewhat off-topic question!). Hats off to those Victorians who were at least trying to use prophylactics, because STIs were endemic, and highly dangerous backstreet abortions were commonplace. Apothecaries and medicine women offered potions that would clear "menstrual blockages," and any herbalist will know the effect pennyroyal tea is meant to have on the female reproductive system.

Roy Porter and Lesley Hall sum up Victorian Britain's seething mass of hypocrisy and repression thus: "all rules had many exceptions, any generalization was readily contradictable."[29] Moral-purity campaigners demanded higher standards while MPs sexually abused exploited children (I refuse to use the term *child prostitute*, as it implies both choice and agency on the part of the child); marriage was held up as sacred, and wives were meant to be sexually ignorant angels, while their husbands visited sex workers "fallen women" in droves. These paradoxes retain great power to fascinate Britons today; period TV dramas such as the lesbian-themed *Tipping the Velvet* or the subtly sexy account of a poor girl working in an Edwardian-era department store *The Paradise* have gone down a treat with 21st-century audiences.

As for what my great-great-grandmother or her daughters might have felt or thought about sex? History does not record it, and I have Lord Campbell to thank for that.

3

Won't Somebody Please Think of the Children?!

"If you believe that sex is dirty, then *everyone* has a dirty mind."—Robert Mapplethorpe[1]

While selling copies of my first book at a roller-derby fund-raiser, I found myself walking the fine line between publicizing my work and not offending the many parents of young children who were in attendance. I decided that as a vendor who had paid for my pitch, I had the right to advertise my book however I wished, so I brought along lengths of purple rope, a pink suede flogger and my favorite bright-red spanking paddle printed with a shiny lipstick mark pattern. I reasoned that if those items didn't catch potential buyers' attention, nothing would. Thankfully they did, and I merrily sold and signed books, chatted with members of the roller-derby community and also attracted the inevitable attention of nearby children. A seven-year-old boy picked up the paddle and asked me what it was.

Being child-free by choice and an introverted curmudgeon, I've never had much time for kids and their endless questions, but I also don't believe in lying to them. So I replied, "It's whatever you want it to be." The boy grinned impishly, waved the paddle around a bit and proclaimed, "It's a sword!" I smiled with relief and said, "En garde!" then chatted with the boy about how to sword-fight properly. That was the extent of the awkward questions from children about my kinky toys not just that day, but ever.

For the rest of the day, my new friend and his five-year-old sister played around on my selling table, coloring in labels, handing out flyers for me and providing me some great free PR. At various times throughout the day, they picked up the paddle, the flogger and the rope, had a merry time playing with them and never once asked me a question that I couldn't answer honestly with a PG-rated statement. It confirmed my belief that children generally consider adult activities boring and have little to no curiosity about them. Children want to play, and all they require me to do is pay them some attention and tell them the truth. It's my fellow adults who are obsessed with placing a sexualized gloss on everything.

Still, if there's one guaranteed argument-stopper in conversations about obscenity, it's "but what about CHILDREN?" Trying to liberalize or remove obscenity law is near-impossible once someone mentions the innocence of under–18s; one wrong step and you've effectively admitted you don't care if young eyes fall on hard-core pornography. Even worse, you'll be painted as an apologist for child abusers and pedophiles, who are viewed by Western society on a par with horse manure or vermin. This emotive, manipulative tactic has been deployed in obscenity debates since the beginning of time; Socrates was accused of corrupting the young, and look what happened to him. The argument may not be based on methodologically sound findings, it may not be based on anything other than instinct and emotion, but *damn* is it persuasive.

Whether it's the British government wasting time, energy and taxpayers' money to try to stop children from accessing explicit images online, or the intimidation of small independent porn producers by ATVOD, wherever reasonable arguments are at a low ebb, we will hear the *Simpsons* character Helen Lovejoy's craven plea: "Won't somebody please think of the children?!"

Children and the Law

> "[A book must be] judged by its effects on an intelligent adult, and not a fourteen-year-old schoolgirl, otherwise English literature would be confined to nursery rhymes."— Mr. Justice Sable, addressing a UK court in the 1950s[2]

This eminently reasonable and sensible distinction was made by a UK judge over 65 years ago. Unfortunately, British authorities have done their best in the intervening time to either forget or obscure Judge Sable's words. At the time of writing, one of the principal factors in deciding whether a work meets the CPS standards for obscenity is "where children are likely to access material of a degree of sexual explicitness equivalent to what is available to those aged 18 and above" and "where publication took place, especially if material can be readily seen by the general public, for example in a newsagents or market, or websites easily accessible to children."

The presumed innocence of all children is a persuasive argument for censoring adult content, but not one supported by available research (courtesy Emily Brady).

This implies that the obscenity of material and its accessibility to under 18 are synonymous, when they're clearly not. It also shows British lawmakers to be influenced with terrifying ease by the force of the hysteria surrounding child abuse. A kind, intelligent father of two small children recently said to me, "When it comes to adults you don't know, you presume everyone's a pedophile." I laughed, thinking he was joking—it turned out he was not. Fair enough, I thought, I'm not a parent and I can only imagine how horrifying the thought of anyone hurting your child must be. However, I did point out to him that, statistically speaking, those most likely to abuse a child are relatives or family friends. He didn't seem very receptive to this fact, and in a world where most parents seem exhausted, depressed and frightened about the future, I couldn't blame him. I do, however, blame a culture that prizes mob rule and vigilante justice over actually protecting children.

3. Won't Somebody Please Think of the Children?!

I also believe that any work should be evaluated for obscenity *regardless* of whether children are able to easily access it. I believe that this is the whole point of obscenity law, given that children accessing material intended for over-18s is already a crime under the 1978 Child Protection Act.[3] Otherwise, we run the risk of conflating "adult" with "obscene," because Lord knows children will instinctively seek out, discover and be attracted to anything grown-ups try to hide from them. It's the eternal pull of the forbidden fruit, and every human being knows what it feels like.

It is frighteningly easy for UK censors to pounce on imagery that they dislike and then bolster their case with the assertion that "children could have accessed it." Independent porn producers Blake and Mistress Megara Furie both found this out to their cost. In addition to the accusations detailed in Chapter 1, the pair were also accused of violating AVMS Rule 11, which demanded their websites have age verification controls in place. This isn't the terrible faux pas it sounds like; we're talking about a tiny technicality unlikely to protect any children.

In a 2017 speech to the Open Rights Group, Blake clarified: "My site accepted debit cards, and at the time ATVOD was of the opinion that the only way you could stop under–18s looking at online porn was to have it protected by credit-card access-only."[4] As Blake has regularly pointed out, accepting credit cards simply increases the financial burden on website owners. Demanding credit-card details from every visitor to your site also encourages fraud and data harvesting, and it is not going to stop any under–18 if they are hell-bent enough on seeking out explicit content. So, hardly a concerted campaign to shove smut in children's faces, but rather an understandable cost-cutting exercise by a small-business provider.

There are, thankfully, activists and technologists speaking out against this illogical situation. Andy Phippen, a professor of social responsibility in information technology who regularly talks to teenagers about online safety, said, "It's a very brave person who tries to say there's no way children could access [their site]." As the ways of sharing online content multiply and fragment, there is simply no watertight way to keep children out.

The jurors in the 1960 *Lady Chatterley*'s trial were unmoved when the prosecution asks, "Would you approve of your young sons, young daughters … reading this book? Is it a book you would have lying around your own house?" By 1979, Geoffrey Robertson had correctly identified that the "what if CHILDREN saw it?" argument "loaded the dice against defendants, who were hard put to convince juries that erotic writing would not affect some little boy or girl, or some mentally disturbed adult, into whose hands it might conceivably fall."[5] If even a pre-internet legal expert could see the futility in trying to keep books and magazines out of children's hands, why are we pretending today that we have any more power to keep the monolith that is the internet from seeping into their lives?

Straw Men

Numerous interviewees for this book described the UK government's attitude towards explicit content as deliberately divisive. Blake, Phippen and Jerry Barnett characterized the polarization thus: either you support online age verification, however ineffective or burdensome, or you must actively want children to see porn. In this climate, who is going to be brave enough to put their head above the parapet? In an email describing her experience with ATVOD, Mistress Megara Furie told me she was horrified to be accused of making her videos available to under–18s: "I had a panic attack. I was sick to my stomach at the thought of someone underage having access to my clips. I instantly saw my name on the sex-offenders register, me writing to my family from prison…"

And who wouldn't feel sick, in a culture that condemns pedophilia so loudly that common sense is regularly silenced? In the year 2000, after now-defunct UK tabloid *News of the World* campaigned to name and shame sex offenders, vigilante violence drove five innocent families from their homes, all incited by on the mistaken belief that they were harboring pedophiles.[6] British pediatrician Dr. Yvette Cloete was driven from her home by some not-terribly-bright individuals who confused her job title with the word "paedophile" and graffitied the front of her house with "PAEDO." No wonder Megara Furie was frightened, if this is the treatment meted out to those *mistakenly* identified as child molesters. Furie was facing *actual* prosecution, as if her website's only accepting debit cards were morally equivalent to child abuse. She added that ATVOD promised not to identify her if she complied with its demands, "but then went ahead and printed a news blog featuring my case, head-on-a-stick style, and my photograph was in all the national papers. I had to move house due to the anxiety they caused for me and the strain it put on the relationship between my landlord and me."

Anxiety is putting it mildly when you're expecting a flaming-torchwielding mob to turn up on your doorstep any second. This is the crux of the issue, though; mention child sex abuse, and sense, especially in the British right-wing media, flies out of the window. It's the ultimate conversation-stopper. People will sympathize with your right to free speech up to the point where you get accused of being a pedophile (or even just a pediatrician). Then you're on your own. Megara Furie knew this, which is why she complied with the request to take down the offending videos. As did Blake and Mistress R'eal. These hardworking businesswomen knew the odds were stacked against them, even though they had done nothing to harm any children. It's hard enough fighting the charge that you're publishing perverted filth online, never mind trying to defend against the accusation that you made that material too easily accessible to young eyes.

"They could take all the porn in the world and bury it on a desert island and I'd still find it," a 14-year-old boy told Andy Phippen during a visit to a British school. Phippen believes this is a common and healthy attitude for a 14-year-old boy to have, and as a former curious teen myself, I'd add it's not that uncommon for 14-year-old girls either. As far back as 1932, Aldous Huxley was bravely putting his head above the parapet when he wrote about children engaged in erotic play with one another in *Brave New World* and did not condemn the idea.

> For a very long period before ... erotic play between children had been regarded as abnormal (there was a roar of laughter); and not only abnormal, actually immoral (no!): and therefore had been rigorously suppressed.
> A look of astonished incredulity appeared on the faces of his listeners. Poor little kids not allowed to amuse themselves? They could not believe it.[7]

Of course, the fact that Huxley's *Brave New World* is read as a dystopia could easily discredit these words as the depiction of a twisted society where human relationships have gone awry. However, seeing as many of Huxley's predictions not only have come to pass but are seen as very beneficial to modern society—contraception, IVF, women's rights, the acceptance of family structures beyond monogamy and heterosexuality—I think he was craftily protesting the way children suffered repression because of adult discomfort with sexuality. In Huxley's *Brave New World*, this leads to arrested development: people who don't discover sex "till they were over twenty years old."

Modern readers may find the idea of people refraining from sex until they're out of their teens sweetly archaic, but it's not actually that unusual in 21st-century Britain. A hysterical media determined to depict the younger generation as having more sex (and having it earlier) than any previous generation won't tell you this. Teen pregnancy rates actually halved in the UK in the years between 2007 and 2014, with experts speculating that social media may be causing teenagers to refrain from risky sexual behavior by keeping them indoors and glued to screens, rather than out getting up to mischief in real life.[8] The continuing insistence on slotting all children into the binary categories of innocent angels or sex-mad delinquents is what makes Huxley's words on the sexuality of children all the more explosive with age. Hysteria regarding the sexualization of children and the specter of child sex abuse makes it ever harder to have any kind of rational debate on whether obscenity law actually protects anyone, and whether children even need or want such protection.

Bad Science

When UK media and government polarize the option so that either you support censorship or you're happy to harm children, few MPs will be brave enough to stand up and support free access to adult material. Yet the threat to children from adult erotica is a mere construct, and one rarely discussed in a rational manner. A 2015 National Society for the Prevention of Cruelty to Children (NSPCC) survey claimed that 10 percent of 12- and 13-year-olds were worried that they were addicted to pornography. The then-culture secretary, Sajid Javid, responded by demanding age-verification controls on all adult websites. I can't cite this survey because it's no longer available on the NSPCC's website, and that's because its findings were completely debunked.

Marketing Today dismissed OnePoll, the organizers of the survey, as totally untrustworthy: "What is reported to be scientific is not in fact genuine research at all, but dishonest marketing concocted by PR firms."[9] In a speech to the Open Rights Group, Myles Jackman added that the NSPCC's methodology was so unscientific as to render the results useless: "It was ridiculous to have a parent who had gone to a site like Money SavingExpert, think, 'I can get a few quid doing some online polls,' sitting their child with them and saying, 'ARE YOU WORRIED ABOUT PORNOGRAPHY, LITTLE CHILD?!' and 'surprisingly' receiving the answer 'What do you think, Mum?' The dimensions of parent-pleasing there are horrific, and it seems incredibly dubious."

One of the most provocative and widely shared statistics used in articles and studies that demand better protection for children from explicit material is that the average age at which a boy first sees pornography is 11 years old.[10] Yet when American journalist Seth Lubove traced this claim back to its origins, he found it had none. The 11-year-old statistic entered the media via a 2005 *Boston Globe* article, which cited a Utah-based organization called Family Safe Media as its source. The owner of FSM claims he got these statistics from Internet Filter Review, a website that recommends content-blocking software—so far, so biased. The IFR is run by

Jerry Ropelato, who, Lubove found, "pens antiporn screeds ... and publishes curious and uncredited stats."[11]

But wait! It gets even more ridiculous. Jerry Ropelato claims to have found the age-11 statistic in a book called *The Drug of the New Millennium*. This was published in 2000, before many of today's teenagers were even born, by a self-described former porn addict, Mark Kastleman. He also comes from Utah, and comments breezily, "I don't remember where I got that from. That is a very common statistic." At this point Lubove gave up, having found nothing to support the claim except one big echo chamber of confirmation biases. The only voices pushing the statistic came from conservative, probably religious proselytizers with an agenda to push and books to sell.

Michele L. Ybarra, Ph.D., and Kimberly J. Mitchell, Ph.D., conducted a study in 2005 looking at 1,500 11- to 17-year-olds and found that 87 percent of them reported first looking for sexual images online at 14 or older: "The majority of youth who seek pornography are simply age-appropriately curious about sex."[12] A 2008 study[13] also gives 14 as the average age at which people first viewed pornography. As Shira Tarrant, a U.S. academic specializing in sexuality studies, adds, "There is a significant distinction between an 11-year-old preteen and a teenager who is 14-going-on-15 years old." Any parent, or indeed any human being, who recalls adolescence—and I regularly do, mostly with horror and relief that it's over—will attest to this important truth.

Granted, these are American, not British, statistics, but given the cultural and legal similarities between the two countries, I would not expect British youth to be much different. A 2012 report by the London School of Economics and Open Rights Group expressed concern at the dubious statistics put forward by the Safety Net campaign, which advocates for placing adult-content filters on all internet services as standard. The report criticizes Safety Net's unquestioning acceptance of the claim that "one in three 10-year-olds has seen pornography online"[14] when this is based on nothing more than "a discussion that *Psychologies* magazine had with an unknown number of 14–16 year old boys at one school."

Instead, the LSE study found that "most children have not experienced sexual images online and, even of those who have, most say they were not bothered or upset by them." It goes on to say that "even assuming some under-reporting, it seems that media hype over pornography is based on unrepresentative samples or just supposition." Also, the notion that children *should* be worried or upset if they see explicit images is something media-savvy youth will pick up on. Then we end up with children telling adult researchers what they think they want to hear, especially when they're aware of how invested many adults are in the belief that porn traumatizes children. Put another way, if your parents caught you watching an erotic film, wouldn't it be easier to dodge responsibility by saying you just stumbled upon it, and what you saw really upset you, rather than saying it bored you or, God forbid, admitting you liked what you saw? Confessing to the latter opens the way for you to be condemned as a pervert; the former allows you to fly under the radar.

As for the studies the British regulations are based on? Ofcom's *own statement on the issue* admits they have found no evidence of a link between seeing porn and harm for children. This information is available in an online report, yet I've never seen the report mentioned or cited in mainstream UK media. It's only thanks to independent bloggers such as Blake that I'm able to quote it here. "1.8 Research does not provide conclusive evidence that R18 material 'might seriously impair' minors' development. Secondly, the research does not provide clear, conclusive evidence of a lesser degree of harm."

The report surveyed 20 countries, 15 from the EU, and "no country has found conclusive evidence that sexually explicit material harms children." Furthermore, the section of the report given over to the question of "Potential harm: what effects does R18 standard material have on under–18s?" could be summarized as "We couldn't find any." These findings are buried in the report, far below justifications for implementing "sufficient safeguards" to keep under–18s from seeing R18 material. This is why I believe it is crucial to question the claims that pornography poses harm to under–18s, and why we must protest laws that invade adult privacy based on this assumption.

A Disclaimer

It's important to state at this point that as a feminist and vocal champion of bodily autonomy and consensual sex between adults, I do know a fair bit about child abuse and its effects. I was a carer for a woman in her mid-30s who, thanks to a man's raping her when she was a child, has suffered debilitating PTSD, chronic pain and MS-like symptoms for the past two decades. We are still great friends, and I have nothing but admiration for her strength and tenacity in the face of severe disability. I do not believe her assailant has ever faced any justice; I can't say for sure, but I know how difficult it remains in the UK to obtain a conviction for rape or child sexual abuse. If I ever met this man, I would happily put a bullet between his eyes for what he did to my friend.

3. Won't Somebody Please Think of the Children?!

A few years before I met this friend, I worked as a carer for a hugely obese woman who could barely leave her armchair, let alone her home. I learned from other carers that this lady had been molested as a child, and then gone on to marry an abusive man. She was now divorced and lived alone in a tiny apartment. Her massive weight gain was an attempt to protect herself from male attention; she would not let any male person in her home, even to read the electric meter. Yet, to us, she was a kind, funny woman who loved her cat, hamster and budgerigar. She welcomed us carers into her cluttered apartment and was always happy to chat with us. She constantly knitted items for charity, even though she herself lived on welfare payouts. The way her life was so hemmed in thanks to child sexual abuse appalled me; it felt so unjust. I hope she's still out there and OK, but this may be very wishful thinking on my part.

I've met and heard stories of people who were beaten black and blue as children; people who've attempted suicide because of abuse they suffered from a parent (one of whom emailed her suicide note to me, but thankfully is still alive); people who grew up in such aggressive, abusive homes that they never raise their voices as adults. In the kink scene, I met a woman who was raped by a man she met at a concert. The man, who also never faced any justice, told her, "You must like it because you're kinky" as he forced himself on her. With terrible predictability, this woman blamed herself, calling it "my fuck-up."

This litany of human misery isn't intended to shock or serve as an excuse for censorship, but it is meant to emphasize that I would happily set fire to anyone who ever violates another human's bodily autonomy. I would watch such people burn and would not even urinate on them to put the fire out. Not all my interviewees seem to feel this way, which, I'll admit, dismayed me. A soft-spoken, intelligent father of three kept dodging my question of whether he intended to raise his kids with a respect for consent, as if this was a minor issue. I suspected that when his infant daughter got a bit older, it would become a *major* issue for him, as I've seen several men have their consciousness raised by parenting girls. Yet this man did not believe that distributing, downloading or viewing child-abuse footage was a matter for the law; he believed that only those who were physically carrying out the abuse should be prosecuted.

I'm deliberately not naming this man because (a) he is entitled to his view and (b) he is a nice person who doesn't deserve a mob descending on his doorstep, but I'd like to contrast his beliefs with a judge's words about a recent case in my city. Sixty-year-old David Minister was jailed for six months after police found that he had used a hidden camera to spy on his lodgers in the bathroom. Minister's computer was then searched, and police found 140 Category A images of children—"the worst possible category"—as well as 399 Category B and C images. Judge Catherine Tulk was unequivocal in deeming the man culpable: "Nobody for one second should think that possessing images of children is a victimless offence just because the images are already there to be seen."[15] Having seen the far-reaching effects child abuse has on people's lives, I can only agree with Tulk, and strongly disagree with my libertarian interviewee.

An Inconvenient Truth

As the Digital Economy Bill made its way through the various hoops of UK government, debate raged about the proposal to introduce ID checks for accessing online porn. Those against the bill pointed out that the very demographic being protected comprised the ones most likely to figure out the get-arounds. Andy Phippen told me that an 11-year-old boy gave him a tip on how to circumvent adult filters: "just type the link in Arabic," apparently! Regardless of our efforts to keep under–18s away from adult content, every child will hit the age of 18 one day and be released into a dizzyingly explicit and liberal world. Wouldn't it be a good idea to start laying the groundwork now? As Phippen reminds us, there is no porn-free utopia where children can somehow be protected from the realities of the world: "You can't make kids safe. What you can do is make them resilient."

Another important point to remember is that once the secretive and authority-phobic teen years begin, the lines between protector and protected rapidly start to blur. One of the more enjoyable moonlighting jobs I've taken in order to support my writing work is tutoring high-school students in English. Working one-on-one with nearly fifty 15- to 18-year-olds in the past decade has given me great insight into life as a teenager in 21st-century Britain, and what has repeatedly struck me is that whether it's regarding sex, drugs or schoolwork, teenagers constantly make calculations about the cost of telling their parents the truth versus telling them what they believe their sweet, naïve, fuddy-duddy folks can handle. You have to ask yourself, who is really protecting whom here? Furthermore, who knows the modern world best: the parental generation who have watched as their values became obsolete, or the young people who have been at the coalface as new values have emerged? As director John Waters says in the 2006 documentary *This Film Is Not Yet Rated*, "All teenagers, because of the internet, have seen more hard-core pornography than their parents have seen. They've seen the most hideous things you can find on the internet, believe me."

Teenagers rejecting their parents' values is a necessary and natural part of the generation gap, which is as old as time itself. Socrates's critics complained that the youths he educated were becoming willful, subversive and anti-establishment: *plus ça change*. What my tutees regularly demonstrated to me was that when young people feel they are being unnecessarily "protected" from something they do not even fear, they will simply find covert ways to get around said protection.

Furthermore, I am living proof that children find risqué material even when there's no broadband connection in sight, and that such formative experiences are not harmful. The first time this author encountered a really explicit image was at the age of 12, in a book of erotic artwork. I found it among the belongings of a deceased relative, as my family was sorting out what could be sold and what needed throwing away. Upon discovering the book—which showed Chinese drawings of cunnilingus, and a black-and-white photo of a woman going down on a man—I remember thinking, "Oh, so *that's* what that looks like." This was 1996, long before internet access was standard in the majority of UK homes. It predated tablets, smartphones, and even the era when everyone owned a mobile phone. I looked at the book, ready to guiltily hurl it back onto the pile if an adult walked in, felt a little aroused, and then put it back and carried on with my 12-year-old business. No permanent scars, no sexual trauma: just some pictures of sex and some natural adolescent curiosity.

Going Offline

Whether it's due to modern erotica's ubiquity, its more graphic nature or the idea that it's all so much nastier, more violent and more gratuitous than porn ever used to be, British lawmakers and journalists continue to act as if digital pornography is automatically more harmful than any pre-internet smut. I would love to know if anyone making this claim ever read *The Story of O*, published in 1959, or any of the Marquis de Sade's work, but I digress. The belief is just not borne out by research. A 2012 LSE study said that while a quarter of UK nine- to 16-year-olds had seen sexual images, only 11 percent were seeing the images online.

So where were the rest of these children seeing risqué pictures or films? Probably on Page 3, where UK newspaper *The Sun* published a full-page picture of a topless woman every weekday from 1972 until 2016, when it finally dropped the practice. *The Sun* is the most popular newspaper in Britain and sells three million copies a day, by the way. I'm guessing a fair few teens also saw such pictures in lads' mags, soft-porn publications popular from the mid–'90s until recently that could be sold to under–18s because they avoided being marked "top shelf" material. I took some covert looks at my brother's copies of *FHM* when I was 14, mostly skimming past the shots of scantily clad, airbrushed glamour models to read some of the surprisingly well-written articles in the hope of gaining an insight into the mind-set that made men create and buy these magazines. As a teen who went to an all-girls school, had only started kissing boys the previous year and wouldn't do much more for another four years, I found lads' mags a fascinating source of real sex education, of a kind that I was never going to get at school or even in any of the fiction books in which I was constantly immersed.

The models in these magazines annoyed me with their moronic, Barbie-like poses, but they melded into a landscape of perky, pouting gloss after a few pages anyway. I was a well read but completely sexually inactive 14-year-old, and while I'd received pretty decent sex education from my school and parents, no adult women had ever talked plainly to me about their sexual appetites. Therefore, it was refreshing to sneak a peek at *FHM*'s reader sex survey, and gape at one respondent saying she would only give up sex "if someone sewed my fanny shut," or another who answered the question "Tell us something about your sex life no one else knows" with "My boyfriend likes to go down on me when I'm on my period."

Thinking back to this also reminds me of the double standards at work with regard to high and low forms of culture. No one has ever explained to my satisfaction why material that would be considered obscene if it weren't in a work of great literature gets a pass from the censors. If it's a crime to expose teenagers to unhealthy constructions of sexuality, why were *The Color Purple* (which contains graphic descriptions of rape, incest and woman-beating) and *To Kill a Mockingbird* (ditto) in my school library and on the GCSE syllabus? How does Angela Carter's *The Bloody Chamber*, with its graphic descriptions of necrophilia, bestiality and vampiric sex, end up being regularly taught to 16- and 17-year-olds?

For this '90s teen, *Sex and the City* and *Queer as Folk* would appear on UK television near the turn of the millennium and answer some of my questions about sex. Unfortunately, *SATC* still danced around subjects way more than lazy journalists of today care to remember. The show has often been feted for its open attitudes to sex and groundbreaking portrayals of female sexuality, yet it never explained how women went from being penetrated to having screaming orgasms in the space of 20 seconds, a misconception for which the media now solely blames pornography. *Queer as Folk* came out around the same time and was a hilarious, sexy and fun look at the lives of young gay men, but it could only teach a heterosexual female so much.

Now I'm in my 30s and have little interest in telling other adults how to parent their children, unless it's about getting them to behave in restaurants. That said, I believe that if you deem it necessary to give an 11-year-old an iPad, then it's up to you to supervise what your child does with this piece of technology. That's not to say that you must violently police their screen time, but you do have to roll with the punches in this world of instant digital access. You can't lead a hungry creature to a smorgasbord and then expect them only to snack on one of the dishes; in the same spirit, it would be nice to see more individual responsibility taken for what children look at online. As Joanne Cantor, a U.S. researcher on ratings systems, points out, "Parental discretion warnings [can] stimulate some children's interest in viewing programs." This, Cantor says, is more about "desire to reject control over their viewing than ... their seeking out violent [or sexual] content." In other words, relying on adult filters and government finger-wagging is no substitute for talking to your kids sensibly about the dark corners of the internet.

I'd add that if your child is intelligent, well behaved and quiet, as this author was for most of her childhood and teenage years, there is no better cover for curiosity. I doubt my parents had any idea of what I was looking at when I was 12 or 14, and I was adept at recording edgy TV shows like the ones mentioned above (onto VHS, so vintage) and then watching them when I was alone in the house. However, knowing I was a bright adolescent with a reading ability beyond my years, my parents took the very wise step of not rendering any particular piece of media more appealing by labeling it forbidden. I spent my teenage years gorging myself on literature and pop culture, with no adult ever saying to me, "You can't watch that" or "You can't read that," and I think that this freedom stood me in good stead for my 20s and 30s. I feel bad that the information-hungry of today won't ever know a world free from adult hand-wringing and reactionary crusades.

All my interviewees agreed that British teenagers want and need better sex education. Andy Phippen reported that many schoolchildren he speaks to are refreshed to find an adult willing to talk to them about sexting, nude selfies and porn without being patronizing or scaremongering: "They need safe spaces in schools for kids to discuss these things rather than just be told, 'Don't do it.' With boys you have about 15 minutes of laughter, giggling and obscene stuff, then they ask serious questions. Girls will have serious questions and are quite angry [about sexual pressure]. They feel, 'Here's someone who's not going to tell us we have to put up with it.' No one's ever had that conversation with them, and that's quite depressing." Phippen isn't portraying a utopia where teenagers are fine with everything they're seeing and have no concerns, but he is proposing something that sadly is still seen as revolutionary in British schools—talking openly with teenagers about dick pics and the pressure to be sexual before you're ready.

Unfortunately, current legislation only obliges British schools to teach the biology of reproduction; all other forms of sex education remain optional. In 2015, the government rejected the Education Committee's call to make sex-and-relationships education compulsory in schools,[16] despite strong evidence from the committee that the vast majority of parents and pupils want this; Britain's Education Secretary Nicky Morgan doubled down on this stance in 2016. Yet the number of young people saying their dominant source of information on sex is school has actually risen, from 27 percent from 1999 through 2001 to 33 percent from 2010 through 2012.[17] Despite a persistent belief that no one gets information from anywhere other than the internet nowadays, real-life discussion and teaching about sex are clearly more vital than ever. As someone who has tutored children growing up in strongly

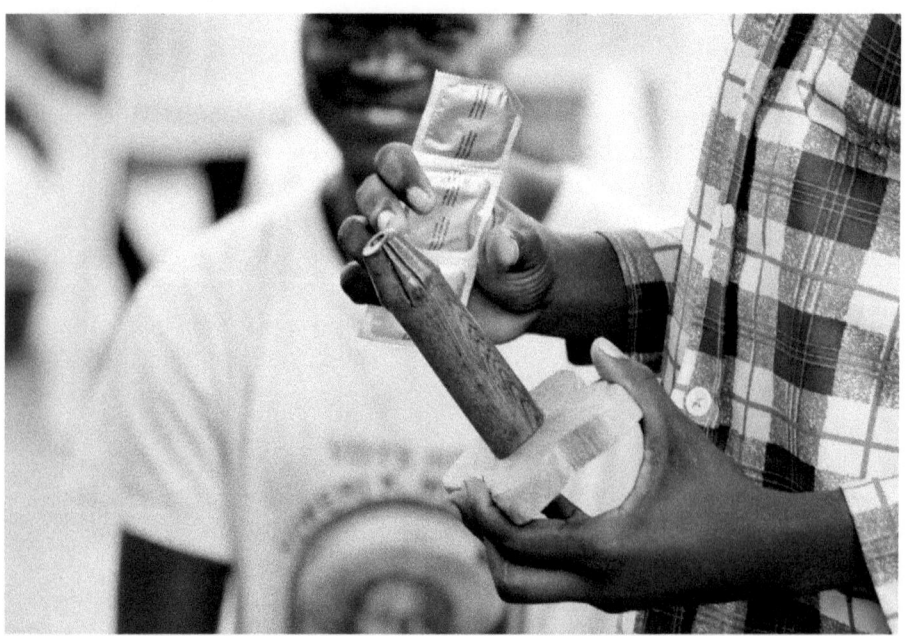

Obscenity laws regularly thwart sex-education efforts, whether in Victorian Britain, 19th-century America, or current UK schools (Pixabay).

religious or conservative households with little to no access to Western media, I can testify to the need for schools to pick up the slack.

As my research on this topic emphasized to me, adults need to ask fewer questions of teenagers, and do a lot more listening instead. The British government could also learn a great deal from its European counterparts' approach to sex ed. Danish professor Christian Graugaard advocates involving 15- and 16-year-olds in critical discussions about pornography: "We should strengthen their ability to distinguish between the media's depictions of the body and sex and the everyday life of an average teenager. They should become conscientious and critical consumers."[18]

The Construction of Innocence

As well as accepting that natural sexual curiosity is part of childhood and adolescence, it would be helpful to acknowledge that the concept of childhood is culturally constructed and historically situated. I always thought Zoë Heller brave to write, "I certainly don't subscribe to any sentimental notion about the innocence of everyone under the arbitrarily imposed age bar of sixteen years,"[19] even if it was in the guise of a fictional narrator. Before Heller's readers can go into outraged paroxysms at this possible condoning of pedophilia, she reminds us that "the people of Britain danced in the streets when the thirty-two-year-old heir to the British throne became engaged to a nineteen-year-old. Is there so much difference between nineteen and fifteen?" I'm sure my readers' conclusions will vary, but they should know that the ceiling placed upon childhood[20] by British law is arbitrary. It is legal for British people to have sex at age 16, but it is not legal to watch other people have sex on film until they are two years older. It is also legal to marry at 16 but not to drink alcohol at your wedding until you are 18.

Until 1929, the legal age for marriage in the UK was 12 for girls and 14 for boys.[21] Interestingly, part of the reason given when the Age of Marriage Bill was read in Parliament was that the low marriage age in Britain was affecting its influence in the rest of the Empire, namely, its "effort to grapple with the social problems arising from the early age at which marriages are contracted in India." In other words, Britons couldn't throw stones at uncivilized tribes elsewhere when we were living in a glass house of our own making. Sixteen has remained the legal age of sexual consent in the UK for straight couples ever since—and as of 2001, gay men were added to the mix—but the clock striking midnight on your 16th birthday doesn't magically confer a sexual and intellectual maturity that you lacked one second before. Likewise, those who saw porn before their 18th birthdays (this author, and I'd imagine most of my peer group, included) or had sex before their 16th birthdays (not this author, as it was a little tricky to "hook up" when you attended an all-girls school, but many of my peer group included) would also challenge the notion that they necessarily lacked all agency, powers of discernment or sexual desire before reaching these landmark ages. Heller adds, "We may have very good reasons for choosing to prolong the privileges and protections of childhood. But let us at least acknowledge what we are up against when attempting to enforce that extension."[22]

The Conservative government took power in 2010 and promised to mandate family-friendly filters from all major internet-service providers. In 2013, Prime Minister David Cameron stated that adult-content filters would be switched on as standard for all new customers by the end of the year, meaning people had to "opt in" and tell their provider that they wanted the filters switched off. At the time of writing, at least two of the four biggest UK ISPs had signed up. Simply put, if you're an adult who wants to watch porn, you now have to tell your ISP, otherwise they will presume you want child-friendly filters on your internet access. Unfortunately, the UK government's beloved filters regularly prevent teens from accessing genuine sex-education sites such as the excellent Scarleteen, as well as non-pornographic LGBT content. I can attest that my own blog—which discusses feminism, sexuality and gender issues, but contains no images or videos and is no more explicit than a school's sociology or English-literature class—gets blocked by the adult filters at my local library. Yet with supreme irony, my book on BDSM, which *does* contain images and explicit descriptions of sex and kink, is only a few feet away from the library computers, on the shelves for anyone to read.

The notion of personal and/or parental responsibility is often absent from arguments about the fragility of childhood innocence. Case in point: the 1994 amendment to the Video Recordings Act, which obliged the BBFC to pay "special regard to any harm that may be caused to potential viewers, or, through their behaviour, to society by the manner in which the work deals with a) criminal behaviour; b) illegal drugs; c) violent behaviour or incidents; d) horrific behaviour or incidents; or e) human sexual activity." This amendment was made following a notorious murder case that shocked and horrified the British public—the 1993 torture and killing of toddler James Bulger by two ten-year-old boys—and what Julian Petley calls "an exceedingly ill-judged remark by the trial judge."

The judge in question publicly stated, "I suspect that exposure to violent films may be in part an explanation"[23] for two children subjecting another child to acts at which many adult terrorists would balk. Thus "video nasties," in particular the horror film *Child's Play 3*, were blamed for inspiring the grotesque violence to which the boys subjected James Bulger. Petley adds that, "not least because of the pervasive popular mythology which insists otherwise, *it does need to be stressed that there is not a scintilla of evidence that the two children who killed James Bulger had ever seen this film, nor even that they watched horror films*" (emphasis mine). It is also worth mentioning that *Child's Play 3* has an 18 certificate anyway, therefore any legislation that presumes two ten-year-olds might watch the film is a tacit admission that the existing ratings system does not work.

Yet the law on what British adults can watch was still tightened in 1994 on the basis of mere speculation about what two children may have watched before they murdered another child. Few were brave enough to point this out in the wake of such a uniquely disturbing case, when people were scrabbling for answers to the futile question of how two children could behave the way Robert Thompson and John Venables did. As Petley puts it, "This procedure is premised on the notion that a medium can in some mysterious way 'harm' not only its spectators but society in general."[24] Incidentally, I was one year younger than Bulger's killers when the story broke. I remember the desperate search for the missing child; I remember the terrible feeling of inevitability when he was found murdered. And I remember the increasing public disbelief as the age of the suspected killers went down and down; initially, a group in their mid-teens was under suspicion, and that was shocking enough.

No one—adult nor child—could believe that two ten-year-old boys were capable of this. But I knew, as one of Thompson and Venables's peer group, that these children were not like the rest of us. Something had gone so severely wrong with the two murderers that, even as an adult, I've always doubted that the roots of their behavior will ever be clearly unpicked. I do not believe that simplistic narratives can offer any answers, nor assuage the grief and terror of the case.

As a nine-year-old, though? I knew right from wrong, I knew films were different from real life, I knew that no piece of media had the power to make me torture another human to death and that to say otherwise would simply be making excuses. Believe me, children definitely know how to make and understand excuses. Regardless, the 1994 amendment set a legal precedent for the government to dictate what content is and is not acceptable—as if having this law in place earlier could have done anything to save James Bulger.

Seeking Votes Through Control

Any attempts to censor internet material will be like trying to contain poison gas with a butterfly net. The UK government's regulations ignore the myriad of ways in which adult content can be accessed—not just on computers but on tablets, phones and smart TVs; not just on porn websites but through blogs, Tumblr, Instagram, WhatsApp, Snapchat and countless other apps; not just inside buildings but potentially anywhere in the world with a decent mobile signal. Instead of acknowledging that violence or sex will always be a few clicks or taps away, Parliament simply brings out a different-size net.

In this media climate, a system that asks people to enter their personal details before looking at porn not only opens them up to increased risk of credit-card fraud and identity theft, but leaves them vulnerable to public annihilation should their details fall into the wrong hands. And make no mistake: anyone with even a toe in the waters of public service *would* be annihilated. Britain's hypocritical, prurient tabloid press—which makes a significant chunk of its income from images of scantily clad women—will bring down the sword of judgment most severely. It happened to Max Mosley, publicly shamed for enjoying BDSM; it happened to Richard Timney, widely mocked for watching porn on a hotel TV. Do not try to tell me that the press interest in these cases was actually about Mosley's alleged Nazism or the fact that Timney's porn tastes were part of the MP's expenses scandal, because I've lived with the British tabloid press for 33 years and I can tell you its priority is *not* justice. It just wants to expose people's sexual practices in order to mock and disapprove of them. When they want to attack a public figure, the British tabloid media and gossip magazines send out a carefully calibrated message—sex is shameful *when we say it is*. As Dr. Clarissa Smith notes in her 2007 examination of British erotic magazines, "*The Sun* patrols the borders of the acceptable, and, possibly to 'protect' Page 3, espouses many of the arguments about sexual exploitation in male pornography."

Despite my being privileged enough to live my life with a degree of openness few are afforded, the "What about the children?!" narrative retains sufficient power over me that I feel nervous about simply having written a book on kinky stuff while moonlighting as a private tutor. I await the day a parent crashes through my door holding my book above his head and condemning me as a vile, corrupting pervert, then calls the police and ends over a decade of this enjoyable, lucrative sideline with one fell swoop. So far, though, parents just thank me, pay and ask how their child is doing.

3. Won't Somebody Please Think of the Children?!

Funnily enough, most parents only seem to care about whether I do a good job in the capacity in which they're employing me; this is apparently a novel concept for the UK's moralistic, scandal-hungry right-wing media. It's also worth mentioning that all my students are over 16 and that, frankly, with the amount of explicit sex and violence that you can find in the books on the approved A Level syllabus, these media-savvy teenagers would be unlikely to bat an eyelid at the fact that their tutor sometimes writes about fisting and bondage.

In fact, they could probably teach me a thing or two. But don't tell the government that.

4

A Very Great Mischief

> "Lesbian and gay activity is [a] clear example of the way in which there is absolutely no consensus in contemporary society about what constitutes the obscene."—Elizabeth Wilson[1]

Language and its uses are a crucial part of the obscenity puzzle, especially for those who identify as a woman, a feminist or a lesbian. In *The Handmaid's Tale*, lesbian separatist Moira says to heterosexual protagonist June that sex between women is completely equal; "even-stevens" is Moira's chosen phrase. June, irritated that she is being condemned as a dupe of the patriarchy by her own friend, retorts, "Even-stevens is a sexist phrase, if you want to get picky about it." This always makes me laugh, but it's given me pause regarding who gets named in dominant discourse, and who gets erased.

Did you know, for example, that the term *homosexual* only applies to men if the *hom* part is pronounced with a long *o* (as in gnome, comb or home)? This is because *homo* with a long *o* means "man" in Latin. Therefore, if you use Bart Simpson's favorite gag name, Homer Sexual, to refer to gay women, I'm afraid your speech is both linguistically incorrect and factually inaccurate. Whereas if you pronounce *homosexual* with a short *o*, as in bomb or Somme, the term's meaning alters to include all people attracted to those of the same sex. This is because *homo* as in *homogeneous* comes from the Greek *homos*, meaning "the same."

You may view this as semantic hair-splitting, but I find it a powerful example of how women, and anyone who doesn't identify as male, have been written out of gay history for as long as homm-oh-sexual relationships have existed. Which is a long time. In fact LGBT folk have always existed, but were regularly erased from Western, white, jingoistic history books. My research into whose sexuality is most represented in UK culture showed me that lesbianism has, at best, been treated as the poor relation of the LGBT rainbow. At worst, it has simply been treated as if it does not exist.

As a supporter but not a member of the LGBT community, I've noticed how the "L" part of the rainbow is rarely, if ever, prioritized. Rather, lesbians are consistently relegated to a subset of the "G" demographic. The initial may come first in the gay rights acronym, but that's the only place where British lesbians are afforded that honor. This feels completely backwards, not least because the gay-rights movement of the 1960s, '70s and '80s regularly aped the tactics of second-wave feminists, as well as borrowed heavily from the civil-rights and Black Power movements.

As a straight woman, I don't have a dog in this particular fight, but I still want to look at how lesbian, bisexual and otherwise women-loving women get relegated to being the cute little sisters of the gay-rights movement, and how they are expected to happily settle for this. As a woman and a feminist, I'm tired of seeing women's issues always rendered a poor second to men's. This is why I'm giving women-loving women their own chapter in this book, and why I'm putting it long before the chapter on gay men and obscenity.

I also speak as a woman who has had my inbox, online space, personal space and bodily autonomy repeatedly violated by older, white, straight men who think that because I'm 5'2" with breasts and a vulva, I automatically owe them something. A few weeks ago, a man followed me to my car on a rainy dark evening and called me a moody cow when I refused to stop and chat. That same day an older white male "Dungeon Monitor" told me I shouldn't come to kink events if I don't want to be touched without my consent and laughed at my furious response. I informed all the other event organizers, but what can you do when *the very event leader* is the one telling women that sexual assault is to be expected? Thanks to experiences like these, I believe that the true test of any society's claims to civilization is how that society treats women. You could view this as a macro version of, say, the Bechdel Test, or my conviction that you can tell if a man is worth the time of day just by how he talks about women. If I watch, read or listen to anything that predominantly seems to be about men—and Lord knows that's easy enough after several millennia of the patriarchy writing history—I automatically ask, "Where are the women?" If there's no adequate answer, I immediately refuse to give another second of my time to a cultural artifact that cares so little for me and my kind, and I switch off.

In the same spirit, why should lesbian women, bi comrades, transgender people, elderly queers and LGBT folk of color care a damn for a gay-rights movement that prioritizes, or exclusively focuses on, the struggles of young, handsome, white gay men? I might not have much interest in Quentin Crisp were I a black working-class lesbian, or even a white one like Jeanette Winterson. For the record, I *love* both Crisp and Winterson, but this isn't about me.

I asked Jill Creighton, who identifies as a bisexual woman and is married to another woman, if there were any Scottish lesbian icons she could refer to when growing up bisexual. Comedian Susan Calman and MP Mhairi Black are two current examples of popular gay Scottish women. Jill ruefully mentioned *Little Britain*'s "Only Gay in the Village" comedy sketch, and also reflected that coming out for her meant putting herself in the firing line for gossip and mockery. "I just knew I didn't want to be spoken about like that…. It was definitely hard being in a little town. You don't want people talking, so you hide it more. I wasn't aware of any Scottish icons at all."

I've also read plenty of fantastic, fearless writing by legendary sex activists Gayle Rubin and Pat/rick Califia, some dating back to the late '70s and '80s, about how women had to fight for a space in the gay and BDSM scenes. I love these two writers and activists for their relentless refusal to be pushed out of communities by entitled men, and if Rubin and Califia have taught me anything, it's that one must lead by example if one wants to see change. There are already plenty of books about how men who love men won their rights, so consider this an attempt to set a precedent wherein women come first, and feel free to form as many smutty innuendos from that statement as you are able.

In *Thinking Kink*, I concluded that while gay male sexuality was viewed by the heterosexual mainstream as a darker form of sexual expression, lesbianism was constantly reduced to some sexy fun engaged in by femme-looking women for the pleasure of a male onlooker. This still winds me up no end, although I'm pleased to see more diverse representations of women-loving women elbowing their way into British mainstream media.

I recently watched the poignant documentary *Whitney: Can I Be Me?*, in which it is strongly implied that the late singer Whitney Houston was in love with Robyn Crawford, her personal assistant and friend for 20 years. Houston's mother, Cissy, even speculates that Whitney would have been happier with a female life partner. However, Cissy qualifies this statement by adding that her own dedication to Christianity would not have allowed her to accept a gay or bisexual daughter. I was surprised to hear an elderly, religious, conservative woman admit that (a) her daughter probably loved women, and (b) she was aware that her child could never come out to her. It seemed so painfully paradoxical to hear the mother of a dead woman confess to alienating her child through her own religious piety. I wanted to yell at the screen, "WHY DIDN'T YOU TELL HER THIS WHILE SHE WAS STILL ALIVE?!" but I'm sure this bereaved mother already lives with that tormenting question every day.

To give Cissy Houston her due, she also states in the documentary that she did not accept Bobby Brown's presence in her daughter's life any more than she would have accepted Robyn Crawford as Whitney's lover. Nor did many of Whitney Houston's fans, who blamed Brown for enabling her spiral into drug abuse. Still, the sad takeaway from the movie is that Houston was probably bisexual, but because of the homophobia rampant in the black community, she was never able to love her female partner publicly and proudly.

What I found particularly fascinating were the words of Kenneth Reynolds, a retired record executive who had worked with Houston in her glory days. I'll admit to some prejudice when I say that this older black man with a shaved head and diamonds in both earlobes was the last person in the world I would have expected to nail why many straight men either dismiss or deliberately eroticize lesbians. "[Straight men] always have a field day with that," Reynolds says to the camera, grinning, "because the first thing heterosexual men say [about a gay woman] is 'Well, she doesn't need me.'" Reynolds also believes that Houston's love of women unsettled alpha-male record executives, who considered themselves indispensable to any woman's success and happiness.

I couldn't have put it better myself. Those who are genuinely unthreatened by women loving women don't feel the need to reduce lesbianism to a sideshow for men. It's a long time since I've wanted to stand up and cheer in the middle of a movie theater, so thanks to Kenneth Reynolds for that!

Loving Women

To preempt any backlash from anti-feminists, gay men or (God help us) "straight pride" activists, let me state for the record: I don't believe gay/bi/pansexual women are necessarily more enlightened or somehow better than any other sexual subculture. Women can identify as lesbian, gay, bisexual and/or transgender and yet still be susceptible to internalized misogyny or capable of lousy behavior. I've heard a lesbian woman say, "It wasn't really domestic violence" about a female ex who punched her in the face. I've heard lesbians talk about straight or femme women in derogatory terms, as if butch or masculine people were automatically higher on the food chain. As the feminist writer and queer activist Julia Serano writes, "There have been gender ... and sexual outlaws of one stripe or another since the dawn of history, yet our mere presence has never once simply made sexism vanish into thin air."[2] Serano has written at length about how wrong it is to presume that queer communities have an edge when it comes to enlightenment; she also details the multiple prejudices she has met with for being a feminine transgender bisexual woman.

Recently, my proposed idea to screen a mildly kinky documentary about BDSM educator Mollena Williams-Haas was turned down by my local bar. The reasoning of the lesbian owner? "I'm really sorry, but we don't want to be known for these kinds of events." So near, and yet so far. At least the bar owner was polite and pleasant about refusing me; we are in Britain, after all. I was disappointed, but I understood why this woman felt uneasy about being associated with the screening. She hadn't owned the bar long and was new in town; naturally, she didn't want to get off on the wrong foot. I felt similarly when my first published writings on sex, porn and feminism appeared in 2009, even though I'd been thinking furiously about such things for at least the previous decade. On the one hand, I wanted to swim to Portland, Oregon, and thank *Bitch* magazine for being the first to publish my work. On the other, I still lived in a small British town, had a day job in an office and worried about the effects that writing about kink, female sexuality and LGBT rights might have on my employability. I was also concerned about how my close and extended family might feel, not to mention what judgment might come down on my head from the wider world.

Jill Creighton's story illustrated exactly why queer people like the aforementioned bar owner feel reluctant to put their heads any further above the parapet. If you already feel like an outlier in your community, you're understandably going to be leery of newcomers, especially if they could bring trouble or unwanted attention with them. I think that's fair enough, which is why I have little time for straight people who demand to be called "queer" just because they're mildly kinky, are nonmonogamous or have same-sex fantasies. It's not my label, and it's not for me to dictate who can use it, but the reason I don't call myself "queer" despite being kinky and polyamorous is that I don't feel I have earned the right. I'm never going to experience lesbophobia, gay bashing or employment or housing discrimination because of who I am and who I love. When asked on the excellent podcast *Black People Kink* what my identity was, I laughed and replied that I am straight, white and vanilla in pretty much every category you could name. Whether it's class, sexuality, economic positioning, skin color or educational background, I'm happy to say that I am average, boring and blah. My hair may be kinky, as may some of my private activities, but that's about as interesting as I get. For me, hard-won identities and names should remain the territory of those who fought for them, not pretenders to the throne like paleface here.

This isn't to say that straight writers should never attempt to deal with gay issues, or that monogamous journalists should never try to write about polyamory. Quite the opposite; writers who are lucky enough to have a public platform should definitely seek out marginalized communities and help those who want to speak out to tell their stories. Not for a scoop, either, but for the betterment of society. I also know that I write most eloquently and accurately when I'm absolutely enraged, which is definitely how I feel when I see my fellow women consistently being erased from dominant media culture. Google "biphobia" if you'd like more examples of how the L and B part of the acronym lose out to the G and T—and I'm not referring to the drink.

Flying Under the Radar

Non-British readers may be unaware that there are no UK laws regarding same-sex activity among adult women. However, I would bet a lot of money that most native Brits don't know this either. The way lesbianism has been treated in UK law and culture has done much to contribute to this bizarre state of invisibility. During the summer of 2017, a letter appeared in the *Big Issue* magazine protesting the inaccuracy of assertions that homosexuality was decriminalized in 1967. "It certainly did not do so for me," sputtered the male author. "I was 17 at the time." The man went on to point out all the ways in which sexual activity among men remained criminalized until 2003, and as I detail in Chapter 8, he is speaking the truth. He finishes the letter with the line "Proper equality, in the law, including an equal age of consent, equal marriage and so on would take a further 50 years of campaigning." This writer is correct as far as gay and bi men are concerned, but his letter fails to mention women in same-gender relationships once, showing yet again how female faces keep getting shoved behind the acceptable (male) visage of the gay-rights movement. Because he is only one step removed from the Western cultural default, Mr. Average Gay enjoys many privileges that his female-identifying, femme, transfeminine, lesbian, bi, pan and cis sisters do not.

This is not to disparage gay men, whose pioneering fights for equality have often required extremes of bravery not seen in their heterosexual counterparts. However, gay males have been welcomed into the charmed circles of 20th- and 21st-century Britain far more often than their women-loving sisters, especially if they're white and middle or upper class. Male homosexuality, if legally suppressed, has also been tacitly tolerated in the upper echelons of British society and its aristocracy for centuries. And if you believe Tom Hardy's depiction of the Kray twins in the 2015 biopic *Legend*, gay men were also tolerated in more working-class circles, provided they had enough guns and knives to silence the homophobes. In the late 1990s, Labor politician Peter Mandelson served in the Blair government and was known to be gay even though he never publicly came out. The British press speculated and printed innuendos about Mandelson's sexuality for a while, but they soon got bored and returned to harassing him about his political moves, not to mention his haircut.

Now, I know there's always a danger of getting sucked into a game of "Oppression Olympics," i.e., pointlessly arguing over which oppressed group has it worse until the rainbow-colored cows come home. Instead, I'm going to simply present some facts of British history.

Women who love other women and wish to spend their lives with another woman were never mentioned in British law until the Civil Partnership Act of 2004.

Women who love women were not mentioned in the 1967 Sexual Offences Act, which only legalized sex between men aged 21 and over.

Women who love women were not mentioned in the 1885 Criminal Law Amendment Act, which criminalized sex acts between men.

Women who love women were not mentioned in any British laws in the 1700s or 1600s, or when the Buggery Act of 1533 was introduced.[3]

Women who love women were omitted from the first recorded mentions of same-sex activity in Britain, thought to be in the 1100s.

Look through British history and you could be forgiven for thinking that LGBT women never walked this green and pleasant land until the 21st century.

There are several theories as to why, in contrast to the constant demonization of gay men, female homosexuals never appeared in UK law. One is that men simply couldn't take the idea of sex between women seriously. Sex with no penis? Now come *on*, how would that even *work*?! Regardless of class or background, our forefathers would have been largely ignorant of the female anatomy thanks to the dearth of sex education mentioned in Chapter 2. To them, the sex act involved one male organ and one female orifice, ended with the man's orgasm and involved none of that suspicious female pleasure malarkey. This phallocentric view of sex was publicly aired in 1811 by a male judge who claimed, "The crime of one woman giving another the clitoris ... is impossible in this country to commit."[4] One wonders how he could be sure, but then overconfident men have rarely let facts get in the way of some good legal blustering.

Another oft-repeated and probably accurate claim is that Queen Victoria was so appalled to hear of sexual activity between women that she refused to believe it existed; she also feared that bringing lady love to public notice via legislation could give women ideas. As a result of this, a late–19th-century proposal to add lesbianism to Britain's list of banned sex acts was quickly and quietly dropped.

By 1921 Victoria was long gone—but her attitude towards gay and bi women had not died. Instead, Victoria's words and attitude had spread to the House of Lords: a group of lawmaking old rich white men. World War I had only ended three years previously, and the face of British gender relations had been permanently altered after a generation of young men were slaughtered in the trenches. Women of all classes had come out of parlors, kitchens and houses to drive ambulances, make munitions, build ships and do many jobs men had previously monopolized. Women over the age of 30 had been given the vote in 1918, although this was a frustratingly hollow victory for suffragists and suffragettes alike; men still had the right to vote from the age of 21. In the upper echelons of Britain's political system, there was also zero female power or influence. It's no surprise, then, that in 1921 the all-male House of Lords voted against a bill criminalizing lesbianism. In case you're wondering, this wasn't because the lords in any way endorsed same-gender relationships. In an address to Parliament, Lord Desart, director of public prosecutions, said, "You are going to tell the whole world that there is such an offence, to bring it to the notice of women who have never heard of it, never thought of it, never dreamed of it. I think that is a very great mischief."[5]

The paradoxical stereotype of women as sexually ignorant wild temptresses has been deployed whenever and wherever men fear that women may be gaining too much power. It has achieved particular traction during debates over obscenity; if a man claims that he's only looking out for the delicate ladies, *surely* no one can accuse him of sexism? As a feminist who knows all too well how chivalry vanishes in a puff of smoke as soon as the man carrying it out doesn't get the smile, compliance or sexual attention he believes he is owed, I will tell you now: this *is* a sexist attitude, if a well-concealed one. If you think women are so easily influenced that the slightest glimpse of unfamiliar sexual activity will drive them to try it, then you must view them as malleable, childlike creatures with no brains, opinions or libidos of their own.

The House of Lords believed that lesbianism had such seductive potential to corrupt that merely *hearing* about it could pollute minds. What the hell does this even *mean*?! If you're going to legislate against something, you need to be able to, first, define what you're actually legislating against and, second, say the term out loud in a room full of other adults. If our lawmakers, whose actions affect millions of people, are afraid of words, what hope is there for us plebes to have free speech? "We do not want to pollute the House with details of these abominations," sniffed one lord in defense of this semantic cowardice.

History does not record whether the 1921 bill even referred to adult lesbians, or if it was ostensibly aimed at preventing sexual assaults by adult women of young girls. One lord claimed a nerve specialist "has told me with his own lips that no week passes that some unfortunate girl does not confess to him ... that she has been tampered with by a member of her own sex."[6] Yet thanks to parliamentary etiquette, which "prevented speakers from using explicit terms to refer to behavior which was regarded as sexually deviant,"[7] we'll never know for sure what the House of Lords was trying to achieve, or for what reasons.

We saw in Chapter 1 how the belief that some things are too obscene to mention resulted in a grown woman being barely able to name her own genitalia. The idea that any factual noun, *vagina* and *lesbianism* included, is too shameful to say infantilizes adults and prevents rational, necessary discussions from taking place. More sinisterly, it erases whole sections of society, and their bodies too.

Still, if you're a sexually threatened old man who doesn't like the idea of women not needing men, you may not even have to legislate against sex acts. Instead, you can ban their depiction. This is what happened in 1928, when Radclyffe Hall's semiautobiographical lesbian novel, *The Well of Loneliness*, was declared obscene. We may have trial by social media nowadays, but in the 1920s it was good-old fashioned trial by print media.

Hall's fifth novel, *The Well of Loneliness* was already skating on thin ice after four publishers turned it down due to its sapphic theme. When it did find a publisher, Jonathan Cape, it was printed inside a discreet black binding and priced highly to avoid scandal. Newspaper reviews were mostly favorable, but all it took was for James Douglas—already notorious as a "brilliant bigot"[8] and the editor of the *Sunday Express*—to condemn the novel and Hall was in trouble.

Douglas had previously shown where he stood on women's rights when

Deeming sexual discussions obscene has only served to disadvantage those without access to education and healthcare (courtesy James Rosen).

he castigated a pro-contraception lord for stating that relentless childbearing was killing women. Hardly surprising, then, that Douglas called *The Well of Loneliness* a "moral poison" in a review titled "A Book That Must Be Suppressed."[9] The editor called upon Home Secretary William Joynson-Hicks, a notoriously religious and censor-happy man, to ban the book. Joynson-Hicks obliged, demanding that *The Well* be proscribed under the OPA.

It's worth mentioning at this point that *The Well of Loneliness* does depict a growing romance between two women, but (spoiler alert) it's not one that ends well. The more femme of the two ends up choosing heterosexual marriage over lesbian love, and the more butch woman, "Stephen," winds up alone, à la the trope of the "tragic homosexual." The book also contains only one very euphemistic suggestion of lesbian activity—"that night they were not divided." I've read the book myself and can attest that the prose is so restrained and unarousing that an uninformed reader could probably miss any hint of lesbianism altogether. I hate to criticize such a legendary author's prose, but the likeliness of one getting randy or having sapphic ideas when reading *The Well* is far outweighed by the danger of falling asleep. I could barely be bothered to finish it, and this is coming from someone who *loves* reading sexy, smutty books. In 1928, though, one hint of two women remaining undivided was enough to have Douglas and Joynson-Hicks frothing at the mouth, and roping in the director of public prosecutions to keep this corrupting literature out of the hands of women.

The idea of a newspaper editor having such influence over the home secretary seems almost quaint to a modern Brit. Nowadays, we accept that politicians don't listen to what the media (or the public) say, scandals involving rent boys or expenses notwithstanding. However, a country where politicians can insulate themselves from public criticism seems equally dangerous, and this seems to be happening more and more in 21st-century Britain.

As for Radclyffe Hall's book, it fell victim to exactly the kind of fear-mongering about lesbianism that had been expressed in the House of Lords seven years previously. Sir Archibald Bodkin condemned *The Well of Loneliness* on the grounds that "women who have not healthy home surroundings are apt to be curious about this disgusting subject and curiosity might lead to practice."[10] The book was deemed obscene and an order for copies to be seized and destroyed followed. Radclyffe Hall could not get her most famous novel published in Britain again for another two decades.

Moral Poison

The idea of any piece of art (or porn) having the power to corrupt seems increasingly old-fashioned in the face of relaxed 21st-century attitudes towards nudity, sex, gay rights and kink. However, scratch the surface and you'll find that the concept of corrupting potential still has a concerning amount of traction in circles across the political spectrum.

Conservative media is as vocal in its support of internet filters and crackdowns on "extreme porn," as it is in its concern about the influence of a heavily sexualized world on children—a concern that is shared, if framed differently, by some branches of modern feminism. Such feminists must have short memories indeed, or perhaps a poor knowledge of history, if they believe that the obscenity law that banned lesbian literature in the 1920s is any friend to 21st-century women and girls. Much as I loathe the way 21st-century media treats the female body as window dressing to sell any product, I've come to the conclusion as a feminist, a woman and a supporter of LGBT rights that censorship, especially of sexually explicit material, never helped anyone—*especially* minorities.

As with every other application of obscenity law, Britain's war against lesbian literature was inconsistent and selective. The same year that *The Well of Loneliness* was banned, Virginia Woolf's *Orlando* avoided any similar condemnation despite depicting lesbian relationships *and* being dedicated to her lover Vita Sackville-West. In fact, *Orlando* went on to become a mainstream best seller. It's been suggested that this was because Woolf and Sackville-West both presented as femme heterosexuals, and therefore appeared unthreatening to the social order, whereas Hall was unapologetically butch (much like *The Well*'s unsubtly named Stephen), was unmarried and lived with a woman. *Orlando* could also be read ambiguously because of the gender-bending nature of the protagonist. One year later, the silent film *Pandora's Box* was cut by UK censors because of a scene so innocent to the modern eye that it could easily be shown to a group of kindergartners. Trust me, I've seen the clip: all that happens is protagonist Lulu dances a very chaste tango with Countess Geschwitz, and then hugs her. This scene has been described as the first sympathetic depiction of lesbianism in film, but it was cut in both the United States and UK.

It is rarely mentioned that some of the first erotic scenes in John Cleland's *Fanny Hill*, censored in the UK in 1964 for being obscene, are between women—one wonders if this made the authorities be harsher on it. The 1968 film *The Killing of Sister George* had to have its lesbian content minimized in order to pass the BBFC's eyes. The BBFC's website explains the decision thus: "While lesbianism had never been illegal in the UK ... the subject remained very much taboo. BBFC principal officers judged that the sex scene would not be harmful, in that it was unlikely to corrupt adult cinema goers, but were concerned that the public was not ready to accept such a detailed lesbian scene."

This is contradictory, to say the very least. If the potential to corrupt is not there, then a quick glance at the OPA should render this movie free and clear. The presence of a taboo subject is not a legal justification for censoring any media. After all, audiences in the late 1960s may not have felt "ready" for movie scenes that depicted interracial relationships, women's liberation or rights for people of color; but so what? The point of art is to provoke, evoke, inspire and push the boundaries of what is acceptable; it's an essential aspect of social and cultural progress. My mother will probably never be ready to hear lots of swearing, but it won't stop me from including profanity in this book, nor swearing out loud whenever she's out of earshot. To pick a much more influential example: *Star Trek* fans can proudly attest to the power of their beloved franchise to outrage bigots, as it was the first American TV show to depict a kiss between a black actor and a white one. In 1968, though, the head of the BBFC quickly rebuffed any progressive notions: "John Trevelyan acknowledged that the BBFC had not been 'ungenerous' when allowing 'passionate scenes of this kind' to be passed in other films 'but only when the relationship was heterosexual.' In explaining the decision for cuts Trevelyan said '…it is a totally different matter when the context is one of Lesbian physical love.'"

Thank Sappho that Britain has finally moved past an era when it was entirely down to men to determine the respectability of depicting sex acts that, by their very definition, excluded men and their pesky prejudices. Incidentally, lesbians of the 1960s did not view *The Killing of Sister George* as a positive or inviting depiction of their sexuality. Scottish author Jeanette Winterson has recalled watching the movie on television in her repressive, homophobic childhood home. Winterson's autobiography *Why Be Happy When You Could Be Normal?* describes in painful detail how the young lesbian was tormented by her mentally unbalanced, fervently religious mother. Far from viewing *The Killing* as an endorsement, Winterson recalls the movie showing lesbianism as the road to pain, violence and damnation.

The British media of the time did little to help Winterson and those like her, isolated young people struggling with their sexuality against the hostile background of a working-class northern town. In the 1960s, British newspapers still refused to carry advertisements that included the words "homosexual" or "lesbian." While the former could be justified because male homosexuality was illegal until 1967, the refusal to acknowledge lesbians had no legal basis. Rather, it reflects that recurrent phenomenon: the personal judgment of the individual masquerading as fact. It also confirms that conflating lesbianism with male homosexuality costs lesbians any separate identity of their own.

Section 28

> "Sexual liberation … figured largely in the Thatcherite construction of the 1960s as a period of moral, national and economic decline."—Jackie Stacey[11]

It's generally accepted that following the 1960s, sexual attitudes in Britain relaxed greatly. It depends partly on whom you talk to—unsurprisingly, women, LGBT folk and those of color are much less likely to agree that British society was particularly progressive in the '70s. It also often gets glossed over that any social progress made in the late '60s and the '70s was no match for the sexual conservatism that fomented in 1980s Britain. The growing backlash against lesbian and gay rights was made public when UK customs raided the London bookshop Gay's the Word in 1984 and seized sex-education literature, plus works by Oscar Wilde, Jean Genet, Thom Gunn and Gore Vidal. Four years later, Margaret Thatcher's Conservative government introduced the most nakedly homophobic piece of legislation of the 20th century.

Section 28 passed with the UK government's full support in May 1988. This law prevented schools and local councils from "promoting homosexuality" or portraying it as "acceptable ... as a pretended family relationship." Those born in the 1990s and 2000s are often unaware that Section 28 ever existed, but it stayed on the books until 2003. The current British prime minister, Theresa May, voted against repealing Section 28 in 2000. Most notably, this piece of hateful propaganda wasn't removed from British law until two years after the age of consent for gay men was equalized with that of heterosexuals, resulting in a situation where 16-year-old boys could legally have sex with one another, but could not be taught anything positive about homosexuality by their schools.

Section 28 was no aberration; it was the culmination of a decade in which the countercultures celebrated in the 1960s and '70s were violently pushed back by the political and social conservatism now dominating the United States and UK. Ruthless individualism had pushed back against collective action and union power; striking miners had been violently and gleefully defeated by Thatcher's government. The Conservative government encouraged contempt for anyone who had the misfortune to be poor, an immigrant, a single parent or non-heterosexual. However, the British government of the late '80s knew it couldn't just ban same-gender relationships, so it resorted to censoring and demonizing them. In this push to return to the mythical, much-talked-about family values of yesteryear, the queer community's only permitted function was to be the "other" against which the straight ideal was constructed.

Section 28 cemented threats to both gay equality and artistic freedom; after it passed, debates raged over whether Wilde's work could be taught in schools or celebrated at literature festivals that received public funding. Although entirely separate from the Obscene Publications Act, Section 28 was simply another obscenity law introduced by stealth. Under the guise of protecting family values and the presumed innocence of children, it gave lawmakers the power to ban the work of any homosexual who refused to be shamed and silenced. Sez Thomasin picks up the story: "In the late eighties/early nineties my older sister was in secondary school. She wasn't actually gay but was widely perceived to be so got the sharp end of some homophobic bullying. She decided to write her sociology coursework about the effects of Section 28 but was banned from doing so on the reasoning that being forced to even discuss it would place her teachers in an impossible position. I found out about this when I had the same teacher nine years later and he loudly wondered if I was going to be a troublemaker like my sister."

Thomasin adds that during their time as a teaching assistant, they met many teachers who were unaware that Section 28 had even been repealed. Furthermore, "even those who had started training after its repeal had had zero training about supporting LGBT kids or challenging homophobia. It was often the teachers who were the worst of all. I complained about one teacher who was openly homophobic and aggressive to kids and the school responded by having me not work with him. There was no question of me being out at these schools, even in the staff room. The last time I worked at a school, in around 2007, I did see one teacher challenge homophobia, and the kids were outraged. Of course they were allowed to say poof and faggot! Nobody else said they couldn't! Of course being gay was wrong."

Thomasin says that in their later job as a sexual-health educator who gave LGBT-awareness workshops in schools, disquieting attitudes persisted up until 2015, when the role was cut altogether. They recall teachers being relieved that an outside speaker was dealing with LGBT issues "so they didn't have to," and recommendations that queer students "get back in the closet because the school couldn't support them. What I really noticed overall was how shocked students would be if I a) mentioned same-gender sex and relationships or b) challenged them on homophobic comments. They were clearly flabbergasted by an adult who would object to homophobic slurs and then talk about the risks and issues around anal sex, oral sex, dildos and fingering as well as penis-in-vagina sex. The fact that I was bothered about homophobia was often taken as confirmation of my queerness. I mean, they weren't wrong, but their logic that no straight adult would ever defend LGBT kids was very telling."

So much for the Conservative government's fear that predatory queer adults would take on teaching careers just to promote their deviant ways to children.

By 1993, the UK had survived its first lesbian kiss being shown in the evening soap opera *Brookside*, and a few years after that, the presence of lesbian characters in soaps, on TV shows and in movies started to become normalized. *Buffy the Vampire Slayer* was originally shown in Britain on BBC2 around 7 p.m. on a weekday evening and featured the sweetly bohemian couple Tara and Willow from about 1999 onwards (as well as plenty of eye candy for all genders and sexualities, but I digress!). This author, a furiously feminist university student in the early aughts, was thrilled to discover an elective module on lesbian culture offered by Warwick's sociology department. I signed up and spent a significant segment of 2004 happily watching films like *Bound* and *Go Fish* and discussing whether Madonna's depiction of lesbian sex was helpful or exploitative.

British cultural awareness of lesbians still lagged somewhat behind that of their gay male counterparts in the early years of the 21st century, but things definitely felt like they were improving. I remember a friend visiting Paris in 2006 and telling me excitedly about a women-only club called Pulp. I was thrilled, even though I was straight, because it felt so daring for lesbians to explicitly state their identity with no reference to gay men. I also remember asking her, giggling, what she saw in this club, and her wonderful response "Oh, nothing much. But there were some women, y'know ... *grinding*!"

For Jill Creighton, the sudden media visibility for women-loving women would have a positive ripple effect for years to come. "I remember the stories of lesbianism in soap operas being splashed across the tabloids and magazines in the '90s. At the time I wondered why it was so important, but now I realize: it brought those stories to rural towns, which even now, are so distant from the rest of the world."

5

20th-Century Smut

Once in place, the Hicklin Act would remain unchanged through the 20th century. It would be reinforced in 1959 and slightly altered in 1964, but the crucial tenet—"a tendency to deprave and corrupt"—would persist. Charles Rembar believes that rather than spelling any new assault on British civil liberties, this was merely the codifying of long-existent attitudes. Rembar adds that pinning the war on obscenity to the beginning of the OPA "suits the notion that there had been a classic age of freedom which ended when a Victorian blight descended upon literature."[1]

Nonetheless, the British discourse on sex did move from a huge fat "nope!" to open discussion of masturbation, homosexuality and female sexuality in less than 100 years. Straddling Victoriana and the new century were the likes of Sigmund Freud, Marie Stopes and Havelock Ellis, followed later by researchers like William Masters and Virginia Johnson, Alfred Kinsey and Shere Hite. Academics, medical researchers and feminists pushed for openness regarding sexual activity and published work written with an explicitness never previously imagined.

In Stephen Frears's 2005 film *Mrs. Henderson Presents*, the bored, recently bereaved protagonist, Laura Henderson (played fantastically by Dame Judi Dench), decides to buy a London theater with her widow's inheritance. The wealthy, upper-class Mrs. Henderson then has numerous debates with male theater managers, government ministers and lords about her right to have naked women appear on her stage. Loosely based on a true story, the movie is designed to demonstrate how uptight and ridiculous British customs were until relatively recently. Much of the dissent that Mrs. Henderson encounters has no legal basis, even in the late 1930s, when the movie takes place. Instead, she is repeatedly told that "standards must be upheld," or that "it's simply not done in England," when she cites the more relaxed Parisian shows as an example. We'll see plenty more examples of how a Chinese whisper regarding law can be given credence even when it has no basis in truth; if you can't wait that long, I encourage you to Google the phrase "Mull of Kintyre myth" right now.

> LORD CHAMBERLAIN: I find that lines have to be drawn somewhere and nudity is on the wrong side of the divide. I have problems enough with the length of skirts; I've had to have inches added to them for the new Offenbach production.
> LAURA HENDERSON: Our production won't have that problem, because we won't have skirts.

In Mrs. Henderson's time, only a tiny segment of UK society actually knew what the laws on obscenity were, or how they functioned. That segment remains minuscule today, although it is a lot less socially narrow; the people I interviewed for this book came from wildly varying class and educational backgrounds, as well as being racially diverse. Still, now as in the 1940s, the vast majority of the UK public believe that whatever is customary must be law, which is patently untrue. This isn't to condemn Brits as incurious or close-minded; you don't put your name to a book about BDSM without discovering just how broad-minded your fellow countrypeople can be. Rather, it shows that all these laws and customs are deliberately guarded in the upper echelons of government power, by politicians who maintain that they are too complex or tedious for the populace to understand, and that the average person is more concerned with survival in these straitened times than spending hours in dusty archives uncovering the truth.

Returning to *Mrs. Henderson*: once the wealthy widow replaces tired music-hall acts with naked female tableaux at her theater, sales promptly go through the roof. The only law to which her performers are required to adhere is that they remain still at all times on stage when nude—presumably because the slightest jiggle of a breast or shaking of a buttock would irreparably corrupt the nation's theatergoers. Bob Hoskins's theater manager circumvents this pesky rule by paying a local scallywag to release a mouse onstage, resulting in much female shrieking, running and wobbling.

These hilarious scenes are contrasted with those that show Mrs. Henderson realizing the limits of her wealth and power. She is constantly called to defend her theater shows to stuffy old men who are unable to even say the words *vulva* or *vagina*. In one scene, a politician refers to women's genitals as "the Midlands," instantly conjuring up strange images for residents of Birmingham. In another scene, the term "pudenda" is hissed by an exasperated statesman, only for Mrs. Henderson to merrily trill, "Oh! You mean the pussy."

This kind of nonsense doesn't just take place in Britain, or in the movies; Lisa Brown, a U.S. state representative, was barred from addressing the Michigan state house after she said "vagina" during a speech from the floor in 2012. Even though Ms. Brown is presumably in possession of a vagina, vulva and the whole kit and caboodle, U.S. custom dictates that she only bring this body part into the political realm so long as she never mentions it by name. What a destructive message to transmit to American children, teenagers and womenfolk. A 2014 episode of *Orange Is the New Black* tackles the squeamishness regarding female genitalia in a funny and explicit episode named "A Whole Other Hole," which shows that women can be just as ignorant as men when it comes to birth canals, urethras, anuses, clitorises, labia and vulvae. Most pointedly, the show's writers leave it up to a trans character, Sophia Burset, to explain to a group of cis women just how their junk works. As well as being utterly hilarious, the episode is a testament to how the fear of frank adult discussions about sex prevents real, helpful education from happening.

In my first book, I described a scene from the movie *The Notorious Bettie Page* in which the trailblazer for pinup models Bettie sits outside a courtroom inside which a group of men is deciding if she should be punished for possessing a female body and allowing it to be photographed. Britons and Americans alike criticize Middle Eastern cultures and religions for treating the female form as an inherent temptation that leads to the downfall of good men. Yet our very language and legal systems betray a similar contempt for women's bodies. We don't blame the candy if children fail to keep their hands out of the jar, but we continually excuse the failure of grown men (and some women) to act like adults when it comes to sex and human bodies.

A few centuries ago, any naked body was the cause of both consternation and fascination. Renaissance master Leonardo da Vinci had to steal or pay for cadavers in order to create lifelike art, because the scandal of a live human disrobing for an artist would result in punishment from the heavily religious authorities. In everyone's favorite '90s tear-jerker, *Titanic*, Leonardo di Caprio's Jack tells posh girl Rose (Kate Winslet) that his nude drawings are of fallen women, drunks and amputees. "In Paris there are a lot of girls willing to take their clothes off," Jack informs a scandalized Rose. When Rose teases Jack, "You draw this woman a lot…. I think you had a love affair with her!" he grins back, "Hardly. She was a one-legged prostitute." The face Rose makes tells us all we need to know about Edwardian attitudes to nudity and sex, although refreshingly for a 1997 movie, she discovers her own sexuality and becomes at ease with her own nude body later in the film.

A New Dawn?

> "The sexual order overlaps with a wide range of institutions and social ideologies. To challenge the sexual order is sooner or later to encounter those institutions as problems."—Michael Warner[2]

Outside the theaters, cheaper printing methods had democratized British pornography by the early–20th century, and the authorities were perpetually one step behind when it came to cracking down on its sellers. The obscenity police were also selective, pursuing the cheaper end of the market while leaving the moneyed and the educated to enjoy erotic books and postcards largely in peace. When Havelock Ellis published his groundbreaking *Studies in the Psychology of Sex* in 1897, he hoped that its explicit content would be excused in the name of science. Instead, he saw both his publisher and his bookseller charged with obscene publication. Even by the 1940s, nudity on stage or even in art school was still seen as an "abomination."[3] As we established earlier, naked bodies could only appear in the theater in tableau form, a bit like a three-dimensional art gallery. You might as well go to Rome or Greece if you wanted to see nude statues, and I expect that any Britons with enough money to travel did exactly that.

In 1906, Harley Granville-Baker's play *Waste* was banned by the lord chamberlain for depicting abortion, even though the termination in question was a botched backstreet fatality. Apparently the rule discussed in Chapter 2—that sins can be depicted in art so long as they are painfully expiated—was not harsh enough for Edwardian London. This furious objection to mentioning contraception or methods of reproductive control that might benefit women would sadly persist well into the 1960s and '70s. The Pill may now be universally available via the National Health Service, but this was a hard-won battle fought in no small part by writers, artists and feminists.

As a 21st-century feminist who is exasperated with modern media's failure to depict abortion realistically, I can see how stories like Granville-Baker's brought us to our current position. All too often, this simple, safe and legal procedure is depicted as a tortuous process women always regret. Never mind that giving birth is 11 times as likely to kill a woman as an abortion; never mind the fact that nature happily killed millions of women in childbirth until very recently, and still kills them every minute in developing countries. For some reason, showing abortion as a simple, consequence-free procedure that one in three women will undergo is a notion that strikes the fear of God into Western media producers.

To give credit where it's due, the 1972 movie *Cabaret* did show the character Sally Bowles choosing to terminate a pregnancy without any fanfare, and made this a mere footnote to the sexy Weimar-era storyline. The movie simply shows abortion as an option that any woman who wanted control over her life and body might choose. Yet in the intervening time, TV and movie creators have tended to opt for grisly complications (see *Vera Drake*), tortured regrets (see *Six Feet Under*, whose depiction of an aborted zygote as a gurgling baby in the afterlife pisses me off even now) or last-minute changes of mind (see *Sex and the City*). Women in 1906 Britain were subject to this same odious combination of condescension and censorship.

Regarding the banning of *Waste*, Paul Ferris writes, "*The Times* praised the play for 'its extraordinary power' in dealing with 'some of the most fundamental facts of human life,' then argued that its very realism made it 'wholly unfit' to be seen by a 'miscellaneous public.'"[4] This nonsensical statement sums up British attitudes of the time. Backstreet abortions *were* a fact of British life pre–1967, but it was a brave playwright who attempted to make that fact public. As Susie Steinbach writes in *Women in England 1760–1914: A Social History*, "Abortion was a widely used form of fertility control" in Britain from the latter half of the 19th century onwards. While the upper and middle classes might be able to obtain a relatively safe surgical abortion by bribing a doctor, the working classes were forced to resort to "folk prescriptions," including taking mercury, lead pills or "a concoction of gin and gunpowder."[5] I remember my aunt hanging a print of an Edwardian apothecary's advertisement in her bathroom in 1998; it promised a clear complexion, menstrual regularity and the clearing of any "blockages." A naïve adolescent, I required further explanation to realize that this was a euphemistic advertisement for an abortifacient. Any midwife or folk herbalist worth their salt will tell you about the magical properties of pennyroyal tea; it's not a coincidence that the firmly pro-choice '90s band Nirvana wrote a song by that same name. In Edwardian Britain, though, a group of men, 100 percent of whom would never be pregnant, decided that it was better for women to poison their bodies in desperation to be rid of a pregnancy than to watch a play about abortion.

The belief that some sexual matters were simply too terrible to mention wasn't just comically ridiculous; it was also deeply harmful. When a bill was put forward to criminalize incest in 1903, the lord chancellor opposed it on the grounds that incest was too disgusting to be talked about. The House of Lords agreed; the bill would not pass for another five years. Perhaps most significantly, incest cases could not be reported on in the media for another 14 years. The distressing side effect of this was that "men were able to claim that they were not breaking the law."[6] The pomposity of an MP helping child molesters to weasel out of responsibility for raping their family members is enraging. Even if the lord chancellor thought that needing such a law was "a sad reflection of the century that was just beginning,"[7] I have to ask: in what century did he imagine incest *wasn't* occurring? It's the moral equivalent of sticking your fingers in your ears because you don't like what you're hearing.

Swinging or Suppressed?

The idea of the sexually liberated Swinging Sixties might have been a reality if you were a middle- or upper-class white male, but women and their sexuality remained under deep suspicion in mid-century Britain. Unaccompanied women, or pairs of women, would not be served in some bars and restaurants after a certain time of night; the lack of male escorts was judged likely to result in the assumption that they were prostitutes. When I complained to a man who was a teenager in the 1960s that I couldn't even order a whiskey at a funeral without my own mother criticizing me, he merrily informed me that in his day, any woman who drank spirits was called a tart.

Far from following a neat trajectory from repression to liberation, 20th-century Britain would see peaks and troughs thanks to a tug-of-war between those convinced the country was in moral decay and those who welcomed radical change. *Lady Chatterley's Lover* was exonerated in 1960; three years later, *Fanny Hill* was found obscene and banned. The distribution of hard-core porn had become more acceptable and mainstream in Europe; the 1959 update to the OPA meant the same was impossible across the English Channel. Literature on sex, even that of an educational rather than salacious nature, remained suspect. In 1953, the Home Office took violently against the publication of Alfred Kinsey's *Sexual Behavior in the Human Male*, which dared to suggest that masturbation and premarital sex might not cause the end of civilization. With the truly bizarre logic now associated with U.S. abstinence-only sex education, the Home Office's spokesman stated that "fear of disease is perhaps the most potent factor in restraining many young men from promiscuous immorality ... and to remove that deterrent gratuitously seems to me to be monstrously irresponsible."[8] One wonders if the official in question would continue to adhere to this belief once the deadly sweep of AIDS began in the 1980s; perhaps he would have doubled down on it, believing that if your nose falling off from syphilis was a fairly effective deterrent, then the threat of death must be an even greater chastity device.

For all the rose-tinted views of the burgeoning youth culture, the London and Liverpool music scenes, high fashion and a new wave of sexual openness, British social conservatism wasn't letting go without a fight. Homosexuality would remain illegal until 1967, even though the Wolfenden Committee had recommended ten years previously legalizing sex acts between adult men, in order to free up UK police to pursue genuinely dangerous criminals. Abortion would remain illegal until the same year. The thrilling advent of the Pill in 1961 is often cited as a game-changer for sexually active women, but it is rarely mentioned that it took another seven years for doctors and the UK's Family Planning Association to agree that they would prescribe it to single women. A 1971 survey found 33 percent of Britons thought that the Pill shouldn't be available to single women.

Women of my generation are rightly appalled by this news, but women who came of age in the '60s and '70s are still likely to consider the Pill a godsend. One pack of tablets instantly freed these young women from dependence on men and having to trust a man to use birth control, from the enforced motherhood and domesticity they had seen shackle their mothers so tightly. It allowed women to remain in education longer, go out to work, earn their own money and buy their own property. Women of the 21st century may complain about the side effects of the Pill, the increased cancer risks and compromised mental health, but their foremothers had little time for such minor issues. Why look for reasons to complain when you were being handed the world on a plate? My grandmother's generation of women, born in the '20s and '30s, were more suspicious of this newfangled contraceptive, believing that all it really achieved was another victory for men's sexual appetites. For them, the Pill took away women's reasons for saying no to sex; the danger of repeated childbearing was the only excuse in an era when wives had no legal right to refuse their husbands. My mother and her generation did not share this view: for them, the Pill meant sexual and personal freedom on an unprecedented scale.

Change inevitably entails discomfort: unmarried couples were regularly refused lodgings by landlords in the '60s and '70s, and women's magazines warned their readers not to give in to sex until after marriage. Motherhood was held up as the raison d'être of all women, and Lord Ailwyn felt no shame in saying to Parliament in 1961, "If I had my way, I would introduce a law forbidding mothers with young children to leave them all day and go out to work. Surely a woman with a husband at work should remain at home and look after her children."⁹ He did at least add that women should be paid for these domestic duties.

My mother worked full-time during the 1970s and remembers raised eyebrows over her wearing trousers (yes, really), as well as regarding her decision to cohabit before marriage. In 1976, she told her boss she was moving in with my dad over the weekend. The older man responded with a jolly but whispered, "Oh, well I won't tell anyone." My mum retorted, "Tell whoever you like," and happily lived "in sin" for the next three years despite pearl-clutching from various corners, not least my maternal grandmother. My mum's three sisters had all married at 21 and had children soon after; Mama Scott did not marry until she was 28, a move that took great personal mettle in the sexist '70s.

The 1963 Profumo scandal (about which my grandfather said, "Before Profumo, people didn't trust most of what politicians said. After Profumo, they would never trust anything a politician said, ever again") showed that for all politicians' claims to be moral guardians of the nation, they were as susceptible to the charms of sexually available women as any man in the street. Members of Parliament, doctors and intelligence agents were all pulled in to the Profumo web, united by a common attitude to beautiful young women who would be "demeaned, if not incriminated, when they showed lust." Historian Richard Davenport-Hines documents this scapegoating in his book *An English Affair: Sex, Class and Power in the Age of Pidum*, reporting that terms like "scrubber ... common tart, prostitute, [and] whore" were used interchangeably with more benign terms such as "girlfriend" during the trial. Public contempt for any female who dares to capitalize on the appetites of rich, arrogant men has always been much stronger than judgment of the philandering men themselves—funny, that.

The tutting mouths of mid-century Britain were, predictably, hiding a huge public appetite for erotica. When *Kamera* magazine, featuring images of nude women, launched in 1957, its weekly sales hit 150,000. Eight-millimeter black-and-white films of women undressing were sold in Soho or by mail order. Pamela Green became the first woman to appear all but naked in a British feature film, *Naked as Nature Intended*, in 1961. Three years later, Green faced an obscenity trial after a schoolboy claimed he had been "ruined" by her nude film *The Window Dresser*.¹⁰ As we will see in Chapter 7, American zealot William Comstock had employed a similar tactic to proclaim contraceptive advice obscene, but Comstock at least had the excuse of operating in a less enlightened time. For adults in 1963 to have given credence to the excuses of that notoriously horny and responsibility-shirking breed, the teenager, is a frightening thought indeed.

Fortunately, the judge in *The Window Dresser* case felt the same—"after thrice viewing the film, [he] dismissed the case and asked for a copy of the film to take home for his own son."[11] Pamela Green highlighted the hypocritical nature of British attitudes towards women who unashamedly took charge of their sexuality when she spoke on the radio show *Woman's Hour:* "I can't understand why a woman should be embarrassed or degraded by looking at a nude body.... We've all got one."[12]

In 2017, the announcement that actor Jodie Whittaker was to play the next Doctor Who in the eponymous long-running BBC series was greeted by right-wing newspapers' publishing photos of the actor topless. How this is meant to shame or intimidate a woman who is presumably aware that she has a pair of breasts I don't know, but I do know that this is a tactic trotted out again and again by woman-haters everywhere. If it weren't, the crime of "revenge porn"—which should really be called "nonconsensual sharing of explicit images"—wouldn't exist, nor would over 80 percent of its victims be female.

The methods of what feminists have christened "slut-shaming" may have altered, but the targets remain constant. When that five-headed colossus the Spice Girls bestrode British pop culture in the 1990s, the women in the group were derided in the UK media for their appearances, their outfits, the way they presented their sexualities. British tabloids and right-wing newspapers continually analyzed the appearances of the five Spices and always found them wanting: too fat, too thin, too busty, too flat-chested. In 1997, I was 13 and considered myself far too cool to like the Spice Girls, preferring instead the indie rock of Pulp, Oasis and Manic Street Preachers. However, even I felt sorry for Geri "Ginger Spice" Halliwell (now Horner) when the British press gleefully mocked and shamed her after it was revealed that she used to work as a topless model and nightclub dancer. I've never particularly liked Ms. H—politically, personally or otherwise—but watching her get excoriated by mostly male journalists for the crime of having a female body and using it to pay the bills was a powerful warning to me. The British media might permit you to be a clever woman who doesn't use her looks or breasts to advance her career, but woe betide any woman who tries to cross the line between bimbo and brainiac.

Where to Draw the Line

In 2016, I visited Amsterdam and made the requisite trip to a sex shop to see how it compared to a UK one. Most aspects were pretty similar, but I did notice that there were DVDs featuring acts that it would be illegal to stock depictions of in a UK sex shop; fecal play was the most obvious one. I didn't feel particularly corrupted or depraved by looking at the cover images; at worst, I felt a bit queasy and was reminded of my days moonlighting as a healthcare assistant. Then I simply conceded that said fetish does not attract me, placed the DVD back on the shelf and left the shop in search of pancakes, a far more tempting and potentially damaging feature of Dutch culture to this sweet-toothed glutton.

Clarissa Smith is a British academic specializing in the depiction of human sexuality, and was called as an expert defense witness in *R v. Walsh*, the 2012 case centering on allegedly "extreme pornography." I was lucky enough to meet Smith in person at the 2016 "Kink Olympixx protest" described in Chapter 1, and told her about the topic of this book. A petite, cheerful lady with glasses, gray hair and a Newcastle accent, Smith looked more like a friendly auntie than an expert in hard-core pornography, but this is exactly why it's foolish to judge people based on appearances. Smith also struck me as extraordinarily brave when she told me she had stood up in a British court and argued that porn that features human feces is not necessarily obscene and/or dehumanizing.

Before you reach for the sick bucket, consider Smith's reasoning: any parent will spend a great deal of time in contact with human excreta when changing their infant's diapers. That doesn't make it degrading or demeaning; it's simply what we do for the vulnerable in our society. I know this firsthand; having worked as a healthcare assistant on and off for over a decade, I've come into contact with every bodily fluid imaginable. As a result, I am one of the least squeamish people I know, and I don't faint, retch or become hysterical when confronted with very young or very old bodies and the messes they sometimes produce. Smith had taken a similar stance in court, saying that when we care for the young, the sick, the elderly and the disabled, we must be willing to come into contact with their feces, urine, vomit, saliva and anything else they care to throw at us. We do not consider ourselves made lesser by these acts; quite the opposite, they are a testament to our caring and nurturing sides.

But bring sex into the equation, and common sense is quickly defenestrated. If an act causes someone arousal, it is immediately viewed as suspect; a British Treasury counsel adviser in the '70s admitted "that he recommended prosecution if a book made him feel randy."[13] If that is the criterion that those trusted by lawmakers to enforce censorship use, then we run the risk of any piece of art being deemed obscene—there are people out there with fetishes for balloons, custard pies and tickling. Run the "It makes me feel randy" test on the right person and you would see a children's TV show about circuses censored as obscene.

On any given day of the week, one need only open a British newspaper to read about a new study about our overly sexualized society that is apparently cause of panic. Porn addiction, children sexting one another and the growing rate of anal sex among heterosexuals are all stories that continue to gain column inches. The latter could, and to my mind should, be viewed as evidence that sexual practices evolve as culture becomes more open. Human beings get curious; they try new things. Yet I don't think I've seen an article—and this applies to both liberal and conservative media outlets—in which a mainstream journalist takes a second to consider this. Instead, the writers of these articles unfailingly operate on the assumption that new or different sex practices are bad and dangerous.

The judge in the obscenity case *R v. Gold*, 1964, felt that there was an unreasonable push to talk about sex acts he found distasteful. In the cross-examination of Margaret Drabble, who spoke in defense of the book *The Mouth and Oral Sex*, the judge intervened to ask, "Why is it important to read about oral sex now? We have managed to get on for a couple of thousand years without it." It's more than a smidge worrying that someone with such a deliberately narrow view of history—presumably the judge had gone his whole life without ever seeing any Ancient Greek vases, or Hindu temple carvings, or ancient Chinese art, or even just reading some of Shakespeare's bawdier lines—was tasked with overseeing a trial in which the freedom to publish works about human sexuality was at issue. Jeremy Hutchinson, in his closing speech, stated, "Disgust is not enough—it is not enough for the Crown to show that [a] book would horrify, shock, disgust or nauseate. In a free society people are allowed to experience all those things without a book being obscene."[14]

Writing about *R v. Gold*, Thomas Grant highlights "the judge's ill-concealed suggestions to the jury that Britain was in terminal decline, and a principal cause of its undoing was too much sex."[15] It certainly seems that a personal agenda was at work, and this demonstrates the danger in allowing any unelected individual or group to dictate what is obscene. Two hundred and fifty-two years previous to this trial, printer James Read found himself prosecuted for publishing *The Fifteen Plagues of a Maidenhead*, an epic poem describing a young woman's wish to be rid of her virginity. Back then, the presiding judge, one Justice Powell, showed a levelheadedness regarding pornographic works that is too often absent from today's judiciary; he concluded that the publication "tends to the corruption of good manners, but that is not sufficient enough for us to punish." Read was duly acquitted. Powell admitted that he was no fan of the work, adding, "There is no law to punish it. I wish there were."[16] However, he respected the limits of the law and was honest about it.

By contrast, the judge presiding over the obscenity trial of *The Mouth and Oral Sex* was on a personal crusade to restore some vision of a "truly moral" society that in fact had never existed. Barrister Jeremy Hutchinson didn't let him off lightly, though: "Was it permissive books that brought the Roman Empire down, or was it something more important, something called Christianity? Was it an Empire which we would all want to preserve? People held in bondage without any rights, without any freedoms? It is terribly easy to think of the past as better than the present and that everything has gone to the dogs."

It's no coincidence that those who romanticize the past tend to be white, heterosexual, middle- or upper-class men. Women, people of color, immigrants and the LGBT community don't tend to have so much nostalgia for a world that treated them as subhuman. Furthermore, the oppression of those parties has never been eased by implementing *more* censorship. Hutchinson urged the jury not to be swayed by the judge's implied request that "you the jury should stand up and find this gentleman here guilty ... not because of the book's obscenity but because it will be in some way a protest against the decadence of our society. I ask you first, not to act on that basis, and secondly *not to accept ... the inference that this world we live in, in England, is in fact more decadent than it was a little while ago*" (emphasis mine). Hutchinson pointed out the many hypocrisies of the romanticized Victorian era: the acceptance of child labor, corporal and capital punishment, the thriving prostitution industry. Voices of reason like Hutchinson's are needed today more than ever, as we remain far too quick to pin the blame for all social ills on the very act that keeps our species going.

A recurring theme in the history of obscene material is how its defenders are forced into trying to attribute literary or cultural value to it in order to save it from the censors. I can see why this tactic was deployed; you might not get very far trying to persuade an old, reactionary, prudish judge of the value of a work on oral sex if you admit that its primary aim is to get its readers horny. Whereas in 20th-century Britain, an era in which social elitism persisted despite politicians' regular claims that the class system was long dead, you might have stood a chance if you could attest to the scholarly value or public benefit of such a work. This resulted in a legal situation wherein a book could be declared obscene, yet if it demonstrated sufficient "artistic merit," this might outweigh its depraving potential and justify its publication as "for the public good." In one sense, this is an admirable attempt to strike a blow for artistic freedom. In another, though, it means only the work of those intellectual enough to play the language games of the courts will be saved.

It also means classism is reinforced; the posh are allowed their porn as long as the plebs never get their filthy hands on it. The Victorian Society for the Suppression of Vice "had no doubts that pornography caused sex crimes, at least when it fell into the hands of the working class."[17] *Lady Chatterley's Lover* was labeled obscene because it might corrupt one's servants (because of course the average Briton kept servants in 1960!). Jerry Barnett adds: "Britain has this entrenched class system, and censorship is an elitist activity. The crackdown on video nasties in the 1980s was about the lower classes getting access to something only the elite had previously had."

In the 1980 comedy movie *Airplane!*, there is a shot of an airport newsstand where a scan of the magazines reveals the labels FICTION, NON-FICTION and WHACKING MATERIAL. I think the scene is funny because it's honest. What else is porn for, really, other than to cause arousal and aid masturbation? Yet our archaic laws force people to tie themselves in knots (no bondage jokes please, that would be obscene) trying to justify the publication of sex-related material on *any* other grounds. Even though masturbation is literally the safest form of sex, is both physiologically and psychologically beneficial and, as long as done alone or only in front of consenting parties, poses no danger to our social fabric, we are still legally prevented from defending media that might make people love themselves.

Dragged Through the Mud

> "Shops complain to Mr. McCaffrey that *The Irish Times* is coming in decorated with bits of ice and dog shit and he mutters to us that's the way that paper should be delivered, Protestant rag that it is."—Frank McCourt, *Angela's Ashes*[18]

A few decades ago, those beleaguered by lurid reports of their sexual activities could at least reassure themselves with the thought that "It'll be fish and chip paper tomorrow." Now, we live with the prospect of having our most thoughtless moments immortalized online forever; more than one of my peers has said how glad they are that our adolescence happened before Twitter, Facebook, Instagram and Snapchat existed to preserve permanent photographic records of our every idiotic, drunken moment. As Jon Ronson reflects in his book *So You've Been Publicly Shamed*, in which he explores the stories of those whose lives have been undone by one idiotic tweet or Facebook picture, the UK is "at the start of a great renaissance of public shaming." While Ronson notes that social-media shaming can be used for positive effect—one example is the withdrawal of lucrative sponsorship deals from the *Daily Mail's* website after its columnist Jan Moir used the death of Irish singer Stephen Gately as a pretext for an attack on gay couples—his book mostly deals with people who have lost jobs, friends, money and their reputation as a result of being exposed online.

As the internet encourages pitchfork mobs to mobilize on the shakiest of pretexts, you would think we could come up with something better than an obscenity law under which even answering the charge entails great risk to one's reputation, employability and safety. As I noted in Chapter 1, people are still opting to plead guilty to obscenity charges rather than risk being outed as a publisher of—or, God forbid, a reader of—filthy works.

The concept of self-monitoring is a key aspect of queer theory, and it applies more than ever in a society where people who are already exhausted from juggling their public and private selves are now asked to add a digital self to the mix. On the day I write this, British news channels are full of the story of Carl Sargeant, a Welsh government minister who was accused of sexual misconduct. Sargeant had tweeted four days previously that he intended to cooperate with the police and looked forward to clearing his name. Today, North Wales police have confirmed that Sargeant was found dead, having apparently taken his own life. Some may say that this indicates Sargeant's guilt; others will counter that his suicide reflects an understandable terror of being tried not just in court, but over social media, in a far-reaching, vicious and non-erasable manner.

I cannot speak to the guilt or innocence of Carl Sargeant, but I do know that social-media wars are fought every minute of every day, at a pace so furious no human brain can keep up. On a daily if not hourly basis I'll catch the unfolding of arguments on Facebook, Twitter or Instagram in which the original post has already been deleted, its author clearly too cowed by the following pile-on to leave their hasty words out in the open. Offending tweets appear, cause a string of outraged responses and are quickly deleted in the time it takes me to make my first cup of tea in the morning. Pre-internet censors could only dream of being able to conceal a displeasing piece of media so quickly. Sargeant's decision to share his statement of innocence online might have seemed unwise to veteran journalists and legal experts, who remain suspicious of the digital world. However, to a younger generation that has been raised on computers, it was an understandable act of damage control. Failure to make a statement would have been viewed as an equally hostile move by those who require constant fuel for their fires of outrage.

When merely being accused of a sex-related crime is enough to ruin your life plenty of times over, it's a brave person indeed who prolongs the experience by fighting the charges. In an email describing their experiences with ATVOD, Blake told me that they pleaded with the regulatory body not to publish details of the case because of the distress it would cause to their family. The fear of being "outed" by a media hungry for any whiff of a sex scandal is valid: Jon Ronson gives the example of Arnold Lewis, a Welsh preacher who killed himself in 1978 after the *News of the World* exposed him as a swinger. The same publication showed no sign of remorse over this needless annihilation of vulnerable individuals when in 1992 it outed another swinger, Ben Stronge. The English man, who worked as a chef, committed suicide as a result of his public shaming. Our media and judiciary seem to learn nothing from these horrific, avoidable cases.

One of UK porn's unsung early stars was Mary Millington, a wholesome British woman who graduated from glamour modeling to making hard-core porn films in the 1970s and remained unapologetic for doing so. Millington also latterly ran a successful sex shop, but it was constantly raided by the obscenity police, and she complained of harassment and threats from the squad. Facing shoplifting charges in 1979 after a struggle with depression and kleptomania following her mother's death, Millington chose to take an overdose rather than risk prison. In her suicide note she wrote, "The police have framed me yet again. They frighten me so much. I can't face the thought of prison." She was 33. Simon Sheridan's 2016 documentary, *Respectable: The Mary Millington Story*, strongly suggests that Millington was singled out for persecution by the police for daring to fight for freedom of sexual expression.

It's unsurprising, then, that many have preferred to self-censor rather than try to fight a powerful and brutal legal machine. I have often heard it said that Stanley Kubrick's 1971 movie *A Clockwork Orange* was censored by the BBFC due to its scenes of rape, child molestation, beating and murder. I did not find out until recently that this is completely untrue—the film was actually passed for UK release without any cuts. It was Kubrick himself who pulled the film from distribution because he and his wife were receiving death threats[19] and negative press attention. One year before this, *A Clockwork Orange* had been cited as a motivating factor during the murder trial of a teenage boy, foreshadowing how rock-music lyrics would be blamed for teenagers murdering teenagers in the 1980s and '90s. Understandably, Kubrick figured it was better to walk away than waste his creative energies trying to win a whole war, and chose simply to remove his movie from the British market.

When UK tabloids attempted to shame Formula One racing magnate Max Mosley for enjoying BDSM, Mosley's defense stated, "Yes, his sex life was strange, but when it comes to sex people think and say and do strange things and only an idiot would think the worse of him for it."[20] If 20th-century Britain teaches us anything, it's that there are plenty of those idiots out there. Furthermore, being publicly judged by them can leave you jobless, childless, unemployable or even dead.

6

Women Don't Want That Sort of Thing

I've long suspected that the reason so much energy goes into repressing female sexuality is the underlying fear that its complex, vivid and voracious nature holds the power to completely unseat male sexual security. Painting female sexuality as the soft, gentle, considerate yin to the thrusting, aggressive, insatiable male yang is an essential tactic in claiming that women don't want to watch people having sex, and it's one that retains a ridiculous amount of traction in a supposedly liberal society. When Clarissa Smith served as an expert witness in *R v. Walsh* (2012) regarding images that depicted fisting and sounding, a prosecutor stated to her that "if the ... pictures were of women they must be degrading and objectifying." Smith refuted this arrogant and patronizing generalization, which presumes no woman could ever enjoy or volunteer for such activities, and I salute her for doing so in open court. The prosecution duly labeled her "disingenuous, self-serving and dishonest." I wonder if the barrister in question has ever watched a woman give birth, and if he considers the orifice-stretching contortions of childbirth degrading too. Hilariously, this is how a bisexual character explains fisting between women in the 1997 film *Chasing Amy*; when her male friend is shocked at the idea, she laughs at him saying, "Our bodies are built to pass a child!"

Women have repeatedly been told that our only relationship with obscene material is to be scared or appalled by it; never to be curious about it, enjoy it or actively seek it out. It struck me from a young age, as odd that I was constantly taught to be either ashamed of, or territorial about, my female body. I didn't understand why, for example, breasts had to be hidden and treated as a source of embarrassment (never more so than during adolescence), when a new pair featured on Page 3 of a major British newspaper every day.

6. Women Don't Want That Sort of Thing

Nowadays one can switch on a TV music channel at any hour and see a dizzying cornucopia of writhing bodies, most of them young, white and female, most of them scantily clad, all of them colorful and pulsating and enchanting. Yet for reasons I have yet to understand, a music channel took it upon itself to bleep out the line "I can feel the heat between your legs" from the Weeknd/Daft Punk's 2017 slow jam "I Can Feel It Coming." I do wonder what damage hearing the line in full is supposed to cause; will a million adolescents spontaneously combust if they hear that vaginas, which presumably some of them possess, sometimes get hot and wet? As a former pubescent girl myself, I can attest that such words pose no harm to adolescent girls. As a grown woman who has sex with men, I can also report that last year I had a lover who didn't like me to talk about my vaginal lubrication. This was an educated, articulate man in his mid–20s who clearly considered himself worldly, but his ambivalence towards my body confirmed to me that plenty of British men could use a few lessons in female arousal. Which doesn't come as a shock when our media has no problem objectifying female sexuality but is afraid to actually celebrate it.

As an intelligent pre-teen growing up in the '90s, I quickly came to the conclusion that what mattered about women's bodies was not women's own feelings and opinions, but everyone else's. When I was ten years old and got lectured for coming home after curfew, I was appalled to hear my father boom, "YOU COULD HAVE BEEN RAPED!" Ewww, I thought. Why is my body and what happens to it considered everyone else's business, especially men's? Not to mention that my family resided in one of the safest, most middle-class neighborhoods on the planet, I was less than a quarter of an hour late and the sun hadn't even set. The overreaction pissed me off because of the possessiveness it demonstrated over my female body: I was sick of seeing breasts, bottoms, legs, vulvas, labia, vaginas and the wonderful clitoris being treated as the property of anyone except women themselves. I was tired of erotica and pornography that seemed aimed only at the straight male gaze, or occasionally at the gay male gaze. Most of all, I was sick of male-bodied people and their presumptions.

Woman's Hour was the first UK radio program to mention male homosexuality on-air. This was a brave act for the BBC in 1955, especially since sex between men would not become legal for another 12 years. The choice to host this watershed moment on a radio program with largely female listeners was very deliberate; the makers figured that women weren't nearly as bothered by the idea of gay sex as straight men were. A 1970 U.S. study on obscenity confirmed this, noting that "women are far more tolerant than men of homosexual erotica, doubtless because they feel less personally threatened by it."[1] Indeed, if the modern woman's porn-search terms are anything to go by, there are plenty of women who feel not just unthreatened but actively aroused by male homosexuality, but we'll come back to that.

Not in Front of the Ladies

The prosecution in the 1960 trial of D. H. Lawrence's *Lady Chatterley's Lover* portrayed women as corruptible innocents in need of protection ("Is this a book you would wish your wife or your servants to read?"), although tellingly the jury disagreed. Yet even after Penguin Books was exonerated for publishing the book, female library assistants in South Wales had the right to refuse to handle *Chatterley*; no such protection was offered to men, of course. This may sound comical to modern ears, especially now that women are creating, consuming and celebrating sexual media despite the nuisance of archaic laws. Yet there remains ample scaremongering about what effect obscene material could have on women: either those directly disturbed by it, or the victims of men influenced by it.

As we've seen with the 2008 Extreme Pornography law, the British legal system treats male sexuality as "a barely constrained appetite that has to be civilized and ought to be kept away from the inflammatory influence of sexual media for its own good."[2] Female sexuality is either framed as completely

Filament magazine aimed to show that erotica for women could be playful, cerebral and sexy (photograph by Andrea Heins).

passive or, more often, is simply absent. For all the progress in how women are perceived in education, the workplace or even the bedroom, we still get labeled as the more practical, less sex-obsessed gender. We're told that women don't need sex as much as men; that women can go without; that women are simply not visual creatures; that women don't objectify men's bodies or consume male beauty. I've heard all these arguments on multiple occasions, and usually from the mouths of men. These excuses aren't merely tiresome; they actively influence discourse on female sexuality while women's own desires get censored or silenced.

"In ignoring whole swaths of intelligent, consenting women who are turned on by acts that turn the authors' stomachs, they have also inadvertently demonstrated their own conditioning by a society that constantly attempts to dictate the parameters of our sexuality." This is from my first-ever printed book review, thanks to *Bitch* magazine's taking a chance on an unknown Brit for their Spring 2009 issue. The subject of my ire? A book written by two men, Carmine Sarracino and Kevin M. Scott, who presumed to tell me, an intelligent and very sexually open-minded woman in her mid–20s, what I liked seeing in pornography. As I hope you can gather, they were dead wrong, not to mention arrogant and misguided. Australian porn producer Ms. Naughty[3] wrote about her "Decadent Decade" spent creating erotica aimed at straight women in the early 2000s, having found that "there wasn't any one thing that all women desired ... women were likely to have different tastes on different days." I imagine that Sarracino and Scott's book would have turned out very differently if these two men had done some fieldwork by speaking to female porn producers and consumers—rather than presuming that three and a half billion people will all be turned on by the same thing. As Ms. Naughty found, those creating erotica for women face an uphill battle in an industry that sees women as "[no]thing other than a minuscule market."[4]

There's been some recent progress in the UK media—a widely reported 2015 survey[5] by *Marie Claire* magazine found that one in three women admitted to watching porn on a weekly basis. I know this because I was one of the reporters covering the story with glee. Finally, there was a comeback to that hoary old "women aren't visual" chestnut—90 percent of respondents said they watched porn online, with only 40 percent saying they read erotic books. It seems pretty clear that once the means of accessing sexually explicit material are in the hands of women, rather than restricted by lawmakers, editors or distributors, we are more than ready to utilize them. So why has there been such a reluctance to treat women as sexual consumers, rather than perpetually the ones being consumed? Is it really just a ploy to protect men from sexual insecurity? Or does it come from a deeper suspicion and fear of female sexuality, a failure to truly credit it as even existing except as a response to male urges?

I found many of the answers to this in the story of *Filament*, an erotic magazine aimed at straight women that was created and published by a British woman. Active from 2009 to 2013, *Filament*'s trajectory exemplifies how obscenity law is still being misused to enforce male prejudices about female sexuality.

Creating Female-Oriented Erotica

> "I liked porn but I really didn't like how most of it was marketed. I hated the way it ignored me as a viewer. It was always aimed at men and spoke only to them."—Ms. Naughty[6]

I first heard Suraya Sidhu Singh speak at a British feminist event in 2010, where she described founding *Filament* a year previously and how she had been constantly met with all the above objections to creating porn for women: it won't sell, women don't like that sort of thing, they're just not into porn the way men are. When I met Suraya again to interview her in 2016, it became apparent that these tired clichés had dogged her throughout the entire run of *Filament*.

As part of her research, Suraya looked at other erotic magazines aimed at women, such as *Playgirl*. She knew that "every time one of these magazines stopped publishing, there would be a postmortem and it would always come down to 'women aren't visual.' They were often edited by men." Suraya preempted men's inevitable claims to know what women want by conducting her own market research, distributing questionnaires through online forums and LiveJournal. She asked women "what they wanted to see, what kind of erotic fiction they wanted to read, what was important to them in the structure of a story." Then she spoke to women who had worked on *Playgirl* and *For Women*, and concluded "early on that publishers were going to be a problem. Because they had been [a problem] for those other magazines, with them being made to publish things they didn't really want to publish." Suraya noticed how *Filament*'s forerunners had often ended up merely imitating women's lifestyle magazines: "If you look at *Playboy* and *Penthouse* they had a lot of political content, whereas women's ones were just sex magazines. A lot of it was just how to be sexy for men. [They suggested that women] do a class on stripping; it was all about how you presented yourself. *There was no idea that you might be a consumer of male beauty*" (emphasis mine).

6. Women Don't Want That Sort of Thing

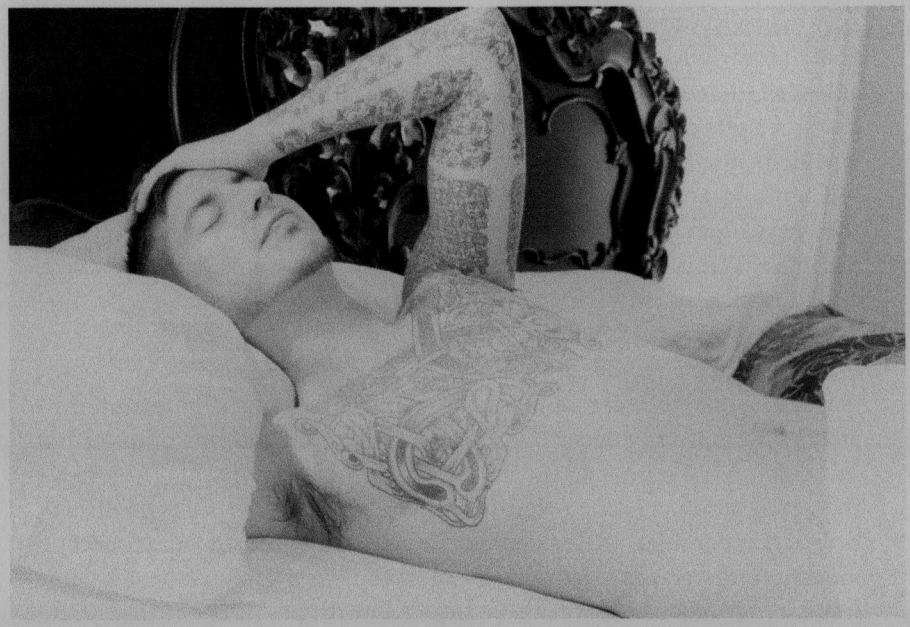

"It was never considered that you might be a consumer of male beauty"—Suraya Sidhu Singh on the erotic-magazine market (photograph by Lily Moss).

Consumers of male beauty were exactly the people at whom Suraya wanted to aim *Filament*, so she self-funded the magazine and initially only sold copies online, before attempting to get the magazine stocked in shops. The results were a massively mixed bag: U.S. bookseller Barnes & Noble agreed to stock *Filament*, and at its most popular the magazine was available at 900 of B&N's nationwide branches, not a number to be sniffed at. Yet distributors in the U.S.'s supposedly more liberal neighbor Canada claimed there wasn't an audience for *Filament* among its 17 million women. Suraya doesn't believe that genuine thought was given to the commercial viability of the magazine, but rather that male distributors simply decided they didn't like the look of it.

Writing about how traditional pornography tropes mark the bodies of women and people of color as "other," Lynne Segal notes that this becomes "a measure of the superiority of those who disown and distance themselves from such bodies"—i.e., those who get to keep their clothes on, usually white straight men. "This is why any naked, eroticized display of the white male body remains taboo outside pornography and, even there, will serve to threaten other white men."[7] This seems much more plausible an explanation than the easily rebuffed notion that women don't want to perv on male beauty. I remember reading an article in a '90s music magazine about an early Elvis Presley concert; a music journalist who was probably still shell-shocked from the volume of adolescent-female screams recalled how the seats of the venue were wet afterwards. Some forty years later, I would sit in a cinema packed with teenage girls sobbing over Leonardo DiCaprio in a wet shirt as our collective purchasing power made *Titanic* the then-largest-grossing film of all time. If your product is young, beautiful and male, and you want to make easy money, you would be insane not to aim it at such an enthusiastic, randy, cash-rich demographic.

Suraya agreed, adding that "the magazine industry is very heavily men-oriented. Their methodology is unscientific." If a female-oriented erotic magazine stops printing, as magazines will do, male distributors immediately point to it as evidence that "women don't want this sort of thing." At its height, *For Women* magazine achieved a circulation of 400,000, a figure that, even in the magazine-centric '90s, was the Holy Grail for publishers. Still, rather considering that markets change, audiences alter and the world moves on, the reason cited for *For Women*'s failure is always that women lack interest in looking at male bodies. It's worth pointing out that nowadays, magazine or newspaper editors can only *dream* of getting their work into 400,000 homes—as print media continues to decline, they're lucky if they achieve one-tenth of that number.

Filament reached Australia, New Zealand, Germany, Romania and Lithuania, but never made it into Canadian or British shops. Suraya presented distributors with her online research, as well as the countless emails she was receiving from women who wanted to know where they could purchase a copy of her magazine. "But they weren't interested, they were only interested in their personal opinion. It was always 'he thinks, he says.'" I asked Suraya if she encountered any women in her battles with magazine distributors. Ruefully, she told me, "Occasionally they'd say they had asked a secretary or female office employee for her opinion; so, she was asked to represent the whole of her gender!" Get the token woman, usually in a much less senior role than any of the men canvassing her, to put her head above the parapet? It sounds like a scene from *Mad Men,* rather than the modern British workplace, where it's emphatically stated that sexism and old boys' clubs are embarrassments of the past.

Erection Objections

> "Penises have adorned our songs and stories for as long as songs and stories have existed. Shakespeare's plays were

strewn with double entendres involving pricks and cocks. Rabelais ... brought up penises whenever the spirit took him; the Marquis de Sade wrote about little else."—Maggie Paley[8]

Whenever I told people what I was writing a book about UK obscenity law, a standard response from my peers was "Oh yeah, you can't show a hard-on on telly, can you?"

Actually, you can, and what's more, you always could.

There is no record of any rule since the 1959 OPA that states it is obscene to show an erection on TV, in movies, in magazines or in books. Take it from someone who has done extensive research. The idea that one cannot show an erect penis in British media is a total myth with no legal basis whatsoever. Yet the legend persists throughout Britain that images of penises in porn magazines or on TV have to meet the "Mull of Kintyre" rule. If this geographical term baffles my non–British readers, allow me to illustrate it using a similar situation in *Australian Women's Forum*, where editors had to check images of penises using a protractor to "measure the angle of the dangle." If your weapon stood to attention, then, sorry, soldier—it had to be hidden.

I checked the most up-to-date version of Ofcom's guidelines just to be sure, and the only mention of erect penises comes when Ofcom says post-watershed TV programs can show an erection if "justified by the context." Though this is still setting the bar higher for male nudity than female—how many shots of female bums, boobs and pubes are *really, truly* necessary to a story line?—it's also not the all-out ban on erections that people believe is in place. So why the persistent belief that an erect penis is the apotheosis of obscenity in British media? Do we truly believe that seeing a boner on TV will cause everyone's grandmother to simultaneously keel over from shock? After all—and I apologize for the mental image with which I'm about to scar every one of my readers, but I think this needs saying—had none of our grandmothers encountered an erect penis, none of us would be here!

Ms. Naughty, a producer of porn aimed at straight women, suggests that mythical boner-bans speak to male fears of both literal and metaphorical exposure: "The penis was a no-go area, a last bastion of secrecy, a final preserve of male power."[9] Whenever I've heard lads' mags and Page 3 defended as "just a bit of fun," I ask the male (inevitably) defending them: Would men be content to open their newspaper every day and be greeted with the image of a tall, broad-shouldered, tanned, clear-skinned, slim yet muscular, chisel-jawed 20-something man with a full head of hair sporting a huge erection? Or would it, just possibly, make a lot of men feel lousy about themselves? The fact that this scenario has never come to pass is our answer: the power to define obscenity still rests in the hands of mostly male censors, publishers and vendors, and of course men are going to protect their interests. There's no better way to achieve this than by ensuring insecurity about their penises won't be exacerbated by pesky concerns like equal access to erotica for both genders.

For Women

Zak Jane Keir, an editor and writer who worked on *For Women* from its launch in 1992 until the early 2000s, told me a similar story: "It's the problem that erotic products aimed at women have always faced in a world where men still have most of the power—the Man in a Suit somewhere up the production chain (a distributor, a head buyer for a chain of newsagents) who says, 'My wife wouldn't buy that, so no normal woman would buy that, so it won't sell.'"

For Women was aimed at straight women, who until that point had been ignored as sexual consumers, while magazine creators aimed their products at straight men and occasionally gay men, too. Women could grab a copy of *Attitude* should they wish to see naked men, but as many readers protested, they weren't

When the tables are turned: would straight men who argue for no limit on pornography be happy if this was the default image (courtesy Sita Mae)?

necessarily interested in seeing stretched out anuses or giant, oiled, beefcake men. They wanted erotica, but they wanted it made with women's eyes, tastes and libidos in mind. This doesn't seem like too much to ask, yet it was treated as a massive and unreasonable demand. I remember ordering myself a copy of *Filament* online after hearing Suraya talk back in 2010, and marveling that while magazines depicting women in various states of undress were freely sold in UK newsagents and bookshops, images of a pretty young man with a boner were so taboo that they were mail-order only.

When I asked Suraya why *Filament* never made it to UK stores, she replied, "The UK market was the hardest one of all. We never got in shops, we never got any official distribution. People were so resistant." Referring to the Mull of Kintyre myth, she added, "The erection thing was an issue. No one knows where [the myth] comes from but people believe it and retailers repeat it."

Zak Jane Keir describes her experience more bluntly: "There was a point, fairly early on, when *For Women* ran a 'General Erection' campaign, asking if readers wanted to see stiff dicks. Of course, the vast majority did, but the printers/distributors/company lawyers all went 'WAAAGH NO YOU CAN'T DO THAT.'" I've often wondered exactly what erotic charge women are supposed to derive from images of non-erect penises; to be blunt, they're not very useful fantasy material. As a straight woman, I can confidently state that I'm not interested in penises unless they stand a chance of bringing me physical pleasure. My partner once quipped, "You don't mind willies, it's just the idiot attached to them that annoys you"; similarly, I don't have a problem with erections, but they shouldn't be making editorial decisions for me and my fellow women.

It seems so contradictory that, at a time when male virility was being so publicly discussed—I remember 1998 in particular as a year when erections never seemed to be out of the news, between Bill Clinton's indiscretions and the launch of Viagra—adult women were still being prevented from seeing an actual image of a man with a hard-on, even when they were quite happy to pay for the pleasure. Aminatta Forna wrote, "For all the claims that women don't really go for visual titillation, when *For Women* decided to abandon full frontals in order to try to get off the top shelf, the magazine had so many letters of complaint that it went back to the old format."[10]

Distributors and the Law

One fascinating thing I learned from speaking with Suraya was how British bookshop chain WHSmith hid behind obscenity law to justify its prejudice against female-oriented erotica. WHSmith is an iconic British bookseller dating back to the Victorian era, and it currently has hundreds of shops on British high streets, in railway stations and in airports. However, when Suraya approached the company to ask if they would include *Filament* in their magazine section, she was told, "WHSmith have their own list of guidelines, and our magazine didn't pass. When we asked where the guidelines came from, they would say it was the law."

It wasn't the law. Suraya emailed me the guidelines that WHSmith had presented to her in 2010. Titled "Adult Policy," they state the following: "No Magazine should on its cover show a photograph of the vaginal area, nipples, penis, testes or anus, nor should it show any sexual activity." So far, nothing too unexpected. However, the wording of the next paragraph requires some unpacking:

> In conjunction with the Obscene Publications Acts, Protection of Children Act and this policy, no magazine should have photographs showing:
> - penetration of the vaginal lips or the anus by fingers, penis, tongue, dildoes, vibrators or other objects.
> - actual sexual contact between two or more people (e.g., sexual intercourse, masturbation, fellatio, cunnilingus or a tongue, hand, or other body part of one person touching the vagina, anus, penis or testes of another).
> - masturbation or mutual masturbation.
> - spermatozoa, ejaculation or unambiguous representation of spermatozoa.
> - excretion or urination.
> - forceful sexual activity (e.g., rape).
> - sexual activity or other involvement (including the use of models) with those apparently under age.
> - bestiality, sodomy, necrophilia.
> - the erect penis.
> - illegal sexual activity.

WHSmith, and indeed any retailer, is entitled to set its own policy on what it stocks. What it cannot do is justify this policy using the OPA or the Protection of Children Act. As has already been well established in this book, the OPA mentions no specific acts, sexual or otherwise. The Protection of Children Act 1978 is only relevant to the clauses about those apparently under age and illegal sexual activity. WHSmith could also be referring to the Children and Young Persons (Harmful Publications) Act, but again, that act only forbids the distribution of any media showing violent crimes, cruelty or "acts of a repulsive nature" that are likely to "corrupt children or young persons." An adult magazine showing adult nudity or consensual sex between adults doesn't fall into either category.

Also, if we want to get pedantic about it, and God knows I love a good spate of pedantry, it's tautologous to mention rape, underage sex, bestiality and necrophilia separately and then also include the clause for "illegal sexual activity." Take it from this philosophy-of-language and -logic graduate—I know tautologies, unsound premises and unjustified epistemic leaps when I see them.

As for citing the OPA, it's a complete red herring, even when we refer to the CPS guidelines. The CPS guidelines explicitly state that they do *not* require the censoring of depictions of consensual vaginal or anal intercourse, oral sex or masturbation unless another aggravating factor was present, such as violence. For WHSmith to imply that the first four clauses on their banned list have anything to do with the OPA is not only dishonest, but the polar opposite of what is legally the case. The CPS does not object to the depiction of those acts—but someone at WHSmith obviously did, and the least they could have done is be honest about that distinction.

Other distributors didn't even try to hide behind cherry-picked laws, knowing that the threat to kill sales would be enough to force magazine staff to self-censor. Zak Jane Keir says that *For Women*'s biggest barrier was not "the law, as we had company lawyers who advised us on stuff and who had to sign off on every page of every issue before we went to print, but the distributors. If someone at the distributors objected to something, it had to be pulled, or you would have the whole issue withdrawn from sale. It was John Menzies[11] whom we used, and they were miserable bastards who disapproved of the whole thing."

John Menzies were the first publishers to serialize Charles Dickens's work, as well as being the founders of legendary magazine *The Scotsman* in the 1830s. Yet, in the 1990s, their idea of a free market did not include anyone who liked men's bodies or looking at them. Writing in *The Independent* in 1996, Aminatta Forna corroborated this account of a media landscape practicing disproportionate censorship on female-oriented erotica: "Women's magazines ... found themselves hamstrung by the double standards of big newsagents and advertisers, who were much stricter when it came to images of men than they were with pictures of women."[12]

In spite of all these barriers, *For Women* was a popular, profitable magazine. Keir recalls, "The first two or three issues sold hugely, possibly topping a million ... the hype and media interest was immense."

What Women Really Want

Having survived an onslaught of male prejudice, *For Women* magazine folded once the internet began to erode sales. While this is a shame in some ways, it also points to the emergence of online female consumers who are finding the explicit content they want without having to worry about mythical erection bans or a man in a suit braying that women don't like looking at naked men. I've been told about the wonderful erotica I can access on Tumblr, Instagram and countless other personal blogs and websites, often run by smart, unconventional women who are tired of being told that they just aren't visual creatures. I can also attest from my own kinky research that FetLife, the BDSM social network, sometimes even features men in bondage or images with a strong female appeal, but these images remain sadly outnumbered by the usual yawnfest of countless slim white young women showing off their bits.

This isn't me being an unreasonable misandrist or hard-line dominatrix; it's a matter of legal clarity. If you're a British woman who wants to watch fem-dom-themed porn, see a woman sitting on a man's face, see women ejaculate or watch bondage or fisting, you're going to have find it in porn from abroad, because these acts have been deemed obscene by our majority-male government. Suraya adds: "It would be so good if people knew that the stuff that women want is the stuff that's being cracked down on. The market is set up to advantage large, heavily funded companies. Independent producers just can't compete." She was referring to the magazine industry, but her words have a direct parallel to the porn world, where, as I recounted in Chapter 1, four independent producers had their businesses annihilated for making videos of naked or submissive men.

Either the law is an ass, or lawmakers need to be honest about who they're really protecting when their decisions directly annihilate female-owned businesses. To make out as if restrictions on pornography only really affect men is to disregard all of the readily available evidence that women like looking at sexually explicit media too.

Web mistress Jackie's sentiment—"Not all women like emotional bullshit. I am just as tough as any guy. I'll watch cum-fuck-slut movies and anal gapings and gang bangs and whatever else is out there all day long. I don't need separate porn for me"—is inconvenient for anti-porn feminists, who deny that any woman can enjoy watching or participating in the production of erotica, or simply dismiss such women as moronic, self-hating handmaidens of the patriarchy. The presumption that women aren't visual, don't like porn, or would like porn better if it contained more soft furnishings and romantic story lines is increasingly belied by the actual erotica women are searching for, enjoying and creating. In an online article titled "Porn for Women: What Do Women Really Watch?" Jerry Barnett writes, "The myth of the demure female is blown away by the realities of porn viewing. By and large, women watch the same content that men do, but [actually] err towards rougher sex rather than away from it."[13] This doesn't surprise me in the slightest.

A glance at Pornhub's 2014 statistics confirms that "bondage," "gang bang" and "rough sex" are the most searched-for terms by the site's female users. So is "squirt," one in the eye (ahem) for the AVMS regulators. Also, despite the cultural myth that all straight men masturbate over lesbian sex, that search term is not even in the top five for men, while "gay (male)" is the second-most-searched-for term for women. Again, I'm not shocked by what real women are searching for, but I am utterly exasperated with Western culture's refusal to acknowledge this. One Sunday during the writing of this chapter, I clicked on PostSecret and read a new submission that stated, "Whenever I want to watch porn, I always go for gay porn movies." The punchline came at the bottom of the postcard—"I'm female and hetero." The fact that the writer felt sufficiently embarrassed about her porn tastes to keep it a secret speaks volumes.

In my first book, I suggested that some straight men like lesbian porn because "there are no other men's bodies to make one feel inadequate, no penises that might be bigger or more satisfying to women than one's own, no worries about having to exhibit similar levels of sexual stamina or competency to a male porn star."[14] I stand by this viewpoint, and would add that male consumers' fear of inadequacy should have no influence on women's access to the kind of erotica they wish to see. Both Suraya and Zak told me how difficult it was to find erotic images of nude men without their being obviously aimed at the gay male market; a photo in which the male subject was bent over holding his buttocks open at the camera got mentioned more than once! The thought of women as sexual subjects and consumers either never occurred to magazine photographers or was too threatening for them to contemplate.

It cannot be stated often enough that the indulgence of fantasy *never* need entail treating our real or prospective sexual partners poorly. Even more crucially, no sex act should be considered obscene just because of the possibility that it could be used coercively; otherwise, every possible sex configuration, from a kiss to double penetration, would have to be banned in one fell swoop. This fear that porn that portrays rough(er) sex or "extreme" acts and sexual violence will result in actual violence against women only patronizes us. Women are viewed as either starry-eyed romantics who only endure sex in order to get love or damaged, untrustworthy nymphos who must have some dodgy reason for wanting to watch two men fucking or sex involving ropes and gags. Either way, as the current regulations confirm, our tastes and desires are not to be trusted.

Perhaps those used to setting the standards for obscenity are concerned that, were female sexual fantasies to be thoroughly acknowledged, given airtime and catered to, groups of drunk women might start cornering pairs of men in bars and goading them on to kiss each other publicly. As a massive fan of the male form myself, I'm pleased to report that my sex drive has never overtaken my senses so strongly that I've behaved like this. Furthermore, I find it sadly revealing when men presume that giving women's sexual appetites free reign would necessarily result in men being coerced, abused and violated. This relies on a presumption that women intend to treat their sexual partners as badly as the worst men have treated theirs; it also brings to mind the phrase "takes one to know one."

A Feminist Issue

One of the major motivations for writing my first book was realizing that the feminist community had massive problems with the notion that women watch, fantasize about and participate in as varied and explicit a range of sex acts as men do. You would think that in the face of condescension from those who want to keep patting women on the head and telling us we couldn't possibly like that sort of thing, feminism would have our backs—and some parts of the community certainly do. However, for other feminists, women's liking porn is a deeply inconvenient truth, which motivates them to align themselves with sexist and conservative groups and dismiss any woman who enjoys or appears in porn as a brainwashed victim.

I used to empathize strongly with this side of the feminist movement. One reason I ended up moving away from it was that I felt anti-porn feminism was bombarding me with *more* explicit descriptions of supposedly degrading acts via books, speeches and articles than I would have encountered by simply watching the porn myself. I don't wish to resort to the sexist tactic of silencing women by accusing them of getting emotional, but it's important to note the parallel between the doom-mongering of anti-porn feminists and that of pro-lifers, or as I prefer to see them (more accurately) described, anti-choicers. Both consider women too weak and stupid to truly make an informed decision. Both believe themselves to be magically immune to all this cultural brainwashing to which other women have fallen prey. And both love shoving Technicolor, gory images in our faces in order to convince us of the validity of their arguments. It's hard to argue with horror.

As professors Feona Attwood and Clarissa Smith note, women "who testify to porn's pleasures or sense of liberation don't count [for anti-porn feminists] in the same way as those who present themselves as addicts, victims or rescuers."[15] See also sex work and women who enjoy BDSM, especially in a submissive role. It's disappointing to this feminist to see my fellow British women endorse the confused beliefs at the root of UK obscenity law, which go something like, "I personally think fisting/squirting/BDSM/face-sitting is disgusting, therefore I must protect all other adults from viewing it." The arrogance of any person presuming to tell another adult which sex acts are degrading to them is flabbergasting, and seemingly rooted in the belief that any sex beyond monogamous, heterosexual, vaginal intercourse is vile and awful for women. Some hardline second-wave feminists go further, claiming that penis-in-vagina sex is something no woman really enjoys. This is a massive and unsupported leap to make, yet it clearly underpins a lot of anti-porn and anti-sex-work feminism.

Gail Dines is a notorious anti-porn feminist who claims that hardcore internet pornography has been conclusively proven to harm women and whose writing is admired by many British and American feminists. Inconveniently, this proof never originates from anything other than Dines's own prejudices about certain sex acts. Analyzing Dines's writing, professors Feona Attwood and Clarissa Smith point out, "For Dines, anal sex, ejaculation on a woman's body or face, and more than one man having sex with one woman are degrading."[16] There is no debate, no further qualification; Dines finds these acts degrading, ergo they must be labeled as such and censored. It seems blindingly obvious to any adult in possession of basic critical-thinking skills that these views are subjective; it will also be pretty clear to any woman who has enjoyed the described acts that Dines has most likely not tried any of them herself.

The reliance of anti-porn censorship on testimony is problematic, not because women's voices are untrustworthy, but because every individual will suffer from some form of confirmation bias. Herein lies the danger in packaging personal opinion as objective fact. I don't have a foot fetish, and I don't expect I would develop one even if I watched hours of feet-related erotica. I might develop a case of boredom, sleepiness or the giggles, but that's about it. Since my time is precious, I'm not going to devote my energy to persecuting foot fetishists as sick, freaky and dangerous, nor to condemning foot-fetish porn as obscene. I therefore challenge Gail Dines and the members of CPS, BBFC and ATVOD to prove how their biases against sex acts enjoyed by millions of consenting adults are any less arbitrary than mine.

For sex-positive feminists, including normal bodies in erotica is part of the fight back against narrow physical stereotypes (courtesy Emily Brady).

Sex Positivity

It's probably a good time to state that for all my frustrations with anti-porn feminism, this book owes much of its existence to the activism and bravery of sex-positive feminists. It was a feminist magazine that commissioned me to write a blog series on BDSM; interestingly, around the same time, a mainstream women's magazine turned down my article about what a night in a fetish club is really like. Feminist-identifying women, men and gender-fluid individuals have provided me with a rich seam of sources, interviewees, illustrations, movies, books and speeches in which I find the complex and diverse nature of female desire is finally being acknowledged.

Anti-porn activists like to dismiss "sex-pozzers" (as they're sneeringly referred to in hard-line feminist blogs) as endorsing the narrow and repetitious nature of mainstream porn. This implies that our choices are neatly divided between believing either that "all porn is great and unproblematic" or that "all porn is evil and harmful to women." In reality, the sex-positive feminism community is a great place to seek more enlightened discussions on the topic, because this is a community in which it has been considered and debated in greater depth than anywhere else. Take it from someone who quite literally wrote the book on kink and feminism, in a climate where many believed the two practices must be diametrically opposed.

Many of those currently fighting for sexual freedom and against censorship identify as feminist—Blake has always described themselves as a feminist pornographer, as do porn producers Nina Hartley, Kitty Stryker, Courtney Trouble and Annie Sprinkle. This doesn't mean their material always depicts women in positions of power (which is what some mistakenly think constitutes feminist porn), or that their material is necessarily softer or "nicer" than other forms of porn (it's not)—but that it's made under fair and decent performance conditions, depicts unaltered, unairbrushed bodies of the type you might easily see on any British high street; and depicts real pleasure, whether from receiving oral sex, being tied up, being caned or playing with strap-on dildos.

7

That Special Relationship

The United States of America is called the Land of the Free, but it's also the Land of the Deeply Strange. Where else in the world can you buy a gun more easily than you can buy a sex toy? Where else does violence, misogyny and sexism go unchallenged on film, yet Colin Firth's wonderful "Bugger, shit, fuck, tits!" swearing scene in *The King's Speech* (2012) get cut by the film censors? And where else will you find the home of Western filmmaking, the site of some of the most fascinating history regarding movies, censorship, sex and scandal, alongside some of the most intelligent, articulate and friendly people you could hope to meet?

That's not me sucking up, either. As a Briton, I *do* feel smug that while we've enjoyed the freedom of sex shops on our high streets since Ann Summers scandalized my grandparents in 1972, some American state legislatures treat sexy lingerie and vibrators as more dangerous than firearms; Alabama's Anti-Obscenity Enforcement Act of 1998—born not of archaic Victorian standards, but rather the era of *Sex and the City*, *Ally McBeal* and watching porn via an agonizingly slow dial-up connection—criminalizes the sale of sex toys. However, the two nations' stances on obscenity merit a more nuanced comparison than these cherry-picked instances provide, and that is what this chapter will attempt to draw.

The smallness of the scale on which British law operates means it can be difficult for my fellow countrypeople to untangle the knot of city, county, state and federal laws that North Americans navigate daily. To that end, let's pause for a quick primer on the legal pecking order of the United States.

Ten states still had anti-sodomy laws on the books as recently as 2014.[1] Same-sex marriage may have been rendered legal by a 2015 Supreme Court ruling,[2] but only because SCOTUS overruled the 14 states that had laws against it. Barack Obama did take a wonderful parting shot at religious

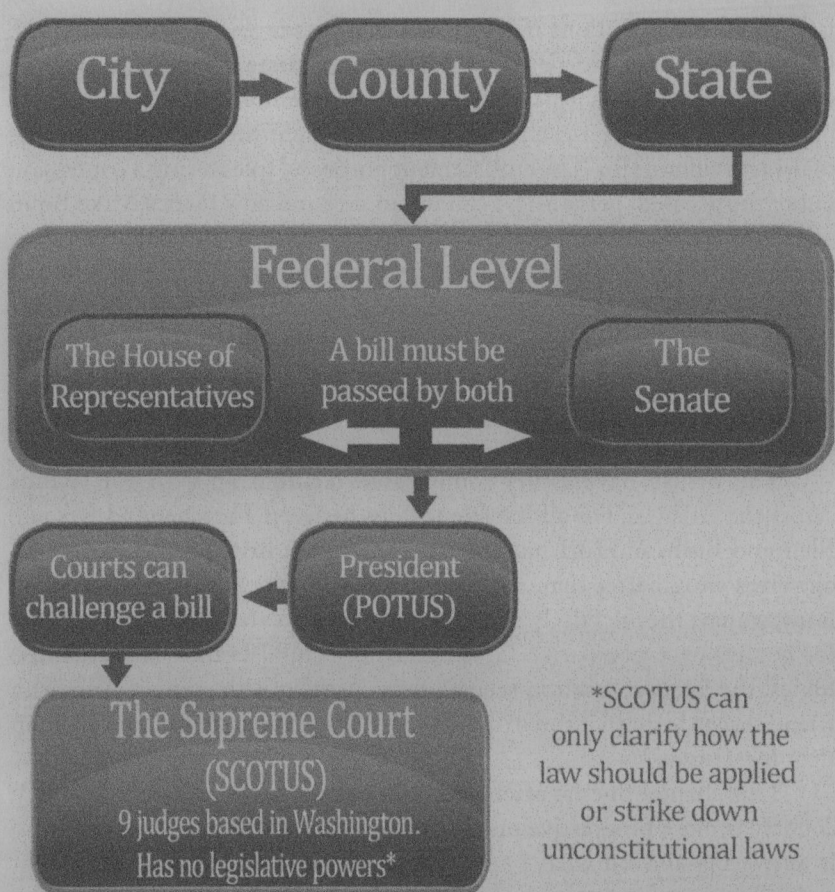

A basic guide to the American justice system (courtesy Emily Brady).

conservatives when he cut all federal funding for abstinence-only sex education, but it took him until 2016 to achieve this, even though it's long been recognized as totally ineffective. Anyone trying to use British tax payers' money for such shenanigans would be laughed off the island in minutes; "Just say no" abstinence campaigns died in Britain as soon as people began dying from AIDS in the '80s. At the time of writing, meanwhile, transgender people have become the scapegoat for all of conservative America's fears, and are being targeted by hateful bathroom bills and military-service bans.

To previous generations of American and British lawmakers, giving pleasure deliberately was a crime, whereas creating art that might arouse someone incidentally was OK. For instance, the aforementioned Alabama law allows for exceptions if you're not using a sex toy to get yourself off. Customers are free and clear if they can demonstrate a "bona fide medical, scientific, educational, legislative, judicial or law enforcement purpose"[3] for buying such an item. Leaving aside for a moment the intriguing concept of using a vibrator for "law enforcement purposes" (pleasuring a confession out of the accused, perhaps?), I cannot understand how Justice Mike Bolin arrived at the conclusion that people buying items to stimulate their own genitals in their own homes "is not a private activity."[4] To be fair, not all U.S. states legislatures are quite so stupid; a Texas court struck down a similar law in 2008, with the presiding judges writing that they had no right to control "what people do in the privacy of their own homes [just] because the state is morally opposed to a certain type of consensual private intimate conduct."[5]

The British have a *very* complicated relationship with our friends across the Atlantic. For all the friendships between Thatcher and Reagan, Blair and Bush, and (if I must) May and Trump, Brits do still like to tell ourselves we're better than our U.S. cousins. Americans don't understand irony, we say; they're falsely cheerful; they have no attention span, no taste for quality over popularity. Given recent electoral events in the United States, the latter accusation seems pretty justified, although an American friend insists I add that three million more people voted for Hilary Clinton than for Trump.

This chapter doesn't offer a straight answer to the question of which country is more progressive on obscenity, because it depends entirely who is answering and on what basis. Silly laws like the Alabama one might make Britain appear more lenient towards explicit content than America, but residents of the UK also accept that our government controls what can be published "particularly in the spheres of 'taste and decency.'"[6] This hardly seems to occur elsewhere in Europe; a quick glance at a Dutch sex shop, a French magazine or an Italian billboard will tell you that much.

To see Britain as inherently more intelligent, cultured and liberal than the USA isn't only arrogant—not to mention self-deceiving, considering the events of June 2016—but when it comes to matters of censorship, it's false. Jerry Barnett told me in no uncertain terms that America has a much stronger record when it comes to freedom of speech: "The First Amendment doesn't stop censorship, but it means that you always have a legal comeback, which isn't the case in Britain. The ACLU will fight stuff that nobody would fight here.... They will defend the Ku Klux Klan and anyone else's free-expression rights. We don't have that culture in the UK."

Barnett was referring to the American Civil Liberties Union, founded in 1920 to protect any American whose rights are under threat. We do have some noteworthy groups in the UK fighting for freedom of expression—Amnesty International, Liberty and the excellent Backlash merit a mention here—but the former is a worldwide organization and the latter two are relatively small. To put it another way, if a British person accused of obscenity tries to cite freedom of speech as their defense, there's no written constitution to protect us, and no guarantee a Supreme Court will back us up.

Still, there were a good couple of centuries during which the UK led in obscenity law and the United States followed. We passed the Campbell Act in 1857; the United States adopted it. British courts banned *Fanny Hill* as obscene; U.S. courts did the same. We had a high-publicity trial over *Lady Chatterley's Lover*; so did America. And as so often seems to be the case whenever Americans adopted British customs, a unique dash of extremist zeal was added to the process.

The effects of the 1857 Campbell Act have reached across time; they also spread across the Atlantic and condemned thousands of women to unwanted pregnancies and resultant poverty, illness and death. If this sounds like too drastic a statement to be true, now would be a good juncture at which to tell the story of Anthony Comstock. This man was not a congressman or a senator, nor did he hold any other significant public office in late–19th-century America. Anthony Comstock was definitely a frothing religious zealot though, and unlike many who meet that description, he was no lone wolf. Using the Campbell Act, plus the Hicklin Test, as his justification, Comstock appointed himself a special agent for the U.S. post office and wreaked havoc on American freedom of communication in the late 1800s. Most frighteningly, he operated with the full backing of the U.S. government.

Comstock's crusade to seize and censor obscene materials and punish their distributors derived from little more than his own demons. In his book *The Birth of The Pill*, Jonathan Eig reports that Comstock masturbated so fervently as a teenager that he considered suicide. I feel some sympathy for the repressed, misinformed teenagers of the 1800s; Irish-American writer Frank McCourt gave much of his memoir *Angela's Ashes* over to his adolescent belief that masturbation would send him to hell (and later, the first girl he had sex with too). The teen McCourt frets, "I can't stop interfering with myself. I pray to the Virgin Mary and tell her I'm sorry I put her Son back on the cross and I'll never do it again but I can't help myself and swear I'll go to confession and after that, surely after that, I'll never do it again. I don't want to go to hell with devils chasing me for eternity jabbing me with hot pitchforks."⁷ To a modern reader, the worries of this Catholic boy are comical, even trivial, but they are also terribly sad accounts of how normal teen boys believed a lake of hellfire and eternal punishment awaited them.

The young Comstock wasn't going to sit and stew in shame, though. He realized that there's no need to blame yourself for your problems when you have a convenient scapegoat. Comstock decided that "filthy books and postcards" were to blame for his addiction to self-love, and set off on his divine mission to purify the U.S. post office. By 1873, the Comstock Act had banned anything "of an indecent character" from being sent through U.S. mail, including not just erotica but information on contraception and contraceptive devices themselves. Comstock paved the way for "every state in the union [to] enact its own anti-obscenity laws, many of which made it illegal to sell or disseminate information on contraception," and even arrested William Sanger, husband of American birth-control activist Margaret Sanger, for distributing pamphlets about birth control.⁸ Comstock seized 200,000 pornographic pictures—which may not sound like a calamity nowadays, but his confiscation of 64,000 contraceptive devices is a lot harder to defend, especially when you consider that American women are still struggling to access decent sex education and affordable birth control today. This is the problem with allowing someone who considers himself "a weeder in God's garden"⁹ to define what is obscene.

Comstock enjoyed the support of the American Medical Association, which wanted the grassroots, women-centric practice of midwifery dissolved and replaced with regulated, hospital-based ob-gyn practitioners (i.e., men). The AMA was happy for information on contraception and abortion to be suppressed—another instance of the male fear of women wielding any power over their own reproductive lives—and "during this period, anatomy and medical textbooks were seized, restrained and re-edited to comply with the strictures upheld in the Rosen decision."¹⁰ If even an association of *doctors* was happy for *actual medical information* to be censored, what hope was there for a sensible attitude towards reproduction from the less scientifically minded? This goes some way towards explaining why, although it ceased to be effective in the mid–20th century, the last Comstock law was not struck down until 1972.

Comstock's actions and motivations parallel the modern campaigns against porn led by those who claim to suffer from porn or sex addiction themselves. Both are concepts that regularly appear in mainstream media, usually as the accompaniment to a celebrity's excusing their infidelity or repeated creeping on women via claims to be a sex or porn addict. Tiger Woods, David Duchovny and Bill Clinton are just a few of the rich, powerful men I can remember being labeled thus over the past two decades, but in their scramble to document a new and scandalous malady, the media left out one important fact; neither sex addiction nor porn addiction have been conclusively proven to exist.

In 2014, clinical psychologist David Ley carried out an extensive study[11] on the literature surrounding porn addiction and concluded that "less than 1 percent of the 40,000 articles that they looked at were ... scientifically or empirically useful." He added that this was because most people who write about porn addiction have an agenda to push, be it conservative, feminist or otherwise. As someone well aware of how divided the feminist community is over the issue of porn, I am not in the least surprised to hear this. I respect that other women feel very differently about pornography, that some consider it at best an unwelcome side effect of sexual liberation, and at worst the exemplification of every evil that men secretly wish to enact upon women. However, I do not believe that personal prejudices have any place in lawmaking, and it's these that infomed both the Comstock laws in the 1800s and feminists' attempted anti-pornography ordinances in the 1980s.

Ley adds that studies on porn addiction are regularly let down by "poor experimental designs, limited methodological rigor, and lack of model specification." United States and UK media, including excellent independent outlets like Everyday Feminism, don't help the matter when they act as if porn addiction were a proven illness. This explains why "the overwhelming majority of articles published on porn addiction *include no empirical research*.... Less than one in four actually have data. In less than one in 10 is that data analyzed or organized in a scientifically valid way."

Unfortunately, those with a moral agenda to push have often been content to ignore the logical flaws in assigning responsibility for one's actions to an already-demonized external factor. This goes some way to explaining how the likes of Comstock got away with it for so long. Not only did Comstock stop women from preventing the unwanted pregnancies that were killing and impoverishing them, he actively caused deaths. At least 15 of the women charged under Comstock's law committed suicide rather than face the public shame of a trial. But hey, what's a little collateral damage when you're on a divinely sanctioned mission to prevent wanking?

While Britons can reassure themselves that such prudish zealotry could never spiral out of control in their country, we should hesitate before considering Britain blameless in the matter; it was our own laws that allowed the Comstock laws to survive an 1896 challenge in the case of *Rosen v. U.S.* This particular defense "cited the precedent of English common law upholding the government's ability to censor material that would tend 'to deprave or corrupt those whose minds are open to such immoral influences.'" Even though 120 years had elapsed since the United States won its independence from the UK, America was still happy to resort to British legal precedent when it suited her ends.

Separate but Equal

So why was America, a country that had proudly declared its independence from British rule in 1776, still happy to ape UK law in the 1800s? For one, the United States was a vast, rapidly growing country whose population was fast outstripping its legal reach. The collective mind-set of 19th-century Americans was one of such libertarianism that it would make Ron Swanson proud. The Constitution was the structure that protected Americans from the "new, suspect central government that a great many ... did not want at all."[12] Which was all well and good, but trying to administer the Constitution across thousands of miles, millions of people and 40-plus state borders was an unenviable task. By contrast, the British powers that be only had to keep their eye on a land area half the size of California, plus a few million tea-drinking malcontents. It's easy to see why U.S. courts in the 1800s often found it easier to borrow from British legal precedent, including "the rule that it was a crime to publish an obscene book."[13] In 1821, two Boston booksellers were convicted for distributing *Fanny Hill*. Then came the Campbell Act in 1857, and the Hicklin Test 11 years later. The unspoken motto was "As the UK leads, so shall the United States follow."

Charles Rembar, the American lawyer who defended *Fanny Hill*, *Lady Chatterley's Lover* and Henry Miller's *Tropic of Cancer* in the 1950s and '60s, was always vehement in his condemnation of the Campbell Act. Obscenity specialist Rembar, who sadly passed away in 2000, scoffed that when the original OPA passed in 1857, "wit was on the side of freedom, and the votes were on the side of suppression."[14] Regarding the Hicklin Test, Rembar points out that "the most common agent of corruption is money. Under the Hicklin Test, could money be described in frank detail? Would we then suppress the *Wall Street Journal*?"[15]

Although his target was Campbell and the British judiciary, Rembar's criticisms retain a much wider application, especially today. The *Wall Street Journal* is currently controlled by Rupert Murdoch, head of a media empire that controls much of what Britons and Americans see on TV, in newspapers and magazines and online. I refuse to buy any media product associated with Murdoch, so strong is my hatred for his grasping monopoly, and I would be happy if his entire output were declared obscene with one stroke.

Furthermore, those of us who lived through the financial crisis of 2007–2008 and its terrible consequences definitely consider bankers and banking institutions both depraved and corrupt for the nonchalant manner in which they toyed with people's lives and livelihoods. They made use of dirty tactics, filthy money and moral codes so low they would get vertigo in a sewer, yet no corporation or individual was arrested under obscenity law. I should add that if anyone mentions the name Bernie Madoff in the presence of my father, the result will be a furious barrage of facts, figures and bile that will pin you to your chair in sheer amazement that Madoff got away with his actions for so long. If you feel brave enough to mention the bankers to the average working-class Briton, consider yourself lucky if they don't spit in your face.

As Bill Bryson details with great humor in *The Life and Times of the Thunderbolt Kid*, an account of his childhood in 1950s Iowa, the United States would continue its push-me, pull-you war on corrupting influences well into the 20th century. Congress enacted 20 different obscenity laws between 1842 and 1956; by that point, all 48 states had some type of law regarding this shape-shifting concept. Organizations clamoring for higher moral standards became the bloodhounds protecting these laws, sniffing out filth and clamping down on it.

Then came Hollywood.

While the rest of the United States was drinking iced tea on a fainting couch and covering piano legs with skirts (or something), a new industry was surging ahead on a tide of morally dubious media: the movies. Those who know Thomas Edison as the man who patented the light bulb may not realize that he applied his skills in the film industry too. Edison had already patented the phonograph and now wanted to add pictures to the mix. During the late 1800s, Edison patented his motion-picture device the Kinetoscope, and with the help of his Scottish employee William Dickson had built the first film studio in the world by 1893. However, despite Edison's fascination with the potential to create moving pictures, they weren't initially a product anyone cared about. This may sound implausible, given that the Western movie industry is now among the most lucrative on the planet, but in Edison's time movies were simply a means to an end. Edison and his rivals wanted to show how amazing their inventions were; hence they needed movies to show on their projection equipment. The pull of the motion-picture industry in the late–19th and early–20th century was down to the inventions, not the art. So next time you're cringing over the latest terrible Jason Statham project, blame Edison and the projection companies for setting this precedent. Movies were never intended to be art; they were intended to be commercial (and if the rash of product placements in recent films is anything to go by, that wish has been thoroughly fulfilled).

I didn't realize until I began researching this chapter that the first movie-production studio was nowhere near Los Angeles; it was in the lush, green Garden State of New Jersey. As a Brit susceptible to the glamorous myths surrounding Hollywood, I was also unaware of why and how the movie industry moved to California, until cinema scholar Brian Dillingham clued me in. The burgeoning U.S. motion-picture industry was centered on the East Coast in the late 1890s and early 1900s, with Edison and the companies Biograph and Vitagraph as its three major players. Edison's habit of suing any company he thought was treading on his territory meant that independent film companies steered well clear of New York or New Jersey, and instead started an exodus towards the West. If this sounds like paranoia on their behalf, bear in mind that Edison maintained his monopoly over the motion-picture industry with furious legal action: he brought twenty lawsuits in as many years against his competitors. You can see why fledgling companies preferred to run and set up shop elsewhere, rather than stay and fight the litigation-happy inventor.

Plus, much as Britain's coastline provided the "pirate radio" stations of the 1960s and '70s with the legal protection they required from broadcasting law, movie producers saw the sense in basing their companies near the golden beaches of America's West Coast. It meant that if patent-law enforcers managed to pursue your company all the way across the country, you still had the option to hop on a boat or leg it down to Mexico so that the Feds could not touch you.

Unfortunately, movie-production companies did not have long to pause for breath after their epic journey away from the long arm of Edison. Anti-obscenity zealots soon caught up to this strange phenomenon of motion pictures, and in 1915, the Supreme Court of Ohio unanimously ruled against the Mutual Film Company, which had argued that movies should be treated as a form of speech and thus protected under the First Amendment. The 9–0 decision that movies were products, and ergo were not protected by the Constitutional right to free speech, was a massive blow not just to the MFC, but to all motion-picture producers. In concentrating on the visual rather than verbal aspect of film, moviemakers had somewhat shot themselves in the foot; since the first "talking picture" would not appear for another 12 years, it was easy for courts to dismiss the free-speech defense. Brian Dillingham picks up the story: "The Ohio decision freaked out everyone! All of a sudden, states were able to create their own censorship boards. There was no federal [countrywide] censorship board and that's the one thing movie studios truly feared. They didn't want the government coming in and cracking down on their freedom of speech."

And create their own censorship boards they did. Thanks to the precedent set by Ohio, 37 states submitted censorship bills in 1921 alone. Fatty Arbuckle and Buster Keaton were some of the earliest entertainers to suffer the consequences of this new morality police taking over the United States. Arbuckle was accused of manslaughter and sexually assaulting an actress, and even though he was acquitted, the media attention to all the sordid details of the case took its toll. Physically and psychologically ruined, Arbuckle died at the age of 33; Buster Keaton, his comedy partner, suffered massive damage to his career simply due to his association with Arbuckle. This was neither the first or the last time the U.S. movie industry would be accused of ushering in a new era of degeneracy.

In a less tragic incident, the legend of stage and screen Mae West paid the price for being a sexually open, fast-talking woman of considerable business acumen in 1927. West wrote and starred in the play *Sex*, which enjoyed a ten-month Broadway run before the obscenity police got word of it. To a modern audience it's a comical tale—the play contains a few double entendres, and nothing more raunchy happens onstage than a man and a woman discussing a birdcage. Yet West actually served jail time for corrupting the audiences who, naturally, flocked to watch *Sex*. A grand jury deemed the play to be "obscene, indecent, immoral and impure," and said that it risked corrupting the young.[16] West—not coincidentally one of my all-time idols, not least because of her refusal to apologize for her sexuality or take any nonsense from men—was sentenced to ten days in jail for bringing *Sex* to the American public. Being a woman who never shied away from confrontation, West traveled to the prison in a limousine, covered herself in roses and wore silk underwear. If she hadn't already been my hero before I read that particular story, she certainly would be now.

Following the Ohio decision, states and cities began to form their own censorship boards as a matter of necessity. Now that movies officially had no protection from the Constitution, it was up to individual states to rule on what material could and could not be shown on the big screen. Much like the confused situation in '50s and '60s Britain, whereby books were banned in one city but available in another, an American in the 1920s could watch a movie at their local cinema, then board a bus to the next town and watch a different version of the same movie.

Jazz music. Rock 'n' roll. Miniskirts. Ozzy Osbourne. Trousers. Marilyn Manson. Bikinis. Cars.

What do all these have in common, apart from providing fascination to American teenagers during the 20th century?

They have all been blamed, at one point or another, for moral decline in the young. Matt Brennan, a music fellow at the University of Edinburgh, writes, "Jazz was simultaneously vilified and valourised. It was a youth culture thought to be subversive and morally corrupt, prefiguring the teenage revolution of the baby boomer generation."[17] Then there were comic books, energetically pursued by anti-obscenity crusaders throughout 20th-century America. Thanks to the efforts of Dr. Fredric Wertham, a psychiatrist who believed that comics promoted, as Bryson puts it, "violence, torture, criminality, drug-taking and masturbation, though not presumably all at once,"[18] 13 states had passed laws restricting the publication and distribution of these inflammatory items. With frightening similarity to the case of William Comstock, Wertham's own sexual obsession seems to have been the root of his tendency to see smut everywhere—in one comic book, he claimed, the shading on a man's shoulder resembled a vulva.

The National Organization for Decent Literature placed Sensation Comics on its list of "Publications Disapproved for Youth" in 1942. Its reasoning was that "Wonder Woman is not sufficiently dressed." Ironically, the issues in question show Wonder Woman relatively covered up, sporting a mid-thigh skirt instead of her more controversial micro-shorts, in an effort by her creators to make her a less sexy, more All-American girl. For children at the time like Bill Bryson, the worst was still to come. Bryson recalls the terrible moment when Fredric Wertham accused two iconic superheroes of not being true men in the "red-blooded, girl-kissing sense." "Batman and Robin in particular he singled out as 'a wish dream of two homosexuals living together.' It was an unanswerable charge. You had only to look at their tights."[19]

A Roll in the Hays

Next came the Motion Picture Production Code, soon abbreviated to the Hays Code after William H Hays, who was president of the Motion Picture Association of America from 1922 to 1945. The Hays Code was intended to prove that the movie industry was capable of regulating itself, and thereby to protect movie producers from the interference of federal or state censors. Film scholars generally view Hays as a quaint, hilarious window into a time when the American authorities were so fearful of moving pictures that they imposed biblical standards upon them, but many also agree that the Code was necessary and inevitable. The industry had to self-regulate or risk the iron fist of federal law smashing it to bits.

To a 21st-century moviegoer, the Hays Code rightly seems ridiculous. It forbade movies from including swearing, nudity, "any inference of sex perversion," interracial relationships, childbirth and any mention of contraception or divorce. If two people were sitting on a bed in a movie, one of the pair had to have their feet on the floor. As pop culture critic Andi Zeisler writes, the Code provided a convenient excuse to push the most conservative vision of America possible. The specificity of its guidelines made sure that any hint of a diverse USA was erased from the silver screen: "Tacit disdain for people of color, homosexuals, transgender people, people with disabilities, that was Hollywood's neat … reality."[20]

The Code was most energetically enforced by Joseph Breen, a self-styled moral crusader determined to stop the flow of filth emanating from America's West Coast. Breen, a devout Catholic and notorious anti–Semite, insinuated himself into the Hays administration in the early 1930s, and "although he never directed a millimeter of film footage himself, [he] left a deep and indelible mark on every movie that Hollywood made between 1934 and 1954."[21] As I've made clear elsewhere in this book, privileged white men with a bee in their bonnet have always been in need of new hobbies, but in this case as with so many others, Breen's misplaced moral crusade led to a creative industry suffocated by personal prejudices. Inevitably, limits on artistic freedom followed. Filmmakers were now obliged to submit their script for checking that it adhered to the Code, which even dictated where the audience's sympathies had to lie. Its first principle was "No picture shall be produced which will lower the standards of those who see it. Hence the sympathy of the audience shall never be thrown to the side of crime, wrongdoing, evil or sin."

The manner in which movie companies were hamstrung by Hays has much in common with the way the Stationers' Guild maintained a stranglehold over English publishers in the 16th and 17th centuries. In both cases, writers faced a surreal choice between submitting their work to the authorities to be stringently checked and then *maybe*, if they were lucky, published in censored form, or taking the illegal step of publishing without permission, which would bring brutal legal consequences with it.

In modern Britain, as the love of management consultants continues to grow, it's entirely possible to become head of a school without any background in teaching or education. Similarly, Joseph Breen had never directed, written, created or appeared in a movie. You may say this made him more objective as a movie censor, as he had no biases toward any particular film or filmmaker. However, the heavy Catholic influence on the Hays Code says otherwise. In fact, movies couldn't be released without a seal from the Catholic Legion of Decency, in case members of the church accidentally stained their souls by watching a movie with sinful themes.

Smooth Criminals

Breen and his Code were at least equal-opportunity offenders, focusing on the sin of crime almost as much as that of sex. The Hays Code stated that movies could show crime as long as it didn't benefit the protagonist, which resulted in directors and writers having to bend their product to fit this bizarre demand. This was problematic if you were trying to draw audiences via a big name like James Cagney, as Warner Brothers found with their 1931 movie *The Public Enemy*. The Code dictated that a movie can show a good-looking chap being a criminal as long as the story arc also emphasized that crime doesn't pay. To stay on the right side of this rule, Warner Brothers had to change the ending of the movie so that Cagney's protagonist ends up a corpse.

The Code also forbade showing or glorifying suicide. Alfred Hitchcock, never one to shy away from a very British dust-up with American authorities, wanted to depict suicide in his 1945 psychological thriller *Spellbound*; the rotund director quietly circumvented the idiocy of the Code by filming the suicide scene from a first-person-point-of-view angle.

If it seemed ambitious to task movies with the responsibility of reinforcing the moral principles of the American public, Breen and the Catholic Legion of Decency weren't fazed. The liberal use of the word "sin" in the Code made it clear whom Breen was batting for; it stated that evil must not be "presented alluringly," and must be punished sufficiently, so that "the audience feels sure that evil is wrong and good is right." The Code's clause concerning "impure love" never even defines this intriguing concept, but instead wriggles out of the uncomfortable question by deeming it "love which society has always regarded as wrong, and which has been banned by divine law." My guess is that extramarital, premarital, nonmonogamous, non-heterosexual relationships were out, as were interracial pairings.

So much for separation of church and state, then—and so much for the First Amendment too.

By the 1950s, film would receive First Amendment protection, further eroding the reach of the Hays Code. A landmark case in 1952, *Burstyn v. Wilson*, saw the Ohio decision overturned. Once SCOTUS had said that movies counted as speech and were therefore protected, the dam that Breen,

Hays and the moral-purity campaigners had built started to crack severely. A flood of sex, violence and profanity threatened ... and the average American welcomed it with open arms.

Many crises end with a whimper rather than a bang. In a similar vein, as one moral panic followed another in 20th-century America, the outdated principles of the Hays Code were not withdrawn but simply superseded. By the 1960s, movie studios were beginning to lose their influence, and Hollywood was turning its money and energy towards the exciting new medium of television. The movie industry could bring in millions of rutting teens in souped-up old cars, if the script of *Grease* is anything to go by. Movies now had the sheen of wholesome, mainstream appeal, and the Motion Picture Production Code was getting diluted to the point of total irrelevance.

The specificity of the Hays Code was its downfall; American society had evolved in leaps and bounds by 1961, when the Code was altered to allow subtle depictions of homosexuality. This was forward thinking indeed, seeing as state law still prohibited sex between men in most of America and, as we've discussed elsewhere, couldn't even conceive of what sex between women might mean.

The British Are Coming

Funnily enough, it was British film that ended up exposing the limits of the Hays Code. For all our buttoned-up squeamishness about sex, there was a brief era in Hollywood when a British movie blazed a trail in the pushback against censorship. Alfred Hitchcock's 1946 movie, *Notorious*, contains a long, passionate kiss between Cary Grant and Ingrid Bergman; the American censors replaced it with a dialogue scene. While researching this movie, Hitchcock also displayed wonderful disregard for America's paranoia about nuclear weapons by asking government officials how much uranium was required to make an atomic bomb. The eccentric British filmmaker was checking his facts, as every good artist does, so that the film's scenes about uranium ore were realistic. The FBI didn't see it this way, and followed Hitchcock for the next three months in case he decided to turn his research into a reality.[22] Given that the Cold War was at its height, you can see why the American authorities were suspicious of the portly, inscrutable director marching into their offices and asking about matters of international security.

Then, of course, came that smuttiest of British imports—the *James Bond* franchise—which my fellow Brits will be pleased to know gave U.S. screenwriters plenty of cause for concern. "You won't believe how film censors freaked out over Pussy Galore," Brian Dillingham told me. "Originally they wanted to call her Kitty Galore!" Indeed, until I started writing this book, I had no idea that the character of Pussy Galore was originally meant to be a butch lesbian. I'm aware that it's a form of British heresy to say this, but I've never read an Ian Fleming novel, or watched an entire *James Bond* film, nor am I particularly interested in the 007 franchise as a whole. Speaking as a left-leaning feminist, I have to say that the sexism, racism and often pure naffness of Bond films will never sit well with me, but I know I'm in a minority among Brits. As for Pussy Galore? From the *Bond* clips I did catch as a child (the movies are rarely off British TV, even today), I recall Honor Blackman looking amazing in a catsuit, her big hair and the way Bond always addressed her in slightly sleazy, crooning tones. I also remember my aviator father proudly announcing that he had flown with one of the pilots in Pussy's all-female flying squadron, so I can see some subtle hints of her being, if not a lesbian, then at least a liberated woman for the time. But she was definitely not butch by any stretch of the imagination, and history does not record why the character was feminized so greatly in the transition from book to screen.

No matter, because it wasn't the possible lesbianism of this great femme fatale that got United Artists' knickers in a twist. It was Pussy—the name, that is. During preproduction on *Goldfinger* (1964), no one in Hollywood thought that the makers could get away with a name that seemed to indicate either a lot of cats or a surfeit of female genitalia; United Artists favored "Kitty" Galore as an acceptable alternative. However, a savvy publicist named Tom Carlisle, who worked closely with Bond legend Cubby Broccoli, avoided this compromise by quietly leaking the original name to the press. Once a public hungry for Hollywood gossip heard that the next *Bond* movie would quite literally contain Pussy Galore, there was no going back. Censors have limited time, resources and money, and they weren't going to waste their energy taking on a franchise as widely loved as *James Bond*.

Evolve or Dissolve

Part of why Britain's Obscene Publications Act has persisted so long is its vagueness—there are no specific taboos in it that might render it dated or irrelevant. By contrast, the Hays Code saw its banned list—swearing, drug addiction, nudity—eroded bit by bit, as more risqué movies were passed for distribution. By 1966, the Code was effectively dead, to be replaced by the film-ratings system, still in place today. Shortly afterwards,

SCOTUS established America's own version of the Hicklin Test. This followed the landmark 1973 case *Miller v. California*, in which the Court ruled 5–4 that obscene material was not protected under the First Amendment. The ruling is famous because one of the justices who voted with the majority, Warren Burger, gave America its first working definition of obscenity. In a statement that would form the "Miller test," still the legal benchmark used today, Burger said that obscenity depends upon:

(a) whether the work appeals to "prurient interest";
(b) whether the work depicts or describes, in a patently offensive way, sexual conduct; and
(c) whether the work lacks serious literary, artistic, political or scientific value.

After Hays, Breen and their fellow anti-obscenity crusaders, the Miller Test may seem progressive, but that's only by contrast with an even more repressive past. In fact, Burger's test forces artists to defend their work as beneficial to the public in a way required of no one else. It raises, yet again, the question of what constitutes a "patently offensive" description of sexual conduct, and who should get to decide. Most crucially, it fails to consider that free expression of sexuality may be a *part* of the public good. Naturally, I can only speak to my own experience, but a vibrator has never made me want to go out and club someone over the head or crash my car into a lamppost, and it also helps with my chronic writer's cramp. To my mind, most music videos, movies, TV shows, songs and hip-hop lyrics lack artistic merit, endorse offensive views of women, people of color and LGBTQ folk, and certainly appeal to nonacademic interests. So do the words of many UK and U.S. politicians, and don't get me started on POTUS. Regardless, I don't see it as my right to prevent other adults from enjoying all these cultural artifacts.

To borrow a few great phrases from Charles Rembar, the Miller test implies that all creative works divide between two mutually exclusive categories: first, proper art and literature, which produces "emotional responses from somewhere above the belt" (HA!), and second, "pornography, which gets you in the groin."[23] While the Miller test may be more specific than the Hicklin Test's vague notions of depravity and corruption, I'm not convinced that it's any more of an aid to defining obscenity than the OPA. Instead, it merely echoes what Sir Alan Herbert said to Parliament during the 1970s: "It is the other man you want to get after, the man who sits down and thinks 'I want to make my readers as randy as I can, as often as I can.'" Justice Burger seemed to inhabit an imaginary world where educated, rich people never masturbate or enjoy erotica, and where work aimed at arousing people must be morally inferior to work aimed at entertaining them. Far from freeing creators of erotica, his test merely forced them to choose sides of a nonsensical binary: staying above the belt or getting hit in the groin.

While researching this chapter, I watched the fascinating 2006 documentary *This Film Is Not Yet Rated*, which claims that the current U.S. movie-ratings system is deeply conservative and highly secretive. The MPAA's criteria definitely echo the UK's AVMS regulations; movies that depict female sexual pleasure, anyone performing oral sex on a woman, female ejaculate (*Boys Don't Cry*) or same-gender sex scenes consistently receive higher ratings (NC-17) than films showing straight sex, oral sex on a man or bloody violence. Although this documentary came out more than a decade ago, I believe that this double standard persists even more strongly today. As an enthusiastic cinemagoer myself, I've seen plenty of thin white women appear naked in mainstream movies, but very little in the way of penises, gay sex, imperfect bodies and women receiving sexual pleasure.

I've recently rewatched the excellent BBC/Netflix series *Peaky Blinders*, a dark English drama that is set between 1919 and 1923. I was not surprised to find that the director of photography on this TV show is a woman, because the wonderfully shot sex scenes—plus other, nonsexual scenes of dressing, undressing, bathing and so on—include loads of naked male bodies. For once, we see more men's bums, chests, shoulders and rippling muscles and a lot fewer female bosoms and backsides. It's sexy, it's realistic and it's refreshing; but it shouldn't even be worth remarking upon in a Western world that considers its media gender-balanced. Hollywood and the MPAA, take note.

For all this, there remains something to be learned from a country that enjoys the protections of the First Amendment. In 1997, parts of the proposed Communications Decency Act were struck down as unconstitutional. The UK government would do well to heed the stated justification: "We have repeatedly recognized the governmental interest in protecting children from harmful materials. But that interest does not justify an unnecessarily broad suppression of speech addressed to adults."

Similarly, the Child Online Protection Act was declared unconstitutional in 2009, whereas the UK government has successfully forced through similar "protective" legislation while I've been writing this book. Outside of the Miller test, there exists no specific U.S. law relating to obscenity; only varying state laws. Unlike the ATVOD and now Ofcom, there is no American regulator dedicated to policing online content, nor any specific

7. That Special Relationship   141

set of rules governing what can be shown. This seems a much more practical approach; minimal legislation, specific regulations replaced by common sense (if it's legal to do, it's legal to show) and no need for shadowy groups who push their personal prejudices on millions of adults' private activities.

The United States wasn't always so sensible, and its stance on obscenity remains unsatisfactory in many ways, but it's telling that America's laws have been most conservative when inspired by her friend across the Atlantic.

8

Shoving It Down Our Throats

"Active homosexuals are potentially murderers and … the act of buggery kills."—George Gale[1]

The year 2017 marked the 50th anniversary of the Sexual Offences Act in Britain, a landmark ruling that legalized homosexual acts between men aged 21 and over. During the summer of 2017, the British media was full of documentaries, dramas, radio programs and online articles celebrating the freedoms brought by the act, but also reminding audiences that the era of repressive homophobia was not so long ago. One article in particular that stayed with me concerned a British naval officer charged with homosexual acts in the 1950s. Not only was the young man dragged through court, shamed, ostracized and encouraged to turn in his lovers to save himself, but he was subjected to a medical examination involving violations that would make anyone's eyes water. When the punishments for being a gay man are clearly so much more despicable than any sex act committed in private, obscenity is reduced to a nonsensical concept. However, in a culture where masculinity is far too often reinforced through sexism and the dismissal of anything remotely feminine, homophobic censorship was never going to die without a fight.

It was only following the release of the 2013 film *The Imitation Game*, which looks at the persecution of Bletchley Park codebreaker Alan Turing, that much of today's British public realized that men could—and did—go to jail for being homosexual. A mathematical genius, Turing struggled with being gay at a time when it was socially unspeakable and legally forbidden, and his arrest for indecent acts with another man led directly to his suicide in 1954. The British judiciary gave Turing the choice between jail or chemical castration, and after opting for the latter, the hero of Bletchley Park suffered such terrible mental and physical effects that he chose to take his own life. Turing was posthumously pardoned by the British government, as were thousands of other men charged with "indecency," but when scores of people have already killed themselves out of shame or gone to their graves hiding their true selves from their loved ones, pardons feel like far too little, too late.

The irony is particularly acute when we consider that Dirk Bogarde, the British actor, who bravely played a gay man in the film *Victim* six years before the passage of the 1967 Act, was himself homosexual but never dared publicly acknowledge it. And why on earth would he have? He would have been arrested. His reputation, and probably his acting career too, would have been destroyed. With eerie prescience, Bogarde's character in *Victim* even says, "I've been to prison four times. I couldn't go through that again."

Not that Bogarde got off lightly; even *playing* a gay man was enough to seriously damage his career. Commentators now conclude that Bogarde's star as an actor was forever tarnished by *Victim*, and he never commanded the same respect in the movie industry again. Rock Hudson, the epitome of Hollywood masculinity in the 1950s, didn't fare much better when he came out in the mid-'80s; Barry Manilow, singer and favorite of my grandmother, has only just come out as gay (and married to a man) at the age of 70.

In 2015, I watched a new British TV series named *Cucumber*, an excellent comedy drama from the creators of the original *Queer as Folk*. I laughed and gasped my way through the first frank, funny episodes, and then I watched in stunned horror as a gay black character was queer-bashed to death by a "confused" straight man wielding a golf club. The vicious, unprovoked attack was shown in full, graphic Technicolor and made for a horrific viewing experience. I admit to being seriously disturbed by the scene, but I applauded the creators of the show for their unflinching look at how homophobia kills, and for reminding heterosexuals how the reduction of gay culture to camp, pink, fluff obscures a fatal culture of shame.

Public Scandal and Private Shaming

> "Lesbians and gay men are particularly vulnerable to the effects of restrictive legislation. There are many people in positions of power who believe that homosexuality is itself essentially 'pornographic.'"—Elizabeth Wilson[2]

The idea that hearing about male homosexuality must have a uniquely corrupting influence has a long history in Britain. Trials in which men were accused of homosexual activity were regularly prefaced with a warning that ladies might find the contents of the trial offensive, which is pretty hilarious given that the demographic most consistently hostile to gay men is—shocker!—straight men. What the ongoing straight-male obsession with sex between men indicates is anyone's guess, although I have a few good theories. But given how the British judiciary has regularly depicted women as paragons of purity and then used this as an excuse to deny them rights, I'm not surprised that "protecting the delicate ladies" was the chosen pretext for dismissing gay sex as simply unspeakable. After all, the supposedly straight men who controlled Britain's law and media until recently would not have wanted to invite speculation about their reasons for despising gays.

Still, it's heartening to learn that as early as 1957 the Wolfenden Committee was trying to inject some sense into the British legal system, recommending that sex between men be decriminalized (although it was less liberal on other issues, recommending harsher punishments for sex work by women). Simply serving on the Wolfenden Committee was a brave act considering that the recent "Lavender Scare" had produced a spate of vindictive prosecutions against homosexuals encouraged by the ultra-conservative home secretary, David Maxwell Fyfe.[3] It was an uphill battle for Wolfenden's recommendations to be heard, let alone heeded, which explains why it took another decade for sex between men to be decriminalized.

Those not directly involved in the fight for gay rights might presume that the 1967 Act ushered in an era of acceptance of homosexuality in Britain, and that the battle was therefore won. In fact, the new law prompted a short-term backlash; during the early 1970s, prosecutions of gay men for indecency went up, not down.[4] Furthermore, this new, public acknowledgment of male homosexuality meant gay men were under a legal microscope more than ever. The fact the act distinguished between sex acts in private and in public left gay men even more frightened to express their sexuality, lest their chosen venue be considered not private enough. Since there were likely to be few gay couples able to live together or even find a safe space to carry out their relationships—we're talking about a time when landlords openly refused to rent to people of color, the Irish, unmarried women and cohabiting straight couples—I do wonder how gay men of this era ever managed to have sex in private. To add insult to injury, the publishers of *Last Exit to Brooklyn* were found guilty of obscenity in 1969 because the book "promoted homosexuality or other sexual perversions," language that would be echoed in 1988 when Section 28 took effect. The jury in the *Last Exit* case was all-male because female jurors were considered too fragile to cope with a book that dealt with homosexuality and drug use. Not only does this support the maddening stereotype of women's being inherently innocent and more easily shocked than men, it raises the question of how obscene materials can ever safely be evaluated if their potential to warp minds is so great. By this logic, no one, not even a juror, is immune to their malign influences!

LGBT people have long demanded that they be recognized and treated as full human beings rather than stereotypes. When the straight community hasn't been responding with outright hostility, it has opted for a grudging admission that gay people may deserve basic rights, but it has also been quick to add that anything more is "shoving it down our throats." This inadvertently homoerotic quote sums up a predominant British attitude towards homosexuality during the past half century. A 1975 poll showed only four in ten Britons approved of gay couples living together openly; while we can presume some respondents simply disapproved of any extra-marital cohabiting, the choice of the word "openly" implies that others would simply rather it be kept secret. The retailer British Home Stores forced a trainee manager to resign in 1976 following a TV documentary in which the man was shown kissing his boyfriend. For a public figure to come out in the 1970s was still a revolutionary and dangerous act, and the British media knew it.

I'm regularly surprised by how few people outside the LGBT community are aware that the age of sexual consent for gay men was not equalized with that of straight couples until the year 2000. I remember reading a fascinating article in the must-have teen magazine of the mid-'90s, *Just Seventeen*, about this very subject. A young gay man had written an articulate protest of the fact British law considered him too naïve to know he wanted to have sex with men until he was 18, whereas straight couples could legally have sex, produce children and marry as soon as they hit 16. I would have been 11 years old at most when I encountered this, but I remember thinking it was a pretty patronizing law even then; it remained on the books with little to no public comment for another five years.

Intriguingly, it became legal to depict homosexuality in British theaters in 1958, one year before the Obscene Publications Act was renewed, and nine years before male homosexuality was legalized. Perhaps campaigners for social change figured that the theater was a good place to start testing the waters, insofar as its clientele was predominantly middle- or upper-class, educated, left-wing and much more accepting of alternative lifestyles. Working in theater meant one could rub shoulders with daring, bohemian characters, and promised access to subcultures where homosexuality was not merely tolerated but actively celebrated. Demonstrating that there really is no business like show business, Sir Ian McKellen says he became an actor in the 1950s "because I thought I could meet other queers."[5]

The belief that any depiction of homosexual activity is tantamount to endorsement persists in some pockets of modern Britain, neatly sidestepping the fact that heterosexual romance and sexuality bombard us everywhere we turn in pop culture. As far as I'm aware, no one has yet wrung their hands about the dangers of "turning straight" from these influences, but conservatives have long believed in the power of homosexuality to recruit the young to its Big Gay Agenda. In 1989, the respected British astronomer Patrick Moore denounced the book *The Milkman's on His Way*, which dared to show a gay teen in a positive light. Using the exact language of the OPA, Moore told the *Evening Standard*, "Our children are being corrupted and depraved by it. [They] will read it and try it out and get AIDS." This was a stunning assertion coming from a man of science, but if Moore really believed that "trying out" gay behavior was so seductive to children, then his call to censor homosexuality as obscene made sense. Being gay wasn't just immoral, the logic went, it was dangerous precisely because of its seductive call to jump on the homosexual bandwagon. During the 1980s, when AIDS was still a mysterious, frightening and fatal condition, acceptance of gay male sexuality suffered greatly from the widespread belief that it was a disease spread (and deserved) by promiscuous gay men.

Such vile attitudes exemplify the 1980s backlash against the liberalization of the 1960s and '70s. The election of Margaret Thatcher in 1979 indicated the most significant rightward swing for British society since the 1940s. Up until this point, Jerry Barnett writes, there was great optimism about the direction of free speech in Britain: "the core of British censorship law looked obsolete: surely it was a matter of time before the OPA was scrapped?"[6] Not only did the OPA remain firmly in place, but an insidious belief that oppressed groups had simply gone too far in demanding equality permeated British culture. A January 1988 editorial from *The Sun* titled "When the Gays Have to Shut Up" ranted that "many [homosexuals] now regard themselves as superior. They believe it is they who are normal, and the rest of society which is perverse." It makes absolutely cringeworthy reading in the 21st century, but I don't exist in enough of a liberal bubble to think that it was an isolated belief, or that it doesn't still persist today.

The homophobia at work in British government and society in the 1980s also legitimated attitudes which obstructed potentially life-saving work in the fight against AIDS. A recently revealed 1986 memo from

The LGBT community has often been caught between proving its respectability and pushing back against homophobia (courtesy James Rosen).

Margaret Thatcher showed her asking if HIV/AIDs educational materials *really had* to mention anal sex (um, yes, they do, sorry, Maggie!), even though it is one of the most high-risk activities for HIV transmission. Crucially, Thatcher asked her advisers if mentioning anal sex would be a breach of the Obscenity Act. Presumably she hoped that it was, because then she would have been able to hide behind legislation and let it solve the awkward conundrum for her. However distasteful, or simply alien, the idea of homosexuality (or anal sex between heterosexuals) is to any individual, to use this as a pretext to deny medically accurate information to people whose lives that information might save is unconscionable. To attempt to do so using obscenity legislation as a protective cloak under which to hide one's prejudices is particularly despicable. Fortunately, common sense and other cabinet members prevailed and the sex education materials were published as planned.

I spoke to several LGBT people who lived and worked during these years; one was Sean Maddison-Brown, a gay British man who was a schoolteacher in the 1980s. Sean told me that the 1988 introduction of Section 28 definitely "pushed people back in the closet. It did feel very intimidating because at that time there was the 'pretty policeman' policy, to entrap gay men. It all felt oppressive; we were being blamed for AIDS, we were being attacked in education, attacked through the council.... And of course there were no out gay people. The only people who were perceived to be gay were John Inman, Larry Grayson and Kenneth Williams, the sort of people who were to be ridiculed."

In 1987, the *Sheffield Star* ran an article with the sensationalist headline "Classroom Clash of 87" regarding a recent visit by the Young Lesbian Group to a local secondary school. Yet the article is refreshingly open-minded, raising objections to the government's plans to erase mentions of homosexuality and contraception from school sex education. It points out the massive flaws in only focusing on "biological facts," and prints a reader's letter that says "all our pupils know gay people as classmates, relatives, friends or neighbours. Perhaps if we started to talk about homosexuality, some of the fear and prejudice would disappear." The article adds that "the topic of homosexuality cannot be avoided in any discussion of AIDS, which the Government itself placed squarely on school agendas earlier this year."

Jane Lee, a now-retired primary-school teacher from South West England, co-authored a book called *Teaching AIDS in the Classroom*[7] as a response to the increasing confusion and paranoia that she was witnessing among her pupils and fellow teachers. After the terrifying campaign of 1986 TV adverts (featuring a huge, looming tombstone marked AIDS), Jane could see that the children she taught were desperate for both reassurance and information. "A lot of kids were hearing about AIDS in the playground, from older kids and older siblings—but they didn't know how you got it," she told me. "This book was a way of dealing with that." In 1991, Jane and fellow teacher Jean Collyer distributed a questionnaire to ten- and 11-year-olds with the aim of discovering what children actually knew about AIDS—and more to the point, what they *thought* they knew. I've read some of these responses, and they are fascinating as well as sweetly amusing. Some children confused the disease AIDS with aid to foreign countries, or hearing aids ("They say you can tell if a person has aids by looking behind their ears"[8]); others found media discussions utterly confusing: "They are saying that you get AIDS by making love. They are talking about using condoms. I don't understand it all!"[9]

As with 21st-century children, the unifying thread among Jane's interviewees was that the current education system was failing to answer their questions and concerns: "One boy wanted to know who was going to show him how to put a condom on."[10] As someone who was in school in the early '90s, I can attest that there simply was no mention of AIDS or

8. Shoving It Down Our Throats

Gay men were blamed for the spread of AIDS in the '80s and '90s; activist groups like ACT-UP were a response to this homophobic shaming (courtesy James Rosen).

homosexuality in the sex education we received. More concerningly, I was 19 when a good friend of the same age casually asked me, "There's a cure for AIDS, isn't there?" I remember sputtering loudly in shock that such a fatal misperception had gone unchallenged during my friend's years of private school. Jane Lee found that, thanks to Section 28, British "schools were terrified, they didn't know what to tell kids."

Teaching AIDS in the Classroom intended to help teachers address AIDS as part of general health education, and to educate children about it in an age-appropriate manner. I've read that book and can categorically state that there is nothing in it I would not show to a child. Although the book advocates a "broad sex education programme," it also recommends basic biological education: learning about germs, viruses, infections and illnesses in general—as well as doing exercises to develop good self-esteem, the ability to say no to unwanted bodily contact and a sense of the value of one's own health. So far, so inoffensive, or so Jane thought. She and several other educators would meet as a working group every six months and feed back their experiences to the government. Unfortunately, "what we were feeding back wasn't what they wanted to hear. They wanted to push 'Just Say No'"—the '80s anti-drugs slogan popularized by Nancy Reagan—

"and we all know that doesn't work." The British government wasn't interested in funding any kind of AIDS education that didn't stick to this party line, and after 18 months they withdrew all support for the project. "They fired us because we wouldn't say what they wanted us to say," Jane concludes. Although Margaret Thatcher was long gone by the time the book was published in 1994, the Conservative government under John Major remained as reactionary and shortsighted on sex education as its predecessor. Once again, it was a case of "not in front of the children"—even when children themselves were the ones asking for information.

Demonizing Deviants

In *Thinking Kink*, I wrote that gay male sexuality is "inextricably connected with darker desires" in the cultural imagination, and that "writing off male homosexuality as deviant meant it could fit nicely in a category alongside the freaky, dirty, warped doings of BDSM practitioners."[11] Images of male homosexual activity are more likely to be considered obscene precisely because of their power to unsettle the heterosexual, vanilla majority. It took two years of living in the same street for my 20-something male neighbor to feel comfortable mentioning his boyfriend to me, and another year before I "came out" to him as the author of a book about kink; at which point he promptly told me he and his partner loved latex and puppy play. It was a fantastically British conversation, which took place across garden fences and which also introduced me to Kazuki James, a British photographer and puppy-play enthusiast whose work features in this book. However, I could easily have missed these opportunities to learn about a gay-male subculture that is pretty opaque to straight females such as myself had my neighbor not felt that it was safe to share these confidences with me. A tour of Britain's major cities might lead you to believe that everyone here is cool with gay men; a visit to a few more-deprived provinces will uncover a segment of British society that sees male homosexuality as synonymous with pedophilia.

While I was working on this chapter, a major scandal broke in the UK involving cover-ups of child sex abuse by dozens of football teams. Despite precisely zero people asking for his view on the matter, British darts player Eric Bristow went on Twitter and criticized the victims for not taking vigilante action against their abusers, tweeting that he "would have went back and sorted that poof out."[12] He later clarified that he "meant paedophile not poof," but it's clear that the two terms occupy a similar space in his mind. Also, the fact Bristow believed "poof" was an acceptable term to use at all says as much about his attitude to gay men as the context in which he chose to deploy it.

Businesses concentrating on the distribution of gay porn were still being prosecuted well into the 1990s—*R v. Philip James McGuigan* (1996) and *R v. Land* (1999) are two examples. A quick glance at the forbidden acts on the CPS's current list shows a persistent prejudice against gay practices such as fisting; and the cases that have been recently prosecuted bear this out. As mentioned elsewhere in this book, Simon Walsh was prosecuted in 2012 for receiving electronic images that depicted fisting and urethral sounding between men at a gay sex party Walsh had attended. Ostensibly the legal concern was whether the acts were likely to cause injury, but I believe this was much less at issue than the fact the acts were kinky and between gay men.

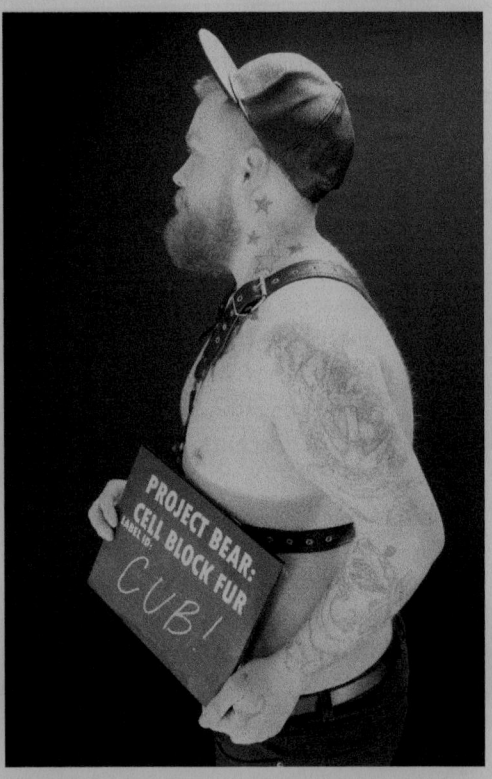

Depictions of male homosexuality became more acceptable in the '90s and aughts; prior to this, it had been considered automatically pornographic (courtesy Kazuki James).

Jerry Barnett points out the ridiculous burden of proof placed upon Walsh: "He could call the 'victims' as witnesses to demonstrate that their anuses had definitely not been harmed by the act, but this was not a defence against online pornography—he had to prove that the act could *never* be harmful."

This did make me wonder why no one is obliged to prove, say, that childbirth isn't harmful before showing videos of it to children (I watched one aged ten, as part of my school's sex education); after all, it involves similar stretching of a similarly sized orifice, and it's also a process that kills millions of women worldwide every year. Given that information, I'm inclined to view gay porn much more favorably than images of childbirth. Unfortunately, as Brooke Magnanti puts it, British law is based on the idea that "sex (and especially sex where commerce is involved) is unique, and uniquely corrupting."[13] The jury in the Walsh case acquitted him, but it's an embarrassment to the British legal system that the case came to trial at all, and unforgivable that an innocent man lost his job and had his private life dragged through the media in the process. Homophobic or anti-kink Britons with no sympathy for Walsh should still be annoyed that public money was spent on his trial.

Walsh's case could have featured a silver lining had it inspired the long-overdue examination of UK obscenity law, because the jury's verdict flew in the face of regulations that render kinky or gay practices automatically obscene. Unfortunately, there has been no change in the intervening time, except for the law's becoming *more* conservative via AVMS and the Digital Economy Bill.

Earlier in 2012, another landmark obscenity case involving gay men would come to court when Michael Peacock was accused of distributing "obscene" DVDs that depicted men engaged in fisting, urination and bondage. Writing about the case, Brooke Magnanti notes, "The rather delicious irony is that not only are such acts relatively common in the kinky community, they're perfectly legal for consenting adults to participate in and watch in person."[14] Unfortunately, those bringing the case against Peacock did not consider this. As Alex Antoniou adds in his study of the case,[15] merely being charged is usually enough to cow the majority of those accused of obscenity: "Most people charged under the OPA plead guilty, since a not guilty plea and a court case resulting in a guilty verdict could lead to a more severe sentence. Nevertheless, Michael Peacock's decision to pursue this case constituted the first test of the 1959 Act before a jury for many years, thereby challenging the so far uncontested views of the police and the CPS on what is obscene."

The CPS claimed that this prosecution was in the public interest because Peacock made no effort to check the age or identity of his clients, implying the issue was *the way* he distributed the DVDs, rather than the content of them. As we have seen elsewhere in this book, the defense that "we're just concerned about who *might* see it" is not adequate grounds to censor a work and often hides a much less innocuous moral agenda.

Fortunately for Peacock, the jury did not believe anyone was going to be depraved or corrupted by the material he was selling. They also demonstrated much-needed rationality by adding that "people likely to see the DVDs at issue were gay men specially looking for this type of material"[16] and acquitting Peacock after a very short deliberation. Again, no change in the legal bias against fisting, urolagnia or BDSM followed, but the case did at least show that the British public is becoming increasingly open-minded about gay sexual practices.

9

Privilege and Platforms
Obscenity in the Modern World

I first heard the word "cunt" when I was 14 years old. A male relative of mine who loves profanity yelled it on the way home from the airport, bellowing, "The cunt's out to lunch!" about some miscreant who had failed to have his rental car waiting for him. I was shocked to hear the "worst word that you can say" thrown about so casually, but it was an important lesson in the power of language. I also remember reading an interview in the mid–'90s with Shirley Manson, the no-nonsense Scottish singer-actor who at the time was fronting the band Garbage. Manson bemoaned how Americans in particular had a problem with "the c-word," and pointed out how stupid it was considering most of those complaining weren't even in possession of a cunt! I knew at the age of 15 that she spoke the truth, but I also knew it wasn't a conversation I could have with my mum, aunts or even most of my schoolfriends unless we found a *very* private locker room—and any schoolchild knows how hard those are to locate!

A few years later, when I was at university, a fellow philosophy student told me in shocked tones that a male student in her literature class had decided to loudly share his description of kicking a woman in the crotch. "I'm not offended by the See You Next Tuesday word," she told me, a claim belied by the fact she was spelling it out. "But he just went on and on! He kept repeating 'I kicked her in the cunt'—urgh!" This charming fellow sounded like the kind of arrogant young male who turns up in higher education and thinks it's his job to shock, as if all the women in his class had never had their bodies insulted, colonized or violated by men before—and as if it ever would fall to a 19-year-old boy to speak on the matter. This point should be borne in mind by those who claim that women, LGBT folk or people of color are just too sensitive when they complain about offensive speech; you can't shock those who've been listening to misogynist/racist/

homophobic crap all their lives. Women KNOW the word *cunt*. We've been called it, had our genitalia called it, and usually in the most pejorative tones. In 1998, feminist Inga Muscio was moved to write a whole book reclaiming the word; yet I still feel the need to hide the cover of *CUNT: A Declaration of Independence* whenever my mother or guests visit. (Do buy it, though. It's a fantastic and essential read.)

In 1785, a man named Francis Grose published a book called *The Classical Dictionary of the Vulgar Tongue*. It contained delightful euphemisms such as "Brother of the Gusset," meaning pimp, and "Brother of the Quill," meaning author (Sisters of the Quill like your author receive no mention, naturally). But guess what Grose defined as a "commodity"? The "private parts of a modest woman, or the public parts of a prostitute." Well, that's bloody charming. Debates on Marxism aside, it confirms that women's bits have long been seen as a product belonging to anyone but women themselves.

I've long refused to use the word *vagina* in reference to my own body not just because it's an inaccurate term rarely used correctly, but also because it's completely sexist. The word *vagina* refers *only* to the birth canal, which renders it irrelevant to those, like myself, who have no desire to use our bodies to bear children. Secondly, the word *vagina* derives from a Latin word for a sheath for a sword. This offends me on the basis that not everyone with a vagina wants to use it to sheath *anything*, and also that, once again, women are supposed to accept that their bodies are defined only in relation to men's. This isn't simply offensive, it's also ass-backwards. Any biologist will tell you that all human bodies start out female in the womb, which is why men have nipples. It's only later on in the gestation period, when hormones are released, that the sex of a fetus is established. Somewhat inconveniently for those who think women being made from a rib is a credible story, female bodies are in fact the human default.

If you're a man and this information discomfits you, consider the following: I've always loathed the term *mankind* precisely because of how it erases 50 percent of the human race. If I happen to mention this, someone inevitably chirps, "Well, OBVIOUSLY that word includes women as well!" I'm a linguist by trade as well as a trained philosopher who understands semantics and logic well, but I don't find it obvious at all. I will never see how a term that *erases* female-bodied people can be said to somehow magically include them. Would *womankind* be acceptable to describe all seven billion human beings on planet Earth? After all, the word *mankind is* actually found within that term, so presumably men should find no cause to complain about their identity being elided into women's for the sake of semantic convenience. But we all know they would, and loudly. In the same spirit, I'll never accept my body's being treated as some kind of cosmic afterthought, or named only as an adjunct to the male body, because I know that language matters.

Separate but equal is an attractive proposition until we look at the reality; as psychology professor Paul Hegarty discovered, "Journal articles and everyday people tend to assume a male, heterosexual norm and explain women/gay differences as deviations from that norm."[1] Therefore we should view anyone who claims that the existence of a binary is the same thing as a level playing field with suspicion. The vast majority of gender-and-sexuality-related binaries in Western society clearly skew asymmetrically. To paraphrase the argument of Diana Fuss's 1991 book on the issue, the dominant groups required propping up by their opposites, as well as the use of supporting terms. Thus, male/female, gay/straight and cis/trans all get aligned with the strong/weak binary, as well as active/passive and rational/emotional.[2] If someone tells you that your group has nothing to complain about, consider from which side of this divide they are speaking.

This isn't just about whose experiences, lives and bodies get first place in the English lexicon and whose are always relegated to a "minority interest," though. Treating the female body and the discourse regarding it as either pornographic or obscene, while the male equivalents are regarded as both superior and the default, holds back our society to a barbaric degree. Shaming and erasing women's bodies from art, law and culture leads to some of the biggest problems in 21st-century Britain. To name a few: female genital mutilation, child sexual abuse, honor killings, sexual harassment at work and the removing of girls from their schools, homes and lives to be married off to much older men. I hesitate to call the latter "forced marriage" because it's really just child rape by another name, but it's seen a 12 percent increase in Britain in the past year, a figure that is expected to rise as more frightened children come forward.

White liberal fears of appearing to dictate how Middle Eastern, African and Southeast Asian communities should conduct themselves can prevent the true extent of the problem from being revealed: demanding that minorities follow British law or leave risks echoing the embarrassing racist chants of the 1970s. However, should fear of being told to keep our white noses out of other communities stop us from trying to help children who are at risk of a lifetime of abuse? In a country where the specter of colonialism and white-savior complexes have only recently become part of the conversation about race, I can see why people are nervous about stepping into the fray, but I'm also wary of this murky concept of cultural sensitivity, especially when it's used to override the bodily integrity of women and girls. Fortunately, I can always look to the writing of Mona Eltahawy if I want to hear from a brilliant Middle Eastern feminist who doesn't pull her punches: "Name me an Arab country, and I'll recite a litany of abuses against women occurring in that country, abuses fueled by a toxic mix of culture and religion that few seem willing to disentangle lest they blaspheme or offend."[3]

Eltahawy was born in Egypt, has lived in Britain, Saudi Arabia and the United States and has been a persistent voice demanding that the so-called Arab Spring include a revolution in women's rights, which were frustratingly absent from the mostly male uprisings. The fearless journalist cannot be accused of armchair politics, either: in November 2011, Egyptian security forces sexually assaulted her, beat her so badly that she sustained two broken bones and interrogated her for 12 hours straight. Eltahawy has no time for cultures that force women to choose between feminism and "the larger goal of solidarity of fidelity to the revolution" and demands an end to "the systemic hatred of women that reduces us to little more than our headscarves and our hymens."[4]

Well-Meaning Whites

> "I used to be the biggest whinger in the world as a kid.... My mother would have to physically restrain me to apply water and Savlon, while the neighbours wondered if those Arabs at number 32 would ever stop beating their children."[5]—Meera Syal, *Life Isn't All Ha Ha Hee Hee*

When I was in middle school in the mid–1990s, I was friends with a girl I'll call M, whose parents were first-generation immigrants from Sri Lanka. M was intelligent, articulate and in possession of a wacky sense of humor, which is why I liked playing with her. She had dark-brown skin and big shining eyes, and she sported black shoulder-length hair that was poker-straight, thick and always slightly messy. We were ten, maybe 11 years old and lived one street apart; as we played on our bicycles in the sunshine, we were pretty much poster children for kids living in racial harmony. However, M was more perceptive than most adults when it came to racial politics. She was already dismissive of white people who were afraid to say what they really meant. She had no time for being called black, as she felt it was inaccurate: "I'm not black, I'm brown!" she would grin at me, before looking at my pale face and laughing, saying, "And you're not white either, you're beige! Or peach…"

9. Privilege and Platforms

I remember playing with M in the hazily lit streets that line my youthful memories, and how sometimes D, a white "friend" of hers, would join us. I didn't like this arrogant boy one bit, especially after I heard him say, "Shut up, Marmite," to M. This flash of racism emerged as it so often does, when D was losing an argument. Seeing that M just laughed at D's insult and didn't stand up for herself, I stepped in and snarled at the boy, appalled by his ignorant bigotry. He certainly never spoke to me again in terms anything other than respectful, but I can't speak to what M went through when I wasn't around. I thought I was waving the sword of justice on her behalf, but I now realize that stopping to yell at every racist remark was a luxury only whitey here could afford. If M took on every stupid preadolescent boy and his commentary about the color of her skin, she would not have had the time to do anything else.

In the above-quoted novel, British-Asian author Meera Syal coins the phrase "glass countertop" to demonstrate how brown-skinned British people never even get near the much-discussed glass ceiling. She also states that racism in Britain is more insidious than fables of shit through letterboxes, spitting and beatings from neofascists would have you believe. She refers to the countless doors, real and metaphorical, that are slammed in the faces of black, Asian and minority-ethnic (BAME) people every day. In the wake of Britain's fateful 2016 referendum, social media and real-life conversations were awash with tales of foul xenophobia and racism against Eastern Europeans, Muslims and anyone else with brown skin or a foreign accent. I heard about a young mother who marched up to a Polish woman who was waiting for her children at the school gate and snarled, "So when are you fucking off home, then?" and this was one of the milder stories that emerged after that unmentionable vote.

It's also only recently that the BBC has even included women of Indian, Pakistani, Bangladeshi or Sri Lankan origin on discussion programs about burqa bans, FGM, child marriage and abuse within the Muslim community. Dial it back a few years and you would see only white men, and perhaps the odd white or brown woman thrown in for the sake of diversity, on such panels. The phrase "Nothing about us without us" springs to my mind.

I hope that I now understand much better why my childhood friend was conserving her energy: because once she hit adulthood, many bigger battles would dog her as a brown-skinned woman in a predominantly white nation. There's probably no more fraught position to occupy in the 21st-century UK. If you're a woman with brown skin, you can expect to be patronized, stared at, spat at, sneered at and have your choice of outfit scrutinized by white people on the street, in books and newspapers and on the news. This is not to say that every woman of Indian, Pakistani, Bangladeshi or Sri Lankan origin has such a tale to tell, or even feels passionately about the intersecting issues of race or gender. But rather that, if we want to have a conversation on the issue, including only white voices leaves us in a progress-free echo chamber.

The Scapegoating of Multiculturalism

Blaming immigrants for all British ills is no new pastime, of course. The economic insecurity of the 1970s was mined by fascists such as Enoch Powell to further their hatred of anyone nonwhite, and the neo–Nazi National Front flourished in the early 1980s. I remember getting one of their flyers through the door as recently as 2005; I read it with morbid curiosity and remember cartoons about murdering IRA "scum," AIDS being referred to as a "queer plague," plus an article about why Britain in 1066 was the perfect society, one that our country should reestablish (!). I don't know if the NF is still active today, but its founders should comfort themselves that plenty of none-too-bright white people with a sense of entitlement are still carrying the torch for thoughtless fascism via groups like Britain First and the English Defense League. Much as with the Mull of Kintyre myth, many modern Brits believe that the skinhead youth culture of the late 1970s and early '80s is synonymous with neo–Nazi beliefs. This is not only false but diametrically opposed to the truth: a quick watch of Shane Meadows's excellent 2006 movie, *This Is England*, shows that skinhead music and culture was actually brought to 1960s Britain by Jamaicans, and that the true skinhead spirit entailed a celebration of diversity (see multi-racial ska band the Specials, who come from Coventry), plus the rejection of jingoistic values.

Still, every hegemony needs a group to blame when things aren't going well, and for most of the 1970s and '80s, Afro-Caribbean and Southeast Asian people were near, if not on, the bottom of Britain's class system, along with poor white working-class Britons ("trailer trash," as their cousins across the pond are dubbed). More recently, middle-class Brits condemned and mocked "chavs," portrayed as feckless, overly fertile, welfare-scrounging white people on council estates. Now they've moved on to tormenting the Eastern Europeans, who get labeled "slavs" and are criticized for wearing tracksuits, speaking with funny accents (a whole series of popular British commercials derive their comedy from the fact a meerkat speaks with a Russian accent) and their inconsiderate habit of

Laws dealing with the explosion of online hate speech, especially by the new "alt-right," have been slow to emerge (courtesy Hannah Crosby).

taking "British jobs." I've never quite seen how fruit picking, car washing, factory or construction labor or sex work can be claimed as exclusively British, but then I inhabit a middle-class ivory tower and have no experience of watching an economic migrant steal employment that I deem rightfully mine. Suffice to say, I've seen plenty of battle lines repeatedly drawn, blurred and hurriedly rubbed out in my lifetime; where my grandmother's generation complained with impunity about "darkies," mine prefers to blame Polish people for filling empty high-street units with their *sklep*s and daring to make use of our world-beating education and health systems. The very nerve.

The other side of scapegoating, of course, is the excising of immigrants from Britain's cultural and linguistic history altogether. This feeds into a rose-tinted view of the world, wherein every British high street contains a rosy-cheeked butcher, a flour-spattered baker and no strange brown-skinned people messing up the picture. Such a belief allows bigots to fly into a rage whenever they hear, for example, that the long-running children's TV series *Postman Pat* now has characters of color in it. Such malcontents will complain that the past is being vandalized in the scurry towards inclusion, conveniently forgetting that there *was* no such perfect past for anyone who wasn't white, male or heterosexual. They also lack the memory of this author, who remembers Panjit Singh, the turban-sporting forklift driver of another popular children's program, *Bertha*. This character featured in the stop-motion-animated series from 1985 onwards, which is inconvenient for those who want to believe there were only white characters in British pop culture until political correctness stuck its oar in.

That's not to say that plenty of movies, TV shows and books aren't guilty of depicting a past Britain where there simply were no people of color until about 1950, but rather that the whitewashing in which they collude is completely inaccurate. There was a black community in Britain during the Tudor period (1485–1603), for Christ's sake, and these people were not slaves, either. So yes, it's definitely problematic that the crucial military role played by the Gurkhas in both World Wars only came to most Britons' attention once plummy-voiced legend Joanna Lumley began campaigning for their recognition. Much as I do adore Lumley, it shouldn't take a white lady to make a nation grateful to brown-skinned men who gave their lives for it in battle. As for the role of Native Americans, Afro-Caribbeans or any other undersung contributors to British war efforts? You will be lucky to find even a passing mention of these heroes, because their faces didn't fit the dominant narratives of the era. British-Indian cultural commentator Sunny Singh has received plenty of abuse for daring to suggest that critically acclaimed juggernauts such as *Dunkirk*, or even the untouchable behemoth that is *Harry Potter*, are whitewashed in order to placate majority-white audiences. The Netflix series *Dear White People* makes similar points with its scathing critiques of well-meaning white liberals, albeit on an American college campus. I've watched the whole series more than once, as it is funny, articulate and true, yet I would bet money that more than one white ignoramus has yelled at their screen, "Why isn't there a show called DEAR BLACK PEOPLE?!"

Incidentally, one of my white male interviewees told me that porn producers are increasingly being accused of racism both when they *do* include actors of color and when they don't; for him, this is a sign that inclusivity has gone too far. I thought it pessimistic to believe our choice limited to either totally whitewashed erotica or that which includes cringeworthy stereotypes of black, Asian and Latinx people, and I also found this statement a bit rich coming from a British man who was nearly as pale as me. If I were black, brown or Latinx, I imagine, I'd quickly become sick of seeing my gender and ethnicity constantly reduced to the trope of hoochie mama/hood rat/big-butted spicy Latina in movies, on TV and in erotica. Furthermore, I don't consider it my right to muffle such protests.

That said, I could see that this man had been in the porn industry himself for decades and didn't feel that many of his critics had paid their dues. I have felt similarly exasperated when my writing has been labeled racist by other white people, which happened to me both during the 2012 *Thinking Kink* blog series and after I published my book of the same title in 2015. I respected these people's right to air their opinion, but I have little time for the opinions themselves, which consisted of little else than demonstrations of how right-on the critics themselves were. This is not to say my work has never offended or pissed off a person of color, only that for whatever reason, not one person from this demographic has ever taken it upon themselves to voice their criticism online, on paper or to my face. The only people who have are other white women. How this is meant to balance the conversation in favor of oppressed groups is anyone's guess.

In a world where self-care and mental health are now fashionable buzzwords, people are being encouraged to stand up and walk away from social-media and online news platforms for the sake of their sanity, although it should be noted that the major social networks make it as technologically stressful as they possibly can to quit them. Even so, I am seeing an increasing number of teenagers, 20-somethings and 30-somethings turn off the digital world, and as a Luddite who loathes the fact that nowhere is safe from Wi-Fi any more—not even airspace, as I found out on an internal U.S. flight in 2015!—I wish to God that social-media self-promotion were not necessary to making my living as a writer. A transmasculine friend of mine quit Facebook altogether a few months ago, so exhausted was he from the abuse that followed Donald Trump's cheap shots at the trans community. I didn't blame him at all; he had tolerated far more ignorant and offensive statements on his feed than I could ever stand.

In 2012, Caitlin Moran expressed extreme irritation at having her journalism accused of racism and ripped to pieces online by "white, 18-year-old sociology students." She added, "Don't tell me how to interview someone, I've been doing this job a long time, young girls." I did empathize with Moran's irritation—I first saw her on TV interviewing the Manic Street Preachers in about 1992, a time when most of those attacking her on Twitter weren't even a twinkle in their parents' eyes. As a working-class woman who elbowed her way into journalism more than two decades ago—a feat now rendered nearly impossible by the current climate of skyrocketing tuition fees and unpaid internships—Moran gives understandably short shrift to keyboard warriors who have achieved very little in their short lives. For the record, Moran has been accused of transphobia and racism in her writing, but I see no point in reproducing these flame wars when there is already adequate space on the internet given over to detailing every criticism of this accomplished journalist and author. Instead, I'll include a statement that was not widely reported in the scramble to condemn her: "If you're going to say someone is racist, simply by not tackling a subject, that's an argument we need to have, because that's not what I believe."[6]

This way in which digital reporting makes mountains out of molehills was exemplified in the summer of 2017, when Irish journalist Kevin Myers saw one of his articles pulled from the Rupert Murdoch–owned *Sunday Times* for anti–Semitic and sexist comments. In the offending piece, Myers speculated upon whether the female British TV presenters Vanessa Feltz and Claudia Winkleman got paid better than other women on the BBC channels "because Jews are not generally noted for their insistence on selling their talent for the lowest possible price."[7] It's important to add that this was included in the Irish version of the *Sunday Times*, which, as you might imagine, is not widely read in mainland Britain. Unfortunately for Myers someone across the Irish sea did notice his words, plus the fact that he had previously denied the Holocaust in the *Irish Independent*. All it took was for Twitter to get wind of Myers's record of unwise bigoted ramblings, and the fur began to fly.

Every online commenter suddenly had an opinion about Myers, a man who had been heretofore unknown outside of the small world of Irish journalism. Myers was labeled anti–Semitic, a Nazi sympathizer and a misogynist; so far, so accurate. Activists from the transgender community tweeted that they had previously identified Myers as a hateful idiot, but no one listened. This all sounds pretty plausible—we all know how long it takes for anyone to listen when cis women make an accusation of rape, and the extra barriers faced by trans women, trans men and non-binary folk mean that they are even less likely to be credited with telling the truth.

However, it's important to bear in mind that the outrage surrounding Myers—and, a cynic might add, the free publicity for such an odious individual—would never have spread so far were it not for the media amplifying and magnifying the story. As print media continues to decline and editors worry about the bottom line, clickbait journalism has become a fast and easy way to shore up a decreasing readership. No outlet with a digital platform, meaning very few publications in modern Britain, is immune to its lure. The *Guardian*, which ran the Myers story, is Britain's last surviving left-wing print newspaper. However, it presently suffixes every one of its online articles with a line asking for donations to help support its rapidly diminishing fortunes. The websites of other British newspapers feature pop-ups pleading with their online readers not to use ad-blockers. Everyone needs clicks to stay relevant, even this increasingly curmudgeonly author. Hence the rise of manufactured outrage, which used to be the purview only of right-wing newspapers such as the *Sun* and the *Daily Mail*, in even the most left-leaning of publications.

It's also worth noting that even the *Guardian* wasn't above resorting to sexism when reporting on the terrible things said by Kevin Myers; it illustrated the story with a large picture of a young, smiling, Claudia Winkleman in a strapless top, and only a tiny image of the older, larger Vanessa Feltz. The older, white, gray-haired Kevin Myers wasn't even given a headshot to go with his foul words. The insidious message is that pretty women still sell newspapers; elsewhere in the same issue, a white male journalist wrote about why *The Handmaid's Tale* is so significant for our society. Am I to believe that such a proudly right-on newspaper really couldn't find a woman or a person of color to take on that particular task?

Cultural Appropriation: The New Obscenity?

In September 2016, best-selling author Lionel Shriver gave a speech[8] on cultural appropriation, fiction writing and diversity at the Brisbane Writers Festival. Before we get to the content, some crucial background: I've loved Shriver's work since 2005, when I read her breakthrough novel (published in 2003) *We Need to Talk About Kevin*. I sat on the bus and mentally punched the air with every page I read, rejoicing in so many fearlessly spoken truths on the matter of childbearing. I loved Shriver for smashing one of the last taboos in Western society, and for listing all my suspicions about motherhood: that it was tedious, unfulfilling, sucked women dry both mentally and physically, destroyed their careers, finances and sex lives. I loved her for saying the unsayable, that reproduction was at best a method for humans to stave off existential dread, and at worst a life sentence most bovinely accepted without question. I even wrote excerpts from *We Need to Talk* on index cards and stuck them on my bedroom walls, as if warning visitors that the inhabitant viewed both life and having children as ultimately futile.

In the intervening 12 years, Shriver's work has never flinched from brutal realities: her novels have dealt with the American healthcare system, obesity and the corresponding obsession with thinness, and in her most recent work, *The Mandibles*, what America might look like if the economic manure truly hit the fan. Her prose is bold, unapologetic and advances a pretty misanthropic viewpoint. However, Shriver's essay in the 2015 anthology *Selfish, Shallow and Self-Absorbed: 16 Writers on the Decision Not to Have Kids* appeared to herald her emergence from the racist closet. Perhaps I should have known something was up from the title of her essay "Be Here Now Means Be Gone Later," which was not the furious defense of a child-free life I had come to expect. Instead, it read like an apology for eugenicists. Lines like "Maybe the immigration debate has sufficiently matured for us to concede that white folks are people, too," seemed disingenuous; I couldn't believe an intelligent author was resorting to such sly, emotive propaganda. As if there has ever been any question that white people are human, nay, the default humans, the dominant type by which all other races have always been measured and found wanting.

The essay bemoaned the fact that if white Euro-Americans like herself continued to refuse reproduction, they might end up a minority, which was obviously a cause for concern. Although Shriver never quite has the guts to spell out *why* this news should worry any white person, it's pretty blatant from her sneering assertion that "liberally minded white Americans are not supposed to care ... that by 2043 whites will constitute a minority in the U.S." She obviously *does* care, enough to write a whole essay on the matter, and in the absence of any other clear explanation, I can only conclude that she's concerned because she feels whites are superior to other races.

Shriver's 2016 speech at the Brisbane Festival took this attitude and proudly doubled down on it. She ridiculed a news story from earlier that year, when two American student officers faced impeachment "for attending a fiesta-themed party where sombreros were worn—conduct some of their peers found racially offensive."[9] Shriver stated that, as a fiction author, she believes any writer should be able to assume the identity of another group for the purposes of fiction, and then she placed a sombrero on her head, live on stage. As shocking acts go, it's not quite Ozzy Osbourne biting the head off a bat, but you can see what Shriver was trying to achieve.

Yassmin Abdel-Magied was in the audience for Shriver's speech, and she wrote about why she walked out.[10] I found Abdel-Magied's words far more powerful and persuasive than Shriver's privileged complaints, but I also knew that, as a brown-skinned woman, Abdel-Magied would be dismissed as a special snowflake, her objections reduced to that catch-all brush-off, identity politics, even though she absolutely nailed Shriver's attitude towards nonwhite, non–European cultures: "I don't care what you deem is important or sacred. I want to do with it what I will. Your experience is

You can leave your hat on: is cultural appropriation just stealth racism or have calls for racial sensitivity gone too far (Pixabay)?

simply a tool for me to use, because you are less human than me. You are less than human."

If one only heard the sombrero speech, one might have defended Shriver as simply intolerant of delicate liberal teens and their hurt feelings, especially since she's an established author who has spent her professional life going against the grain and never been afraid to shock with her words. However, once you know that this writer also feels, "oh, a little wistful about the fact that my country of birth, the U.S., will probably in my lifetime no longer be peopled in majority by those of European extraction like me,"[11] and that she gives considerable passages of *The Mandibles* over to "the Lats" becoming the dominant population, there's simply nowhere left to hide. I have to concede that someone who was once my torchbearer against pro-natalist, anti-feminist pressures has slotted herself into an ugly stereotype: the protectionist, immigrant-blaming, past-romanticizing closet racist. It's that feeling you get when someone you previously thought was an intelligent, compassionate individual comes out with "Why isn't there a Straight Pride day?" or "What about White History Month?"

In our scramble to find people of color who support whatever narrative we are promoting, we must be careful not continue the terrible track record of dominant groups: i.e., trying to excuse our prejudices by finding the one woman, gay person, person of color or other "exotic" human being who doesn't feel oppressed and then asking that person to speak for their entire race, gender or other demographic. I would hate for Lionel Shriver to be held up as emblematic of how all white, European, child-free women feel; similarly, it's important to note that Yassmin Abdel-Magied does not represent anyone but herself.

In summer 2017, I met a man who fell somewhere between these two extremes, and I found his story fascinating; not because it proves whether cultural appropriation is "a thing" or not, but simply because his was a viewpoint I hadn't heard before. This 30-something man identifies as mixed race: his mum is white and British, his dad black and Jamaican. One night we were in a Turkish restaurant setting the world to rights when he told me the white obsession with cultural appropriation leaves him utterly baffled. He added that he doesn't care if white people wear dreadlocks, cornrows or Afros, reminding me what a huge part hair now plays in race-related debates. In America, arguments have long raged over whether black people wearing their hair naturally is a personal choice or a political imperative—the Black Panther movement epitomizing the determined celebration of natural Afro hair—but in Britain, not so much. So I was intrigued to hear my friend's perspective on this new and knotty issue, which he happily shared as we tore up blackened pitas and dipped them in a colorful array of sauces and spices.

What I learned from that particular evening is that one mixed-race British person has neither the time nor the inclination to trawl the internet in search of white people emulating African, Caribbean or Native American culture in ill-advised ways. There may be many more like him, but he is the one person from whom I have heard it direct, therefore I'm telling his story rather than leaving bickering internet hordes to be treated as authorities on this subject. My friend's springy hair has the reddish hue of cinnamon and stands straight up in a mini flat top that reminds me of the early '90s TV show *Kid 'n' Play*. Freckles are scattered across his face, which is light brown. None of this should matter, but it would be untruthful of me to pretend that I don't "see race" or notice any of our physical differences. What also merits a mention are this man's priorities: finishing his degree, working part-time to fund his studies, making sure his parents are OK and looking after his disabled younger brother. Castigating strangers online or swarming the Instagram accounts of celebrities who derive much of their income from clickbait anyway does not feature on his list.

Whatever middle-class white students get up to online isn't of interest to this mixed-race man; he's more concerned about staying alive and sane during a cutthroat, economically terrifying time, and I don't blame him for feeling no compulsion to wade into such arguments. He did add to me later that those on his father's side of the family, especially the cousins with whom he is close, may feel differently about whites aping black culture, but that it's simply not a discussion they've ever had. This epitomizes to me how wrong it is when intra-white arguments end up drowning out all attempts to listen to the voices of oppressed groups. My friend happens to feel cultural appropriation is a nonissue; Yassmin Abdel-Magied feels the opposite; millions of other people of color's feelings will vary. The only lesson white people need take away here is that *we do not have a dog in this fight.*

Soon after that pleasant dinner date, I was accosted in Birmingham city center by an older black woman who demanded to know why I was wearing a dog collar with SLAVE emblazoned on it. The short answer was that I had just purchased it and couldn't wait to scurry back to the meet-up of kinky bloggers I was attending that day, and show off my new piece of kinky jewelry, but I didn't want to be flippant. I explained that it was not worn to shock or offend, but was rather part of a costume, one which celebrated sexual freedom. I also acknowledged the woman's point that it could be viewed as an insult to her ancestors, who were actually enslaved. I told her that, as she was my elder, I had to respect her experiences and viewpoint. She was mollified by this to the extent that she asked me for a hug. We embraced in the middle of a cloudy June day, and then parted ways contentedly. Disagreement over words and meanings doesn't always have to end with mudslinging; perhaps more time spent IRL and less in front of screens is needed to remind us of that.

As a white, straight, cis writer I endeavor to share my platform with those who aren't afforded the same privileges as me. If someone starts debating me on Twitter, I use a simple test to work out if they're genuinely passionate about the subject or just looking for a fight—I ask them if they would like to write a guest post for my blog. This stops dogmatic armchair activists in their tracks. Few actually follow through and take me up on my offer, which tells me everything I need to know about how invested they really are in their viewpoint. However, I'm pleased to report that several women of color have, and I'm thrilled to finally be in a position where I can use my platform to amplify other women's voices. Other women have been touched that I've even offered, rather than just hurling abuse, and consequently we've ended whatever debate we were having in wonderfully polite, British tones. Not many online debates end so nicely, but if I've learned anything from my time as a writer and a carer, it's that people in general just want to feel like someone is listening to them. Therefore once you actually prove that you're willing to cede your platform to marginalized groups, a lot of voluble aggression against your white, middle-class ass disappears like vapor on the wind. Jacq Applebee, a British disability activist and writer, wrote an excellent guest post for my blog on how black British people are regularly presumed to be African-American. Jacq made impassioned points about the erasure of black British people in favor of their more media-friendly American counterparts, especially when Britain has a fantastically diverse history of West Indian, Caribbean and African immigration. I silently agreed with every point as Jacq eloquently castigated black America for claiming Idris Elba, Nelson Mandela and athlete Kriss Akabusi as their own. I have also learned a great deal from Jacq about bisexual erasure and biphobia, experiences to which I cannot personally speak.

One of my favorite quotes regarding manufactured outrage comes from a little-known man named Cass. He was speaking long before the popularization of the internet, which explains why I can't even tell you his second name. All I know is that Cass was a drummer with the Senseless Things, an indie band who were moderately big in Britain in 1993. Cass was asked to comment on the case of Nicky Wire, bassist with Manic Street Preachers—who were and are my favorite band of the 1990s and 2000s—publicly wishing AIDS on Michael Stipe of R.E.M.

Cass's words to *Melody Maker* still ring true, over two decades on: "Who cares? We fall for it every time. Nicky said it to 2,000, you said it to 200,000, but it ain't changed anyone's opinion of Michael Stipe. More publicity for the Preachers, more publicity for us, more for R.E.M., you keep your jobs. Everyone's a winner, baby."[12] I'd venture that were the Wire-Stipe furor to happen today, it would burn 100 times as bright but for one hundredth of the time it took for Wire to cause such a scandal and be forgotten within days as the churning cycle of 24-hour news moved on. I don't know if that's a good or a bad thing. But it's how the modern world deals with foul behavior; loudly, quickly and with a very short memory.

I recently watched the full-length music video for Michael Jackson's 1992 single "Black or White." That itself is not unusual, as I have been a fervent MJJ fan since I was five years old and am grateful for the advent of free online streaming, since it allows me to watch all my favorite Jackson videos at the touch of a button. The video in question was directed by horror-comedy legend John Landis, who had also directed the trailblazing *Thriller* video nine years earlier.

What was peculiar on this particular occasion was that the version of "Black or White" I watched had not been cut, as most versions usually are.

The last five minutes, where a panther-like Jackson dances in a grimy backstreet, grabs his crotch a lot and smashes up a car with a crowbar, are never usually shown on music channels or in online versions. Those with long memories or a similar thirst for music trivia know that this is because the single was released days after the 1992 Los Angeles riots, in which over 80 people died, thousands more were injured and property was trashed in the aftermath of the Rodney King acquittals. John Landis, and presumably countless others at Jackson's record label, Epic, felt that such a violent ending to a song with such a positive message about racial harmony wasn't really appropriate at the time.

I can understand their reasoning, although I imagine that, in 1992, the mostly black and Latinx residents of downtown Los Angeles had a lot more to worry about than the contents of a music video. Such as not dying, being beaten or having their property set on fire. But I digress. Since the LA riots are now 25 years old, and standards for what can be shown in music videos have relaxed, no one will mind if the smashy-smashy ending to the video is now shown.

Yet this is where I saw the epitome of our paradoxical attitude to censorship and obscenity. What I noticed about this version of the video (included on Jackson's posthumous 2010 DVD *Vision*) was that it is actually still censored! Granted, only the most eagle-eyed of music dorks will be able to see how it has been cut, but I am that dork, and I can tell you that the car Jackson smashes up (and indeed his very motivation for smashing it up) originally had racist graffiti spray painted upon its windows and bodywork. "WOGS OUT," "NIGGERS OUT," that kind of charming slogan. This detail is the crucial factor in explaining Jackson's sudden burst of violence against an inanimate object—he was hardly known for being thuggish, after all—and yet 21st-century racial politics are considered too explosive to allow for the unveiling of these words.

"Black or White" is a song whose lyrics vehemently reject racism, excoriate the KKK (see the lyric about not being scared of any '"sheets"), and address the crap that people of color go through every day in America and the world. Watch the middle eight of the video and you'll see Jackson in a white T-shirt against a background of burning crosses and riots. The King of Pop's own relationship with race and his African-American background may be questionable, but in this video he makes a clear statement: "Words like *wog* and *nigger* are bad. If I see them sprayed on a car, I will smash that car because I am a proud black man." A 2010 audience was apparently deemed unable to handle that. Just as a 1992 audience supposedly couldn't handle seeing a smashed-up car, even though countless low-income people had seen their whole communities smashed up thanks to the LA riots.

Incidentally, this very white author lived in Los Angeles for three months in 2012. I had no car and no spare money, as I was doing an unpaid internship, so I explored the city on foot. I can testify that if you start in the center of downtown Los Angeles and work your way south, you'll see the effects of the riots everywhere, even two decades on. Vacant lots still sit where shops and buildings were burned to the ground. Groups of men, usually men of color, congregate aimlessly on street corners and shout at passersby; one yelled at me, "How does it feel to be so white and so beautiful?" and I still don't know if this was intended as a compliment or a racial slur. I would guess, though, that few of these people cared about the content of a Michael Jackson video then, and I can't imagine they care much now either. Yet majority-white censors persist in framing racist epithets as obscene, as if that could somehow protect people of color from their impact.

Now seems an ideal moment to pass the mic to Sara Vibes, 25th International Ms. Leather, who said the following when I interviewed her for *Thinking Kink*:

> Racism isn't over, just like incest isn't over, but kinky people still openly flaunt their Daddy/girl relationship. That could be just as "triggering" but no one is demanding that couple no longer be allowed to play in a public BDSM space.
>
> I don't get to consent to hearing the N-word so if you happen to hear it in the dungeon and that's triggering to you, think about what it's like for me every day, in the street. I'm sorry you have to be reminded of your whiteness and shared American history, but that's how I want to do kink play.
>
> It actually makes me hot to know that anyone within earshot has to stop what they are doing and take a second to think.

Afterword

In 2014, Japanese artist Megumi Igarashi was charged under her country's obscenity law for creating vulva-themed art. Igarashi lambasted the Japanese authorities for their hypocrisy, writing on her website that vaginas had always "been such a taboo in Japanese society. Penis, on the other hand, has been used in illustrations and has become a part of pop culture." Japan is a country where the media won't even use the term *rape* when reporting on sex crimes, but instead sticks to the bland catch-all verb *assault*. Quite how this is meant to protect anyone from the realities of sexual violence I cannot say. I'm also at a loss to explain why it's obscene if a woman in her 40s creates some images and sculptures based upon her own body, although I'd speculate that females taking ownership of their genitals is the part that unsettles those in charge. Although she now lives in Ireland, Igarashi is still appealing against court rulings[1] regarding her Japanese exhibitions.

This is one of the many examples of how, when tested, obscenity law inevitably defaults to protecting the interests of the most privileged. Just this week, an American woman is in the news after she was sacked for being caught on camera giving the middle finger to Donald Trump's motorcade. Akima LLC, Juli Briskman's employer, claimed the 50-year-old had violated company policy by making the picture her Facebook-profile image—even though she was not at work at the time of the incident, nor were her employer in anyway implicated in her flipping Trump the bird. Juli Briskman described Akima's stance to the *Huffington Post*: "basically, you cannot have 'lewd' or 'obscene' things in your social media. So they was calling flipping him off 'obscene.'" However, Akima hasn't been consistent in applying this policy: Briskman alleges that "a male colleague kept his job after recently posting lewd comments on his Facebook page that featured Akima LLC as his cover photo. She said this colleague was reprimanded for calling someone 'a fucking Libtard asshole,' but was allowed to delete the post and keep his job. 'How is that any less "obscene" than me flipping off the president?' she asked. 'How is that fair?'"[2]

It doesn't seem very fair at all, and if I were Briskman, I'd be outraged at my employer's selective memory, not to mention its misuse of the language of obscenity when the situation in no way merited it. Her case exemplifies how an impulsive, harmless gesture of defiance towards a rich and powerful man can be magnified through the lens of online dissemination, and how quick HR departments and pundits alike are to move from "flipping the bird to someone who's not even looking" to "an obscene gesture."

However, it's important to be even handed when considering these cases of online outrage. A year before Briskman's trial by social media, elementary-school aide Jane Wood Allen was fired after it was revealed that she had made racist comments and had referred to then–First Lady Michelle Obama as a "gorilla" on Facebook. A hashtag was formed calling for Allen's immediate dismissal, and within a few days her school district confirmed that she had been sacked. Whether you find the actions of Briskman or the Facebook posts of Allen more offensive depends entirely upon your political leaning, attitudes towards race, and beliefs about freedom of speech. Personally, I'm more appalled by the latter, as well as stunned that Allen thought she could get away with being racist so publicly, but I'm also cautious about sanctioning the online witch hunt that followed.

I do not want to inhabit a world where no public servant is allowed to have a private life, and where teachers feel unable even to go for a drink and air their views among friends, lest a malevolent journalist be sitting at the next table recording their every word. Yes, both these women could have been a lot more circumspect about how they used social media to demonstrate their feelings towards those in power, but we should not mistake the swift condemnation of both Briskman and Allen for a real or effective form of justice. To me, it's just another form of the reactionary cherry-picking that has previously claimed movies, jazz music or violent video games were the real threats to our social fabric. All it does is reassure the public that the enemy is identifiable and can easily be brought down, when even a passing acquaintance with how government, big business and the financial markets function demonstrates that this is not the case.

Still, I recognize that I am lucky to live in an era when I can detail my country's wrangles with depravity and corruption and sleep easy knowing that armed guerrillas aren't going to break down my door and spirit me off for torture and interrogation. The freedom to tell the bizarre, non-linear and at times near-nonsensical story you've just read is a luxury that has only recently become available. Prior to the modern age, the masses were expected to shut up, keep their heads down and not question what religion, the upper classes and autocrats told them. Now that the internet has democratized—and some may say devalued—journalism, photography, art and the creation of erotica, it's a lot harder to keep raunchy content out of the hands of the masses. It's also difficult to convince many Brits, especially those of the tech-savvy generation versed in the European Declaration of Human Rights, that the government has any right to control what media they consume. That doesn't stop it from being the case, and I hope this book has provided some insight into just how many laws silently control adult media consumption, but no one likes admitting they've been duped by the authorities. We all like to think we're cleverer than that; I certainly thought I was, until December 2014. Plus, in a world where leaving Facebook or deleting WhatsApp (which I have recently done due to too much time spent on devices giving me Repetitive Strain Injury) is viewed as striking a major blow for privacy, it can be difficult to explain how concepts of obscenity or censorship are still relevant.

At least in D. H. Lawrence's era, you could simply refuse to walk into the bookshop stocking the offending tome, or perhaps send a letter of disgust to your favorite newspaper. That letter might take a week or two to appear, if ever, and by the time it reached print you may well have forgotten precisely what you were so pissed off about in the first place. Now? Foulness is everywhere, and you have to make a very deliberate decision to switch off from it, especially if you are any kind of public person.

That's not to say I've ever felt exercised to the extent that I would step away from pop culture altogether, but rather that trying to declare one form of art more obscene, dangerous or influential than another is like trying to nail jelly to the ceiling. It certainly disappoints me to hear singer the Weeknd refer to women as "bitches" in his hit song "Starboy," but it pisses me off equally that UK TV channels bleep these words out even after 9 p.m., the watershed for profanity. As a law-abiding, tax-paying, TV-license-paying adult, I believe I have earned the right to hear a singer refer to women in derogatory terms, not least because it helps me decide if they're worthy of my attention or patronage. The Weeknd certainly went down in my estimation when I looked up the lyrics to "Starboy" and found a parade of hoary hip-hop clichés about money, cars and treating women like crap. Perhaps his words were intended to be ironic, but if he really was trying to blur the distinction between mocking sexism and endorsing, it was too subtle an effort. Also, as a lifelong fan of Michael Jackson's work, I must point out what a massive debt the Weeknd's music owes to the

King of Pop, not least for his love of falsetto and fancy footwork. I also nostalgically recall how MJJ never called women bitches in his songs; I can't even think of a cuss word in a Jackson song, apart from one lone f-bomb in the 1995 song "Scream."

Nevertheless, in the interest of fairness, I must acknowledge that what Michael Jackson said in his songs and what he did in private are two very distinct issues. The latter topic has been covered authoritatively by the excellent biographer J. Randy Taraborrelli,[3] and much as it pained me to read parts of Taraborrelli's account, I've concluded that Jackson definitely engaged in some seriously questionable behavior with young boys. The extent of the inappropriate behavior has never been legally proven, but there's enough casual misogyny elsewhere in Jackson's biography to disgust any feminist. Jackson referred to women as "bitches, wenches and hos" in his interactions with his young friend Jordy Chandler, as well as dismissing Madonna as "a nasty heifer." Not very clean-cut behavior from the cleancut, self-styled Peter Pan of pop music—not to mention someone whose music and dancing I have adored for nearly three decades. That's the occupational hazard of loving pop culture, though: all our idols will inevitably have feet of clay. Also, one person's moronic misogyny is another person's favorite hip-hop tune. I'd certainly like to see the Weeknd's lyrics punch upwards rather than revert to hackneyed clichés, but that doesn't stop me appreciating his dancing, singing, pretty eyes and lickable face.

I definitely count it as a victory for the average Brit that all types of media are now accessible on a level that would have been impossible to predict in 1959, and I'm thrilled to see sex-positive feminism, LGBT culture and the explosion of erotic literature gaining degrees of mainstream acceptance. As someone who still encounters bouts of terribly British nerves when asked what my first two books are about, I'm relieved to report that the vast majority of those I tell don't even bat an eyelid. If anything, they show curiosity and enthusiasm for the subject, and sometimes share their own stories or opinions. This, to me, is social progress. This is why I keep writing.

The conundrums presented by sexism and censorship will probably always be my personal hot-button topic. I can accept that some liberal groups are in danger of eating their own tails if they persist in nitpicking about language, tone policing and virtue signaling (not to mention the derailing of which they often accuse their opponents) instead of offering any practical assistance to oppressed groups. That said, I remain very glad to see a much bigger, more vocal call-out culture than there was ten or 15 years ago, when I felt deeply alone as a feminist alienated by the tacky, lowest-common-denominator depictions of the female form I saw all around me. I signed the No More Page 3 petition, not simply because I have always loathed Page 3 and everything it represents (I do), but also because as a relative of Liverpudlians, a distant relative of a Hillsborough victim and a left-leaning feminist, I loathe the *Sun*, the Murdoch empire that owns it and everything for which *those* institutions stand. Page 3 is now gone, although the *Sun* likes to claim that its decision had nothing to do with feminist protests but was simply a coincidental choice to modernize and put the breasts online. I don't really care what the reason was, I'm just happy I no longer have to see this cringeworthy relic of British sexism lying on train seats or in workplaces. If I can live without looking at glossy pictures of penises in public, then I'm sure British men are surviving fine without Page 3.

I did, however, balk at signing a later petition to remove soft-porn lads' mags from UK supermarkets altogether, because it felt like feminism was starting to become a pretext for both censorship and bullying. I didn't see how I and other middle-class, university-educated feminists had the right to stand in judgment of the women who posed for lads' mags; they deserved fair pay and decent work opportunities just like the rest of us, and relegating their product to sex shops would only have the opposite effect. Ultimately, this debate was academic; the internet has since killed off the last of the print lads' mags, and their classier counterparts like *GQ* have

The aging female body is conveniently forgotten by those who claim naked women are "just nicer to look at" than men (courtesy Emily Brady).

begun to opt for more sophisticated covers, often depicting men instead of women (clothed men, of course, because men are permitted that particular privilege) and not going for the tedious, lazy, done-to-death "sex sells" option. This also feels like progress, however small.

I've covered the scaremongering regarding children elsewhere in this book, and I hope I've also made it pretty clear that I don't care what any adult man or woman fantasizes about, or looks for in porn, so long as all parties consent. I do care that pictures of sex workers are used without their consent in patronizing articles about how terrible it is to be a porn actor or escort; I'm also highly suspicious of a condescending "rescue industry" that hijacks sex workers' stories for pay. As a freelance writer who is still all too regularly asked to write or give my time for free, I'm always going to side with workers who are getting trodden on. Especially when it's by those with too much time and money on their hands, who are offering "help" that was never requested in the first place; where were these saviors when I was stuck in the low-paid female-dominated field of care work?

Wherever you land on the issue of obscenity, I hope this book has at least informed your journey, taught you something you didn't know before and made you laugh. I hope it's been effective in unpacking the acts and regulations that have loosely cohered to create Britain's current legal landscape. I hope it has opened your eyes to the silent ways in which speech and sexuality can be restricted, and at times made you angry at how often governments, the media and even the medical establishment have illegitimately claimed the right to say who is a sick pervert and who an upstanding citizen. I hope it's made you think about how race, gender, class and sexuality map onto our personal beliefs about what is obscene, and made you question your own convictions about where reasoned debate ends and hate speech begins.

By turns, it's been exhausting, hilarious and arduous to create this work, but every step towards publication has felt like a triumph. Starting and finishing this book were both intensely solo tasks, but the vast bulk of *To Deprave and Corrupt* should be viewed as a group effort, and I must pay tribute to all those who provided me with media resources, legal information, eloquent viewpoints and hilarious anecdotes. I must also thank you for staying with me on this journey until the bitter, filth-spattered end.

Chapter Notes

Introduction
1. Ummni Khan, *Vicarious Kinks: S/M in the Socio-Legal Imaginary* (Toronto: University of Toronto Press), 18.
2. Sylvia Patterson, *I'm Not with the Band: A Writer's Life Lost in Music* (London: Sphere, 2016) 416.
3. Gayle Rubin, quoted in Meg-John Barker and Julia Scheele, *Queer: A Graphic History* (London: Icon, 2016), 50.

Chapter 1
1. Myles Jackman: Obscenity Lawyer website, accessed November 1, 2017, http://www.mylesjackman.com/index.php/my-blog/107-pornography-is-the-canary-in-the-coalmine-of-free-speech.
2. Guy Phelps, *Film Censorship* (London: Gollancz 1975), 49.
3. Brooke Magnanti, *The Sex Myth: Why Everything We're Told Is Wrong* (London: Orion, 2012), 30, emphasis my own.
4. "The Following Content Is Not Acceptable," *Myles Jackman: Obscenity Lawyer*, November 2014, accessed November 1, 2017, http://mylesjackman.com/index.php/my-blog/106-the-following-content-is-not-acceptable.
5. *Ibid.*
6. Mollena Williams-Haas, *The Toybag Guide to Playing with Taboo* (Emeryville, CA: Greenery Press, 2010) 36.
7. The Crown Prosecution Service, *Legal Guidance: Extreme Pornography*, accessed November 2, 2017, http://www.cps.gov.uk/legal/d_to_g/extreme_pornography/#an02.
8. Ian Ruben, "Extreme Porn," *New Statesman*, May 10, 2008, accessed October 19, 2017, https://www.newstatesman.com/politics/2008/05/extreme-rights-pornography.
9. *The Adam Smith Institute*, 2015, accessed November 5, 2017, https://www.adamsmith.org/nothing-to-hide/.
10. Magnanti, *The Sex Myth*, 134.
11. *Ibid.*
12. "The Following Content Is Not Acceptable."
13. Holly Watt, "Spanking and Caning—Just Two of the Sexual Acts Now Banned in British Porn Films," *The Telegraph*, December 2, 2014, accessed October 19, 2017, http://www.telegraph.co.uk/culture/film/film-news/11269271/Spanking-and-caning-just-two-of-the-sexual-acts-now-banned-in-British-porn-films.html.
14. Jerry Barnett, *Porn Panic! Sex and Censorship in the UK* (London: Zero Books, 2016), 17.
15. As of October 2017, Pandora Blake publicly stated their wish to be addressed as Blake, and also requested the use of gender-neutral pronouns when referring to them. I emailed Blake on October 4, 2017, for clarification on how to refer to their past activities and they responded, "'They' and 'Blake' would be lovely, but you could [include] a note about how I was going by Pandora Blake and she at the time."
16. Ofcom, "Final Determination on Mistress R'eal," April 20, 2015, accessed November 1, 2017, https://www.ofcom.org.uk/_data/assets/pdf_file/0028/84772/20150420_mistress_real_determination_-_rule_14_20_april_2015.pdf.

17. "Pink Flamingos," date and author not known, BBFC online, accessed November 1, 2017, http://www.bbfc.co.uk/case-studies/pink-flamingos.
18. Ofcom, "Final Determination on Mistress R'eal."
19. Ms. Tytania, "How Backlash UK Helped Me Beat ATVOD's Bullying," August 2014, accessed November 1, 2017, https://mstytania.net/2014/08/.
20. ATVOD/Ofcom, "Dreams of Spanking Determination," July 30, 2015, Dreams_of_Spanking_Determination_-_Rule_14_30_July_2015.pdf.
21. Ms. Tytania, "How Backlash UK Helped Me Beat ATVOD's Bullying."
22. Michael Warner, "Fear of a Queer Planet," *Social Text* 9, no. 14 (1993): 3–17.
23. Charles Rembar, *The End of Obscenity: The Trials of Lady Chatterley, Tropic of Cancer and Fanny Hill by the Lawyer Who Defended Them* (New York: Simon & Schuster, 1968), 21.

Chapter 2

1. Jesse Bering, *Perv: The Sexual Deviant in All of Us* (London: Transworld, 2013), 10.
2. Geoffrey R. Stone, "Origins of Obscenity," *University of Chicago Law School Journal*, 2007, accessed November 1, 2017, http://chicagounbound.uchicago.edu/cgi/viewcontent.cgi?article=2980&context=journal_articles.
3. *Ibid.*
4. Roy Porter and Lesley Hall, *The Facts of Life: The Creation of Sexual Knowledge in Britain 1650–1590* (New Haven: Yale University Press, 1995), 92.
5. Magnanti, *The Sex Myth*, 100.
6. Margaret Atwood, *The Handmaid's Tale* (London: Hachette, 1985), 242.
7. Catherine Scott, "Does Kinkphobia Color Criticism of Fifty Shades of Grey?" *Bitch*, February 17, 2015, accessed November 4, 2017, https://www.bitchmedia.org/post/does-kinkphobia-color-criticism-of-fifty-shades-of-grey.
8. House of Commons, Home Affairs Committee, "Hate Crime: Abuse, Hate and Extremism Online," accessed November 4, 2011, https://www.publications.parliament.uk/pa/cm201617/cmselect/cmhaff/609/609.pdf.
9. "I've left Twitter. It is unusable for anyone but trolls, robots and dictators," January 3, 2017, accessed November 4, 2011, https://www.theguardian.com/commentisfree/2017/jan/03/ive-left-twitter-unusable-anyone-but-trolls-robots-dictators-lindy-west.
10. Vonny Moyes, "Chimamanda Ngozi Adichie Doesn't Deserve the Mainstream Feminist Slush Pile," March 3, 2017, https://femigre.wordpress.com/2017/03/17/chimamanda-ngozi-adichie-doesnt-deserve-the-mainstream-feminist-slush-pile/.
11. Harriett Gilbert, "So Long as It's Not Sex and Violence," in Lynne Segal and Mary McIntosh, *Sex Exposed: Sexuality and the Pornography Debate* (London: Virago, 1992), 227.
12. Sue Carter, "Women's Libraries and Bookstores Deal with Historic but Problematic Second-Wave Feminism," *Quill and Quire*, April 17, 2017, accessed November 8, 2017, http://www.quillandquire.com/omni/womens-libraries-and-bookstores-deal-with-historic-but-problematic-second-wave-feminism/.
13. Catherine Scott, *Thinking Kink: The Collision of BDSM, Feminism and Popular Culture* (Jefferson, NC: McFarland, 2015), 58–59.
14. Richard Davenport-Hines, *An English Affair: Sex, Class and Power in the Age of Profumo* (London: HarperCollins, 2013), 138.
15. "Damian Green Says Computer Porn Allegations Are 'PoliticalS,'" *BBC News*, November 5, 2011, http://www.bbc.co.uk/news/uk-politics-41874026.
16. Porter and Hall, *The Facts of Life*, 80.
17. Joan DeJean, *The Reinvention of Obscenity: Sex, Lies, and Tabloids in Early Modern France* (Chicago: University of Chicago Press, 2002), 82.
18. Catherine Scott, "Why Is Breast Cancer Awareness Made So Sexy?" *Independent Voices*, September 14, 2012, accessed October 19, 2017, http://www.independent.co.uk/voices/comment/why-is-breast-cancer-awareness-made-so-sexy-8135480.html.
19. DeJean, *The Reinvention of Obscenity*, 83.
20. *Ibid.*
21. Geoffrey Robertson, *Obscenity* (London: Weidenfeld and Nicolson, 1979), 27.
22. *Ibid.*, 28.

23. *Ibid.*, 29.

24. Charles Rembar, *The End of Obscenity: The Trials of Lady Chatterley, Tropic of Cancer and Fanny Hill by the Lawyers Who Defended Them* (New York: Simon & Schuster, 1968), 20.

25. Scott, *Thinking Kink*, 131.

26. Susie Steinbach, *Women in England 1760–1914, A Social History* (London: Hachette, 2005), 130.

27. *Ibid.*

28. *Ibid.*, 33.

29. Porter and Hall, *The Facts of Life*, 132.

Chapter 3

1. Quoted in *Mapplethorpe: Look at the Pictures*, BBC documentary, Fenton Bailey/Randy Barbato, 2017.

2. Robertson, *Obscenity*, 41.

3. Protection of Children Act, 1978, Chapter 37, last accessed October 10, 2017, http://www.legislation.gov.uk/ukpga/1978/37.

4. "ORG London: Stop Censorship of Legal Content," https://www.youtube.com/watch?v=Om0x9bQBjwg&feature=push-u-sub&attr_tag=DddHXuCijGBcF4Z9-6.

5. Robertson, *Obscenity*, 55.

6. "Doctor Driven Out of Home by Vigilantes," *The Guardian*, August 30, 2000, accessed October 26, 2017, http://www.theguardian.com/uk/2000/aug/30/childprotection.society.

7. Aldous Huxley, *Brave New World* (London: Chatto & Windus, 1932), 6.

8. "Social Media Might Actually Be Reducing Teen Pregnancy," *The Daily Dot*, March 10, 2016, accessed October 26, 2017, http://www.dailydot.com/irl/uk-teen-pregnancy-rate/.

9. NSPCC accused of risking its reputation and "whipping up moral panic" with study into porn addiction among children. *The Independent*, April 12, 2015, accessed October 26, 2017, http://www.independent.co.uk/news/uk/home-news/nspcc-accused-of-risking-its-reputation-and-whipping-up-moral-panic-with-child-porn-addiction-study-10171195.html.

10. Shira Tarrant, *The Pornography Industry: What Everyone Needs to Know* (Oxford: Oxford University Press, 2016), 146.

11. Seth Lubove, "Sex, Lies and Statistics," *Forbes* (2005), accessed May 3, 2016, http://www.forbes.com/2005/11/22/internet-pornography-children-cz_sl_1123internet.html.

12. *Exposure to Internet Pornography Among Children and Adolescents: A National Survey*, University of New Hampshire, 2005, accessed October 26, 2017, http://www.unh.edu/ccrc/pdf/jvq/CV76.pdf.

13. Chiara Sabina, Janis Wolak and David Finkelhor, *The Nature and Dynamics of Internet Pornography Exposure for Youth*, 2008, University of New Hampshire, accessed May 3, 2016, http://scholars.unh.edu/cgi/viewcontent.cgi?article=1283&context=soc_facpub.

14. Response to DFE Consultation on Parental Controls, Open Rights Group & LSE Media Project, 2012.

15. "Former Firefighter Jailed After Installing Spy Cam in His Lodgers' Bathroom Which They Thought Was a Towel Hook," *The World News*, September 29, 2017, accessed November 11, 2017, https://theworldnews.net/uk-news/former-firefighter-jailed-after-installing-spy-cam-in-his-lodgers-bathroom-which-they-thought-was-a-towel-hook.html.

16. Commons Select Committee, "Government Response to Sex Education Report Is 'Feeble,'" July 16, 2015, accessed November 9, 2017, http://www.parliament.uk/business/committees/committees-a-z/commons-select/education-committee/news-parliament-2015/comment-sex-education-15-16/.

17. "Why Teach PSHE and SRE in Schools?" accessed November 9, 2017, http://www.publications.parliament.uk/pa/cm201415/cmselect/cmeduc/145/14505.htm#a17.

18. Helen Russell, "Pornography Belongs in the Classroom Says Danish Professor," *The Guardian*, March 16, 2015, accessed November 9, 2017, http://www.theguardian.com/culture/2015/mar/16/pornography-belongs-classroom-professor-denmark.

19. Zoë Heller, *Notes on a Scandal* (London: Penguin, 2003), 83.

20. Hansard, "Age of Marriage Bill," April 30, 1929, accessed November 9, 2011, http://hansard.millbanksystems.com/lords/1929/apr/30/age-of-marriage-bill-hl#s5lv0074p0_19290430_hol_108.

21. "The Law of Marriage," accessed November 9, 2011, http://www.parliament.uk/about/living-heritage/transformingsociety/

private-lives/relationships/overview/lawof marriage-/.
22. Heller, *Notes on a Scandal*, 83.
23. Julian Petley, *Censorship* (Oxford: Oneworld, 2009), 91.
24. *Ibid.*, 92.

Chapter 4

1. Elizabeth Wilson, "Feminist Fundamentalism," *Sex Exposed: Sexuality and the Pornography Debate* (London: Virago, 1992), 26.
2. Julia Serano, *Excluded: Making Feminist and Queer Movements More Inclusive* (Berkeley: Seal Press, 2013), 132.
3. LGBT Archive, "Timeline of UK LGBT Legislation," accessed November 9, 2017, http://lgbthistoryuk.org/wiki/Timeline_of_UK_LGBT_Legislation.
4. "What Can They Do in Bed Anyway: Lesbian Sexuality and the Law," LGBT History Month online, February 15, 2017, accessed October 21, 2017, http://lgbthistorymonth.org.uk/but-what-can-they-do-in-bed-anyway-lesbian-sexuality-and-the-law/.
5. Jeffrey Weeks, *Sex, Politics and Society: The Regulation of Sexuality Since 1800* (London: Longman, 1989), eBook edition.
6. Rebecca Jennings, *A Lesbian History of Britain* (Oxford: Greenwood World, 2007), 112.
7. *Ibid.*, 111.
8. Ferris, *Sex and the British*, 126.
9. *Ibid.*, 150.
10. *Ibid.*, 152.
11. Jackie Stacey, "Promoting Normality: Section 28 and the Regulation of Sexuality," *Off-Centre: Feminism and Cultural Studies*, edited by Sarah Franklin, Celia Lury and Jackie Stacey (London: HarperCollins Academic, 1991), 286.

Chapter 5

1. Rembar, *The End of Obscenity*, 17.
2. Warner, "Fear of a Queer Planet."
3. Ferris, *Sex and the British*, 18.
4. *Ibid.*, 16.
5. Susie Steinbach, *Women in England 1760–1914: A Social History* (London: Weidenfeld and Nicolson, 2004), 131–32.
6. Ferris, *Sex and the British*, 20.
7. *Ibid.*, 21.
8. Davenport-Hines, *An English Affair*, 138.
9. Hansard, May 1961, accessed November 3, 2011, http://hansard.millbanksystems.com/lords/1961/may/01/criminal-justice-bill-1.
10. Pamela Green, Obituary, *The Guardian*, May 17, 2010, accessed November 3, 2011, http://www.telegraph.co.uk/news/obituaries/culture-obituaries/film-obituaries/7734345/Pamela-Green.html.
11. *Ibid.*
12. *Ibid.*
13. Robertson, *Obscenity*, 112.
14. From his closing speech defending *The Mouth and Oral Sex*.
15. Thomas Grant, *Jeremy Hutchinson's Case Histories* (London: Hachette, 2016) 177.
16. *R v. Read*, 1708.
17. Robertson, *Obscenity*, 27.
18. Frank McCourt, *Angela's Ashes* (London: HarperCollins, 1996), 414.
19. Alan Travis, "Retake on Kubrick Film Ban," *The Guardian*, September 11, 1999, accessed October 20, 2017, https://www.theguardian.com/uk/1999/sep/11/alantravis.
20. Jon Ronson, *So You've Been Publicly Shamed* (London: Picador, 2015), 135.

Chapter 6

1. Robertson, *Obscenity*, 118.
2. Feona Attwood and Clarissa Smith, "Emotional Truths and Thrilling Slide Shows: The Resurgence of Anti-Porn Feminism," *The Feminist Porn Book: The Politics of Producing Pleasure*, edited by Shimizu Taormino et al. (New York: The Feminist Press, 2013), 53.
3. Ms. Naughty aka Louise Lush, "My Decadent Decade: Ten Years of Making and Debating Porn for Women," *The Feminist Porn Book: The Politics of Producing Pleasure*, edited by Shimizu Taormino et al. (New York: The Feminist Press, 2013), 73.
4. *Ibid.*, 75.
5. "More Women Watch (and Enjoy) Porn Than You Ever Realized," *Marie Claire*, October 19, 2015, accessed October 11, 2017, http://www.marieclaire.com/sex-love/a16474/women-porn-habits-study/.
6. Ms. Naughty, "My Decadent Decade."
7. Lynne Segal, "Sweet Sorrow, Painful Pleasures: Pornography and the Perils of

Heterosexual Desire," *Sex Exposed: Sexuality and the Pornography Debate* (London: Virago, 1992), 73.
 8. Maggie Paley, *The Book of the Penis* (London: Fusion Press, 1999), 77.
 9. Ms. Naughty, "My Decadent Decade," 72.
 10. Aminatta Forna, "For Women or For Men Only?" *The Independent*, April 27, 1996, accessed October 12, 2017, http://www.independent.co.uk/life-style/for-women-or-for-men-only-1307073.html.
 11. Scottish bookseller established in the 19th century, now a distribution company mostly serving airport newsstands.
 12. Forna, "For Women or For Men Only?"
 13. Jerry Barnett, "Porn for Women: What Do Women Really Watch?" *Sex and Censorship*, March 2015. Accessed November 3, 2011. http://sexandcensorship.org/2015/03/porn-women-women-really-watch/.
 14. Scott, *Thinking Kink*, 147.
 15. Attwood and Smith, "Emotional Truths and Thrilling Slide Shows," 54.
 16. *Ibid.*, 50.

Chapter 7

 1. Associated Press, "12 States Still Ban Sodomy a Decade After Court Ruling," *USA Today*, April 21, 2014, accessed October 25, 2017, https://www.usatoday.com/story/news/nation/2014/04/21/12-states-ban-sodomy-a-decade-after-court-ruling/7981025/.
 2. "U.S. Supreme Court Rules Gay Marriage Is Legal Nationwide," *BBC News*, June 27, 2015, accessed October 24, 2017, http://www.bbc.com/news/world-us-canada-33290341.
 3. Smriti Sinha, "One Woman Is Fighting for the Right to Buy Sex Toys in Her State," *Policy Mic*, May 19, 2014, accessed October 25, 2017, https://mic.com/articles/89589/one-woman-is-fighting-for-the-right-to-buy-sex-toys-in-her-town#.uWns3twEe.
 4. *Ibid.*
 5. *Ibid.*
 6. Petley, *Censorship*, 160.
 7. McCourt, *Angela's Ashes*, 341.
 8. Jonathan Eig, *The Birth of The Pill* (London: Macmillan, 2014), 45.
 9. *Ibid.*
 10. *Ibid.*

 11. David Ley, Nicole Prause, Peter Finn, "The Emperor Has Clothes: A Review of the 'Pornography Addiction' Model," February 12, 2014, accessed October 25, 2017, https://link.springer.com/article/10.1007/s11930-014-0016-8.
 12. Rembar, *The End of Obscenity*, 47.
 13. *Ibid.*, 18.
 14. *Ibid.*, 19.
 15. *Ibid.*, 20.
 16. Charlotte Burns, "Sex, the Play That Put Mae West in Jail, Returns to New York," *The Guardian*, September 29, 2016, accessed November 9, 2017, https://www.theguardian.com/stage/2016/sep/29/sex-play-mae-west-new-york.
 17. Dr. Matt Brennan, "Land of the Free," *The Big Issue* August 7–13, 2017.
 18. Bryson, *The Life and Times of The Thunderbolt Kid*.
 19. *Ibid.*
 20. Andi Zeisler, *We Were Feminists Once: From Riot Grrl to Cover Girl, the Buying and Selling of a Political Movement* (New York: Public Affairs, 2016), 6.
 21. John Patterson, *DGA Quarterly*, Fall 2007 edition, review of *Hollywood's Censor: Joseph I. Breen and The Production Code*, accessed November 6, 2017, https://www.dga.org/Craft/DGAQ/All-Articles/0703-Fall-2007/Books-Hollywoods-Censor.aspx.
 22. *Ibid.*
 23. Rembar, *The End of Obscenity*.

Chapter 8

 1. *The Daily Mail*, July 21. 1989.
 2. Wilson, "Feminist Fundamentalism," 26.
 3. Thomas Grant, *Jeremy Hutchinson's Case Histories* (London: Hachette, 2015), 123
 4. Dominic Sandbrook, *State of Emergency: The Way We Were: Britain, 1970–1974* (London: Penguin, 2011), 406
 5. Patrick Higgins, ed., *A Queer Reader* (New York: Fourth Estate, 1993), 268
 6. Barnett, *Porn Panic!*, 27.
 7. Jean Collyer and Jane Lee, *Teaching AIDS in the Classroom: A Skills Based Programme of AIDS Education for Key Stages Two and Three* (London: Forbes, 1994).
 8. *Ibid.*, 23.
 9. *Ibid.*, 20.

10. *Ibid.*, 23.
11. Scott, *Thinking Kink*, 132.
12. http://www.bbc.co.uk/sport/darts/38139647.
13. Magnanti, *The Sex Myth*, 133.
14. *Ibid.*
15. Alex Antoniou, "R v. Peacock: Landmark Trial Redefines Obscenity Law," *Graduate Journal of Social Science* 10 (2013), 89.
16. *Ibid.*, 90.

Chapter 9

1. Antoniou, "R v. Peacock," 96.
2. Barker and Scheele, *Queer: A Graphic History*, 91.
3. Mona Eltahawy, *Headscarves and Hymens: Why the Middle East Needs a Sexual Revolution* (London: Orion, 2015), 5.
4. *Ibid.*, 32
5. Meera Syal, *Life Isn't All Ha Ha Hee Hee* (London: Transworld, 2000), 73.
6. "I Don't Believe You're Racist by Omission: Caitlin Moran Defends Lena Dunham and 'Girls,'" *The Huffington Post*, September 30, 2014, accessed November 6, 2017., http://www.huffingtonpost.co.uk/2014/09/30/lena-dunham-caitlin-moran-girls-racist-omission_n_5905078.html.
7. Kevin Myers, quoted in Robert Booth, "Anti-Semitic Column Pompts Apology from Sunday Times," *The Guardian*, July 31, 2017, accessed November 10, 2017.
8. Lionel Shriver, "I Hope the Concept of Cultural Appropriation Is a Passing Fad," *The Guardian*, accessed October 10, 2017, https://www.theguardian.com/commentisfree/2016/sep/13/lionel-shrivers-full-speech-i-hope-the-concept-of-cultural-appropriation-is-a-passing-fad?CMP=share_btn_tw.
9. Eric Russell, "Sombreros at Bowdoin 'Tequila Party' Ignite Controversy on Campus and Beyond," *Press Herald*, March 4, 2016, accessed October 29, 2017.
10. Yassmin Abdel-Magied, "As Lionel Shriver Made Light of Identity, I Had No Choice but to Walk Out on Her," *The Guardian*, September 10, 2016, accessed October 29, 2017, https://www.theguardian.com/commentisfree/2016/sep/10/as-lionel-shriver-made-light-of-identity-i-had-no-choice-but-to-walk-out-on-her.
11. Lionel Shriver, "Be Here Now Means Be Gone Later," *Selfish, Shallow and Self-Absorbed: 16 Writers on The Decision Not to Have Kids*, edited by Meghan Daum (London: Picador, 2015), 93.
12. "Manic Depression," *Melody Maker*, January 2, 1993.

Afterword

1. Daisuke Kikuchi, "'Vagina Artist' Megumi Igarashi Continues Her Battles with Japan's Definition of Obscenity," *Japan Times*, April 18, 2017, accessed November 2, 2017, https://www.japantimes.co.jp/news/2017/04/18/national/vagina-artist-megumi-igarashi-continues-her-battle-with-japans-definition-of-obscenity/#.Wd3qo2hSzIU.
2. "Woman Fired for Flipping Off Donald Trump's Motorcade," *Huffington Post*, November 6, 2017, accessed November 8, 2017, http://www.huffingtonpost.co.uk/entry/woman-flips-off-donald-trump-fired_us_59fe0ab4e4b0c9652fffa484.
3. J. Randy Taraborrelli, *Michael Jackson: The Magic, The Madness, The Whole Story* (London: Pan, 2013).

Bibliography

Attwood, Feona, and Clarissa Smith. "Emotional Truths and Thrilling Slide Shows: The Resurgence of Anti-Porn Feminism." *The Feminist Porn Book: The Politics of Producing Pleasure.* New York: Feminist Press, 2013.
Atwood, Margaret. *The Handmaid's Tale.* London: Hachette, 1985.
Barker, Meg-John, and Julia Scheele). *Queer: A Graphic History.* London: Icon, 2016.
Barnett, Jerry. *Porn Panic! Sex and Censorship in the UK.* London: Zero Books, 2016.
Bering, Jesse. *Perv: The Sexual Deviant in All of Us.* London: Transworld, 2013.
Brennan, Dr. Matt. "Land of the Free." *The Big Issue.* August 7–13, 2017.
Bryson, Bill. *The Life and Times of The Thunderbolt Kid: Travels Through My Childhood.* New York: Random House, 2006.
Carter, Angela. *The Sadeian Woman: An Exercise in Cultural History.* London: Virago, 1979.
Davenport-Hines, Richard. *An English Affair: Sex, Class and Power in the Age of Profumo.* London: HarperCollins, 2013.
DeJean, Joan. *The Reinvention of Obscenity: Sex, Lies, and Tabloids in Early Modern France.* Chicago: University of Chicago Press, 2002.
Eig, Jonathan. *The Birth of the Pill: How Four Pioneers Reinvented Sex and Launched a Revolution.* London: Macmillan, 2014.
Eltahawy, Mona. *Headscarves and Hymens: Why the Middle East Needs a Sexual Revolution.* London: Orion, 2015.
Ferris, Paul. *Sex and The British: A Twentieth Century History.* London: Mandarin, 1994.
Gilbert, Harriett. "So Long as It's Not Sex and Violence." *Sex Exposed: Sexuality and the Pornography Debate,* edited by Lynne Segal and Mary McIntosh. London: Virago, 1992.
Grant, Thomas. *Jeremy Hutchinson's Case Histories.* London: Hachette, 2016.
Hall, Lesley, and Roy Porter. *The Facts of Life: The Creation of Sexual Knowledge in Britain 1650–1950.* New Haven: Yale University Press, 1995.
Heller, Zoe. *Notes on a Scandal.* London: Penguin, 2003.
Higgins, Patrick, ed. *A Queer Reader: 2500 Years of Male Homosexuality.* New York: Fourth Estate, 1994.
Huxley, Aldous. *Brave New World.* London: Chatto & Windus, 1932.
Jennings, Rebecca. *A Lesbian History of Britain.* London: Greenwood World Publishing, 2007.
Jeff, Leonard J., and Jerold L. Simmons. *The Dame in the Kimono: Hollywood, Censorship and the Production Code.* Lexington: University of Kentucky Press, 2001.
Khan, Ummni. *Vicarious Kinks: S/M in the Socio-Legal Imaginary.* Toronto: University of Toronto Press, 2014.

Lee, Jane, Jean Collyer, and Jane Leg. *Teaching AIDS in the Classroom: Skills-Based Programme of AIDS Education for Key Stages Two and Three*. London: Forbes, 1994.

Lush, Louise. "My Decadent Decade: Ten Years of Making and Debating Porn for Women." *The Feminist Porn Book: The Politics of Producing Pleasure*. New York: Feminist Press, 2013.

Magnanti, Dr. Brooke. *The Sex Myth: Why Everything We're Told Is Wrong*. London: Orion, 2012.

McCourt, Frank. *Angela's Ashes: A Memoir*. London: HarperCollins, 1996.

Paley, Maggie. *The Book of the Penis*. London: Fusion Press, 1999.

Patterson, Sylvia. *I'm Not with the Band: A Writer's Life Lost in Music*. London: Sphere, 2016.

Petley, Julian. *Censorship: A Beginner's Guide*. Oxford: Oneworld, 2009.

Phelps, Guy. *Film Censorship*. London: Gollancz, 1975.

Porter, Roy, and Lesley Hall. *The Facts of Life: The Creation of Sexual Knowledge in Britain 1650–1950*. New Haven: Yale University Press, 1995.

Price, Simon. *Everything: A Book About Manic Street Preachers*. London: Virgin, 1999.

Rembar, Charles. *The End of Obscenity: The Trials of Lady Chatterley, Tropic of Cancer and Fanny Hill by the Lawyer Who Defended Them*. New York: Simon & Schuster, 1968.

Robertson, Geoffrey. *Obscenity*. London: Weidenfeld & Nicolson, 1979.

Ronson, Jon. *So You've Been Publicly Shamed*. London: Picador, 2015.

Sandbrook, Dominic. *State of Emergency: The Way We Were: Britain 1970–1974*. London: Penguin, 2011.

Scheele, Julia, and Meg-John Barker. *Queer: A Graphic History*. London: Icon, 2016.

Scott, Catherine. *Thinking Kink: The Collision of BDSM, Feminism and Popular Culture*. Jefferson, NC: McFarland, 2015.

Segal, Lynne. "Sweet Sorrow, Painful Pleasures: Pornography and the Perils of Heterosexual Desire." *Sex Exposed: Sexuality and the Pornography Debate*, edited by Lynne Segal and Mary McIntosh. London: Virago, 1992.

Serano, Julia. *Excluded: Making Feminist and Queer Movements More Inclusive*. Berkeley: Seal Press, 2013.

Shriver, Lionel. "Be Here Now Means Be Gone Later." *Selfish, Shallow and Self-Absorbed: Sixteen Writers on the Decision Not to Have Kids*, edited by Meghan Daum. London: Picador, 2015.

Smith, Clarissa. *One for the Girls: The Pleasures and Practices of Reading Women's Porn*. Bristol: Intellect, 2007.

Stacey, Jackie. "Promoting Normality: Section 28 and the Regulation of Sexuality." *Off-Centre: Feminism and Cultural Studies*, edited by Sarah Franklin, Celia Lury and Jackie Stacey. London: HarperCollins Academic, 1991.

Steinbach, Susie. *Women in England 1760–1914: A Social History*. London: Hachette, 2005.

Syal, Meera. *Life Isn't All Ha Ha Hee Hee*. London: Transworld, 2000.

Tarrant, Shira. *The Pornography Industry: What Everyone Needs to Know*. Oxford: Oxford University Press, 2016.

Warner, Michael. *Fear of a Queer Planet: Queer Politics and Social Theory*. Minneapolis: University of Minnesota Press, 1993.

Weeks, Jeffrey. *Sex, Politics and Society: The Regulation of Sexuality Since 1800*. London: Longman, 1989. eBook.

Williams, Mollena. *The Toybag Guide to Playing with Taboo*. Emeryville, CA: Greenery Press, 2010.

Wilson, Elizabeth. "Feminist Fundamentalism." *Sex Exposed: Sexuality and the Pornography Debate*, edited by Lynne Segal and Mary McIntosh. London: Virago, 1992.

Zeisler, Andi. *We Were Feminists Once: From Riot Grrrl to CoverGirl, the Buying and Selling of a Political Movement*. New York: Public Affairs, 2016.

Index

Abdel-Magied, Yassmin 164, 166, 167
abortion 5, 6, 7–8, 13, 52, 93–94, 96, 128; anti-abortion/pro-life 43, 120; pennyroyal tea 52, 94; pro-choice 94
Abortion Act (1967) 7
abuse 2, 23–24, 26, 30, 41–42, 63, 77, 120, 150, 156; *see also* child abuse
Acquired Immune Deficiency Syndrome (AIDS) 5, 95, 125, 146–50, 158
addiction, porn/sex 60–61, 100, 128–29
Adichie, Chimamanda Ngozi 42, 43
age of marriage 69, 145, 157
Age of Marriage Bill (1929) 69
age play 23
agents, sexual 8
AIDS *see* Acquired Immune Deficiency Syndrome
Ailwyn, Lord 96
Akima, LLC 171; *see also* Briskman, Juli
Al-Qaeda 5
Albutt, Henry: *The Wife's Handbook* 51
Allen, Jane Wood 172
alt-right/far-right 12, 41, 42, 159; media 58, 73, 98, 163
American Civil Liberties Union (ACLU) 126, 127
American Medical Association (AMA) 128
anal sex *see* sex, anal
anti-bigotry 5
anti-feminism/anti-feminist 6, 41, 77, 165
anti-gay laws 2
anti-immigrant 34
Anti-Obscenity Enforcement Act (Alabama, 1998) 124
Anti-Semitism 40, 135, 162
anus/buttocks 25, 31, 91, 92, 11–16, 119, 140, 151
Applebee, Jacq 168
Arab/Arabic 6
Arbuckle, Fatty 133
aristocracy 38, 80
artwork, erotic 49–50, 65, 84, 100, 125, 171, 173
asexual 14, 46

Ashley Madison 20
Asia/Asian 155, 157–58, 160; art 100, 171; Chinese 65, 91, 100; Japanese 171
assault 26–27, 75, 82, 133, 156, 171; sexual 75, 82, 133, 156
atheism 8, 14
Attwood, Feona 121
ATVOD *see* Authority for Television on Demand
Audio Visual Media Services (AVMS) regulations 1–3, 19–22, 27–28, 31, 57, 119, 140, 152
Authority for Television on Demand (ATVOD) 2, 20, 28–32, 55, 57–58, 104, 121, 140; 2015 Blitz 30
AVMS *see* Audio Visual Media Services regulations

Barahona, Ana 6; *Bearing Witness: Eight Weeks in Palestine* 6
Barker, Meg-John 14; *Queer: A Graphic History* 14; *see also* Julia Scheele
Barnett, Jerry 21, 27–28, 32, 34, 58, 102, 118, 126, 127, 146, 151
BBC *see* British Broadcast Corporation
BBFC *see* British Board of Film Classification (BBFC)
beauty, male 97, 109–12, 115
Belle de Jour *see* Magnanti, Brooke
Besant, Annie: *The Law of Population* 51
bestiality 24–25, 66, 116
The Big Issue (London) 79
bigotry 6, 11, 82, 85, 157, 159, 162
bisexual 8, 75–79, 81, 85, 106, 168; biphobia 79, 168
Bitch Magazine (U.S.) 2, 78, 109
black people 24, 33, 43, 76–78, 143, 155–56, 158, 160, 166–69
Black People Kink 78
Black Power movement *see* civil rights movement
Blair, Tony 32, 126; Blair government 80
Blake, Pandora 21, 28, 30–32, 57–59, 62, 104, 123; *Dreams of Spanking* 31

185

Index

Bodkin, Sir Archibald 84
body, female 8–9, 84, 92, 94, 98, 106–7, 111, 154–55, 175
body, male 9, 109, 11–12, 119, 140, 154–55
Bogarde, Dirk 143
bondage 22, 73, 118, 119, 152
bondage and discipline, domination and submission, sadomasochism (BDSM) 2, 1–24, 29–30, 46, 70, 72, 76, 78, 91, 105, 123, 150, 152, 170; anti–BDSM 28, 44
The Bondage Mistress Club (TBMC) 28, 30
Boys Don't Cry 140
breasts 9, 13, 14, 25, 34, 47, 75, 91, 98, 106, 107, 113, 116, 140175
Breen, Joseph 135, 136, 139
Brennan, Matt 134
Brexit 18, 19, 21; see also European Union
Brighton 8
Briskman, Juli 171–72
Bristow, Eric 150
British Board of Film Classification (BBFC) 20, 22, 23, 24, 27, 28, 29, 30, 32, 70, 85, 86, 104, 121
British Broadcast Corporation (BBC) 30, 31, 35, 45, 51, 88, 98, 107, 140, 157, 162
British legal system 10
Brown, Bobby see Houston, Whitney
Brown, Lisa 92
Browne, Cass 168
Bryson, Bill 131, 134
Buffy the Vampire Slayer 88
Buggery Act (1533) 80
Bulger, James 70–71; see also Thompson, Roberts; Venables, John
Bundy, Ted 26, 27
Burger, Justice Warren 139
Burstyn v. Wilson (1952) 136

Cabaret 94
Cagney, James 136
Califia, Patrick 14, 76
Cameron, David 70
Campbell, Lord Chief Justice John 21, 49–50, 53, 130; see also Obscene Publications Act (1857)
Catholic Legion of Decency 136
Catholicism 5, 128, 135–36; anti–Catholic 50; see also Church
Chamberlain, Lord 91, 93
child abuse 24, 26, 55–56, 64, 155, 157; sexual 42, 53, 58, 60, 62–63, 95, 104, 116, 150, 155
Child Online Protection Act 140
The Child Protection Act (1978) 57, 116
children 8, 12, 13, 15, 39, 54–73, 87, 99, 134 140, 146, 148–51, 155–56, 159, 160; protection of 8, 56–57, 60, 64–65, 70, 116, 140; sexuality of 60, 100
Child's Play 3 71
Christianity 5, 8, 38, 76, 101
Church 5, 38, 46, 136
cisgender 79, 92, 155, 162

Civil Partnership Act (2004) 80
civil-rights movement 75; Black Panther movement 166
class 1, 38–40, 49, 80–81, 91, 102, 176; lower 33, 38, 51, 80, 86, 94–95, 102, 131, 158, 170; middle 38, 51, 80, 94, 101, 107, 145, 158–59; upper 37–39, 51, 80, 90–91, 94–95, 101, 129, 140, 145, 172–73, 175
Cleland, John: *Fanny Hill* 85, 95, 127, 130
Cockburn, Lord Chief Justice Alexander 21, 50
colonialism 10, 155
Communications Decency Act 140
Comstock, Anthony 127–29
Comstock, William 97, 129, 134
Comstock Act 128–29
The Confessional Unmasked 50
consent/consensual 22–24, 26, 30, 62–63, 69, 75, 79, 87, 102, 109, 116–17, 121, 126, 145, 152, 176; lack of 22–23, 29, 98
contraceptives/birth control 5, 7, 8, 13, 47, 50–52, 59, 83, 93, 96–97, 127–28, 135, 148, 181, 183; condoms 5, 52, 148; the Pill 7, 93, 96, 127
Copley, John Singleton see Lyndhurst, Lord
Coxe/Tartar, John 47
CPS see Crown Prosecution Service (CPS)
Crawford, Robyn see Houston, Whitney
Creighton, Jill 76, 78, 89
crime/criminal 4, 22–23, 25–27, 30, 40–41, 45–46, 48–49, 57, 66, 70, 79, 80–81, 94, 96, 98, 102, 104, 116, 124–25, 130, 134–36, 171
Criminal Justice and Immigration Act (2008) 25
Criminal Law Amendment Act (1855) 80
The Crown 50, 100
Crown Prosecution Service (CPS) 21–24, 28–29, 55, 117, 121, 151–52
cultural appropriation 7, 163, 165–67
Cumberbatch, Benedict 10
cunnilingus 65, 116
"cunt" 11, 40, 153, 154
curiosity, sexual 8, 61, 69
Curll, Edmund 47–48

Davenport-Hines, Richard 45, 97; *An English Affair* 97
deep-throating 27
degradation 22
DeJean, Joan 47
de Sade, Marquis 65
Desart, Lord 81
deviance/deviants 35, 48, 82, 88, 150
DiCaprio, Leonardo see *Titanic*
Digital Economy Act (2017) 1, 18–21, 32, 45, 64, 152
Dillingham, Brian 132, 138
Dines, Gail 121
disability 27, 99, 135
diversity 7, 44, 76, 91, 123, 135, 157–58, 163, 168

Index

divorce 38, 135
Doctor Who 98
dominatrix/dominatrices 13, 18, 22, 27–29, 118; Mistress Megara Furie 28–30, 57–59; Mistress R'eal 28–29, 31, 59; Ms. Tytania 31, 32
Douglas, James 82–84
Drabble, Margaret 100
drugs 64, 70, 77, 134, 138, 145

Eastern Europeans 157–59
Edison, Thomas 131–32
education 38, 40, 65, 83, 92–93, 96, 107, 109, 135, 139, 145, 148–49, 153, 159
Education Committee 68
Edwardian London 53, 92, 93, 94
Eig, Jonathan: *The Birth of the Pill* 127
ejaculation/orgasm: female 21, 22, 27, 66, 118, 140; male 27, 30, 80, 116, 121; squirting 119, 121
the elderly 76, 99
Elizabeth II, Queen 12
Ellis, Havelock 90, 93
Eltahawy, Mona 156
erotica 1, 49, 72, 93, 107, 109–12, 140, 174; for women 9, 39, 108–10, 112–13, 115–19
European Declaration of Human Rights 45, 173
European Union 19
expression, freedom of 6, 7, 126, 127; *see also* First Amendment, U.S. Constitution; speech, freedom of
expression, sexual 1, 28, 76, 104, 126, 139
Extreme Pornography (2008) 1, 25

face-sitting 21, 23, 27, 30, 118, 121
Facebook 35, 40–41, 102–3, 161, 171–72
"faggot/poof" 11, 88, 150
Family Safe Media (FSM) 60
fellatio 116
Feltz, Vanessa 162–163
female pleasure 22, 27, 81, 115, 140
feminism/feminist: anti-porn 13, 43–44, 118, 120–22, 129; anti-sex work 44, 121; second-wave 44, 75, 121; sex-positive 27, 122–23, 174; trans-exclusionary 44; writers 28, 40, 42, 76, 78, 114, 154, 168
fetish 24–25, 99, 121–23
FHM see For Him Magazine
Filament (UK) 108, 110–16
fingering 88, 116
First Amendment, U.S. Constitution 126, 132, 136, 139, 140; *see also* expression, freedom of; speech, freedom of
fisting 17, 22, 26, 28, 30, 73, 106, 118, 121, 151, 152
For Him Magazine (*FHM*) 66
For Women Magazine 110, 112, 114–15, 117
freedom, sexual 4, 8, 14, 18–19, 23, 28, 47, 96, 123, 167
Freud, Sigmund 90
FSM *see* Family Safe Media

gay rights 10, 75–76, 79, 84, 86, 124, 144
gay visibility 8
Gay's the Word raid (1984) 86
gender 2, 4, 8, 13, 44, 78, 81, 85, 109, 112, 123, 140, 155, 160, 166, 176; issues 70, 158
Genet, Jean 87
genitalia 2, 9, 10, 25, 126; female 6, 82, 91–92, 138, 154–55, 157, 171; male 9, 30, *see also* clitoris; penis; vagina
Gonosologium Novum see Marten, John
Google 40–41, 79, 91
Granville-Baker, Harley: *Waste* 93, 94
Greece 37, 50, 74, 93, 100; art 93, 100
Green, Damian 45
Green, Pamela: *Naked as Nature* 97; *The Window Dresser* 97–98
Greer, Germaine 10
Grose, Francis 154
The Guardian 162–63
Gunn, Thom 87

Hall, Radclyffe: *The Well of Loneliness* 82–85
The Handmaid's Tale 38, 74, 163
harassment 41, 45, 104, 155; sexual 41, 45, 155
hate/harmful speech 7, 10, 41, 153, 159, 176; *see also* expression, freedom of; First Amendment, U.S. Constitution; speech, freedom of
"Hate Crime: Abuse, Hate and Extremism Online" 40
healthcare 9, 36, 83, 163
heterosexuality 9, 24, 40, 59, 69, 76–77, 79, 85–86, 88, 100, 107, 119, 121, 140, 143–46, 155
The Hicklin test 20, 21, 90, 127, 130, 139; *Regina v. Hicklin* 21
Hillsborough football-stadium disaster 35, 175
Hindu/Hinduism 5, 8, 100; art 100; *see also* India/Indian
Hitchcock, Alfred 136–37
Hite, Shere 90
HIV *see* Human Immunodeficiency Virus
Holland, Andrew 25–26
Hollywood 131–32, 135, 137, 138, 140, 143
Holocaust *see* Judaism
Holywell Street 49
homophobia 5–6, 10, 20, 24, 34, 77, 80, 86–88, 142–43, 146–47, 149, 152–53
homosexuality 5, 48, 74, 79, 83, 86–87, 96, 135, 137, 140, 142–48; couples 17, 79, 81, 87–88, 103, 144–45; homosexual men 20, 69, 79, 80, 86–87, 89, 96, 107–8, 119, 124–52; *see also* lesbians
The House of Commons 49
The House of Lords 49, 81–82, 84, 94
Houston, Cissy *see* Houston, Whitney
Houston, Whitney 76–77
Human Immunodeficiency Virus (HIV) 5, 6, 147
humiliation 23

188 Index

Hutchison, Jeremy 100, 101
Huxley, Aldous 59–60
hypocrisy 7, 9

Igarashi, Megumi 171
immigration 10, 87, 101, 156, 158–59, 164–65, 168
in vitro fertilization (IVF) 59
incest 24, 66, 94–95, 170
The Indecent Advertisements Act (1889) 51
India/Indian 5, 157–58, 160, 168; art 5; *see also* Hinduism
insecurity, male 77, 81, 106, 110, 113–14, 119, 128
Instagram 72, 102–3, 118, 166
internet 1, 3, 4, 11, 12, 32, 38–42, 51, 57–58, 61, 64–65, 67–68, 70, 72, 84, 103, 117, 121, 166, 168, 173, 175; *see also* social media
Internet Filter Review (IFR) 60
internet service provider (ISP) 70
intolerance 7
Ireland/Irish 8, 39, 102, 103, 127, 144, 162
Islam 5, 6; *see also* Muslim
Islamophobia 6, 40
isolationism 41
ISP *see* internet service provider
Israel 6
IVF *see* in vitro fertilization

Jackman, Myles 17, 21–23, 60
Jackson, Michael 168–70, 173–74; "Black or White" 168, 169
James, E. L.: *Fifty Shades of Grey* 39
James Bond 137, 138; Pussy/Kitty Galore 138
Javid, Sajid 60
jazz 133–34, 172
Johnson, Pete 31–32; *see also* ATVOD
Joynson-Hicks, William 83–84
Judaism 42, 162

Keaton, Buster 133
Keir, Zak Jane 9, 114–15, 117, 119
The Killing of Sister George 85–86
kink 2, 18–19, 24, 30, 54, 63, 72, 75, 78, 99, 150, 152, 167, 170; kinkphobia/ anti-kink 24, 152
Kinsey, Alfred 90, 95; *Sexual Behavior in the Human Male* 95
Kubrick, Stanley: *A Clockwork Orange* 104

lads' mags 13, 65, 66, 113, 175
Last Exit to Brooklyn 144–45
Latinx 160, 169
Lawrence, D. H. 173; *Lady Chatterley's Lover* 4, 102, 108, 127, 130; 1960 obscenity trial 14, 57, 95, 108
Lee, Jane 148–50; *see also* Teaching AIDS in the Classroom
The Leeds Vigilance Association 51
left-wing/liberal 12, 43, 45, 51, 55, 64, 106, 111, 126, 144–46, 155, 160, 162, 164–65, 174; media 100

Legally Bland 44, 45
lesbians/gay women 8, 74–86, 89, 138, 143, 148; butch 78, 83, 85, 138; literature 84–85, 138; film 53, 74, 86, 88–89, 138; sex 48, 74, 79–81, 85, 88–89, 119, 137
Lewis, Arnold 104
LGBTQ 11–12, 74–76, 78–80, 84, 86–88, 101, 139, 145, 147, 153, 174; content/literature 8, 14, 70, 82; rights 78, 84; women 80; youth 88
Lister, Kate 37
London 8
London School of Economics (LSE) 61, 65
Longhurst, Jane 25
Los Angeles 132, 169, 170; LA riots 169, 170
LSE *see* London School of Economics
Lubove, Seth 60–61
Lumley, Joanna 160
Lyndhurst, Lord 49–50

Maddison-Brown, Sean 147
Magnanti, Brooke 26–27, 38, 151, 152
The Malthusian League 51
Manchester 8
Mandelson, Peter 80
Manson, Shirley 153
marriage, forced 6, 155, 157
marriage rights 8, 79, 124
Marten, John 47
Masters and Johnson 90
masturbation 46, 49, 90, 95, 102, 116–17, 119, 127–28, 134, 140; female 48; male 119, 127–28
May, Theresa 87, 126
McCourt, Frank: *Angela's Ashes* 127
mental health 31, 57, 86, 96, 143, 161, 163
Menzies, John 117
MFC *see* Mutual Film Company
Middle East/Middle Eastern 6, 11, 64, 92, 155, 156
Miller, Henry: "The Miller test" 139–40; trial 139; *Tropic of Cancer* 130
Millington, Mary 104
Milton, John 38
Minister, David 63–64
misogyny 2, 5, 6, 8, 13, 33, 38, 40, 48, 77, 124, 153, 162, 174
monarchy/royal power 14, 3, 46
monogamy 5, 17, 40, 59, 79, 121
Moore, Patrick 146
Moran, Caitlin 43, 161, 162
Morgan, Nicky 68
Mosley, Max 72
Motion Picture Association of America (MPAA) 140
Motion Picture Productions Code/The Hays Code (U.S.) 48, 134–39; William H. Hays 134–35, 139
The Mouth and Oral Sex 100–101
Moyes, Vonny 42
MPAA *see* Motion Picture Association of America

Mrs. Henderson Presents 90–91
"Mull of Kintryre" rule 91, 113, 115, 158
murder 6, 11, 24–27, 35, 48, 70–71, 104, 133, 142, 158; *see also* Bulger, James; Longhurst, Jane; Pistorius, Oscar
Murdoch, Rupert 130, 162, 175
Muslim 6, 8, 157; *see also* Islam
Mutual Film Company (MFC) 132
Myers, Kevin 162–63
The Mysteries of Conjugal Love Reveal'd 46

the "n-word" 24, 169, 170
National Organization for Decent Literature 134
National Society for the Prevention of Cruelty to Children (NSPCC) 60
Native American 160, 166
Nazism 24, 72; anti-Semitism 162; Nazi sympathizers 42, 162; *see also* neo-Nazis
necrophilia 24–25, 66, 116–17
neo-Nazis 12, 41, 158; National Action 41–42, National Front 158
Netflix 140, 160
New Jersey 132
News of the World 104
Nirvana 94
NSPCC *see* National Society for the Prevention of Cruelty to Children
nudity 9, 37, 40, 84, 90–93, 97–98, 113, 115–16, 118–19, 135, 138, 140; selfies 8, 11, 67; sexting 8, 67, 100

OB/GYN 128
Obscene Publications Act (OPA, 1857) 3, 20–21, 28–29, 32, 37–38, 41, 44, 48–50, 83, 85, 90, 95, 113, 116–17, 127, 130, 139, 146–47, 152, 164
OfCom 20, 28, 31, 32, 62, 113, 140
online streaming 22
OPA *see* Obscene Publications Act (1857)
Open Rights Group 57, 60, 61
oppression: of women 11
Orange Is the New Black 92
overly sexualized 8

pain 23
Palestine/Palestinian 6
Pandora's Box 85
pansexuality 77, 79
parent(s) 26, 54, 56, 60–68, 70, 72–73, 87, 99, 100, 124, 156, 161, 166
patriarchy 13, 44, 47, 74, 75, 118
Patterson, Sylvia 12, 43
Peacock, Michael 152
Peaky Blinders 30, 140
pedophilia 13, 24, 34, 44, 55–56, 58, 69, 150
penis 9, 11, 14, 38, 80, 88, 112–16, 119, 140, 171, 175; erection 112–13, 115, 118 sex 80, 88, 116, 121, 140
Penthouse magazine 110
people of color/minorities 39, 84–85, 101, 111,
135, 139, 144, 153, 155–61, 163–67, 169–70; interracial relationships 85, 135, 136
perversion 22
Petley, Julian 70–71
Phippen, Andy 57–59, 64, 67–68
Playboy magazine 110
Playgirl magazine (U.S.) 110
poison 49, 72, 94; moral poison 83, 84
polygamy/polyamory 17, 78–79, 121, 136
pop culture 2, 4, 43, 67, 98, 135, 146, 160, 171, 173–74
porn performers/stars 9, 13, 17, 21, 27, 91, 119
porn producers 2, 4, 19, 22, 28, 55, 57 109, 123, 160; Ms. Naughty 109–10, 113
porn, revenge 98
Pornhub 119
"Possession of Extreme Pornographic Images" 25
Powell, Enoch 100, 158
pregnancy/childbirth 51–52, 59, 93–94, 96, 106, 127, 129, 135, 151, 163; reproduction 50, 68, 93, 128, 145, 163–64
prejudice 6, 27, 30, 39, 40, 77–78, 86, 110, 116–17, 121, 129, 135, 141, 147–48, 151, 166
President of the United States (POTUS) 34, 125, 139; Barack Obama 33, 124; Bill Clinton 115, 126, 128; Donald Trump 18, 41, 126, 161, 171
Profumo political scandal (1963) 4, 97
protest 2, 14, 17–19, 21, 24, 27, 42, 44, 59, 62, 79, 99, 101–2, 114, 145, 161, 175
prudery 9
psychiatry 24, 134; Wertham, Fredric 134
psychology 24, 27, 61, 93, 103, 129, 155; Ley, David 129; Hegarty, Paul 155

queer 76, 78, 87–88, 103, 143, 146, 158
Queer as Folk 66, 143

R v. Gold (1964) 100
R v. Walsh (2012) 26, 99, 106, 151–52; *see also* Walsh, Simon
R18 certificate 20, 22–23, 28, 45, 62
race 1, 155, 158, 164, 169, 172, 176; mixed race 11, 166–67
racism 7, 10, 11, 33, 40, 43, 138, 153, 155, 157, 160, 161, 162, 164, 165, 169, 170, 172; Ku Klux Klan (KKK) 126, 169
rape 11, 24, 26–27, 40, 43, 46, 62–63, 66, 95, 104, 107, 116, 155, 162, 171
ratings system 22–24, 55, 64, 67, 71, 138, 140
Read, James: *The Fifteen Plagues of Maidenhead* 100
religion 5, 6, 8, 11, 31, 46, 47, 50, 76, 77, 86, 92, 124, 127, 156, 173
Rembar, Charles 35, 50, 90, 130, 139
responsibility 27, 57, 62, 67, 70, 95, 97, 129, 136
Reynolds, Kenneth 77
right-wing/conservative 8, 9, 46, 61, 69–70, 76, 84, 86–88, 96, 100, 120, 125, 135, 140–41,

144, 146, 150, 152; government 70, 87, 88, 150; media 58, 73, 84, 98, 100, 163
Robertson, Geoffrey 3, 4, 49, 57; *Obscenity* 3
rock 'n' roll 104, 133–34
role play 24
Ronson, Jon: *So You've Been Publicly Shamed* 102–4
Ropelato, Jerry 61
Rosen, James 128, 129
Rowling J. K. 12
Rubin, Gayle 14
Rule 11 57
Rule 14 28, 30
Rushdie, Salman 11; *The Satanic Verses* 11

Sable, Justice 55
sadomasochistic material 22
Safety Net campaign 61
Sappho/Sapphic 82, 83, 86
Sargeant, Chris 103
Saudi Arabia 11
scandal 4
Scarleteen 70
scat play 22, 24, 98
Scheele, Julia 14
The School of Venus (*Écoles de Filles*) *see* Coxe/Tartar, John
Section 28 86–88, 144, 147, 149
Serano, Julia 78
sex: anal 30, 37, 88, 100, 117, 121, 124, 147; extramarital 128, 136; heterosexual 88, 100, 121, 140; homosexual 7, 26, 79–80, 107, 116, 140, 142, 144–46, 150–52; oral 27, 37, 65, 88, 100–101, 116–17, 123, 140; premarital 95, 136; vaginal 37, 88, 116–17, 121
Sex and the City 66, 94, 124
sex education 14, 66–70, 80, 87, 95, 125, 128, 147–51; early guides 46–47, 87
sex work/prostitution 13, 17, 37, 43–44, 48–50, 53, 92, 95, 97, 101, 121, 159, 176; anti-sex-work groups 44, 121
sexism 2, 7–10, 24, 31, 39, 46, 74, 78, 81, 97, 112, 120, 124, 138, 142, 154, 162–63, 173, 174, 175
sexual activity 23, 70, 79–80, 82, 90, 116–17; gay 26, 79, 81, 144, 146, 150
Sexual Offences Act (1967) 80, 142, 144
sexual threats 23
sexuality, female 47, 66, 78, 90, 95–96, 106–10, 120, 123, 133
sexually transmitted disease/infection (STD/STI) 52; *see also* AIDS; HIV
Shakespeare, William 100, 112
shame 20, 30, 35, 58, 72, 87, 98, 102–5, 129, 142–49
shop, sex 98, 104, 124, 126, 175
Shriver, Lionel 17, 163–66; *The Mandibles* 163, 165; *We Need to Talk About Kevin* 163
sin 93, 97, 135, 136
Singh, Suraya Sidhu 9, 110–12, 115–16, 118–19

"slut-shaming" 43, 98
Smith, Clarissa 72, 99, 106, 121
SnapChat 40, 72, 102
social media 21, 24, 40, 41, 43, 45, 59, 82, 103, 157, 161, 171, 172; *see also* Facebook; Instagram; SnapChat; Tumblr; Twitter; WhatsApp; YouTube
The Society for the Formation of Manners 49
The Society for the Suppression of Vice 49
Socrates 55, 65
Soho 49, 97
speech, freedom of 6, 8, 11, 17, 34, 40, 58, 44, 126–27, 132–33, 172; *see also* expression, freedom of; First Amendment, U.S. Constitution
The Spice Girls 98
Star Trek 85
The Stationers' Guild 37, 38, 135
STD/STI *see* sexually transmitted disease/infection
Steenkamp, Reeva 35
Stipe, Michael 168
Stopes, Marie 90
The Story of O 65
"straight pride" 77, 165
strippers 13
Stronge, Ben 104
submissives (sub) 22, 25, 30, 118, 121
Sudan 11
suffragettes/suffragists 51, 81
suicide 20, 63, 103–4, 127, 129, 136, 142–43
The Sun (London) 65, 72, 146, 163, 175; Page 3, 65, 72, 106, 113, 175
The Sunday Express (London) 82
suppression 4
Supreme Court of the United States (SCOTUS) 124–25, 127, 132, 136, 139
Syal, Meera 156–57

tabloids 13, 58, 72, 89, 98, 105
Taraborelli, J. Randy 174
TBMC *see* The Bondage Mistress Club
Teaching AIDS in the Classroom 148–49
teen pregnancy 59
teenagers 12, 13
terms, derogatory 11, 24, 40, 77, 88, 150, 153–54, 169–70, 173
Terrorism Act (2006) 41
testes/testicles 30, 116
Thatcher, Margaret 32, 86–87, 126, 146–47, 150
This Film Is Not Yet Rated 64, 140
Thomasin, Sez 87, 88; sexual-health educator 88
Thompson, Robert 71; *see also* Bulger, James; Venables, John
Timney, Richard 72
Titanic 92, 112
torture 11, 43, 70, 71, 94, 134, 172
toy, sex 23, 30, 49, 88, 116, 123–24, 126, 139

Index

trans visibility 8; *see also* transgender
transgender 42–44, 75, 77–79, 92, 125, 135, 155, 161, 162; *see also* LGBTQ; trans visibility; transphobia/anti-trans
transphobia/anti-trans 10, 41, 44, 162
Tulk, Catherine 64
Tumblr 72, 118
Turing, Alan 142–43
TV shows 8
Twitter 12, 13, 40–41, 43, 47, 102–3, 150, 161–62, 167; tweets 41, 43, 47, 102–3, 150

U.S. Constitution 130, 132–33
urethra 26, 92, 151
urethral sounding 26, 106, 151–52
urine 22, 27, 99, 116, 152

vagina 31, 82, 91–92, 107, 116, 154, 171; clitoris 81, 92, 107; labia 92, 107, 116; vaginal sex 37, 80, 88, 92, 116–17, 121; vulva 75, 91–92, 107, 134, 171
Vagrancy Act (1824) 49
vanilla 5, 24, 78, 150
Venables, John 71; *see also* Bulger, James; Thompson Robert
Venus in the Cloisters see Edmund Curll
Victim 143
victim: female 8, 9, 26, 43, 98, 108, 120–21; male 151; murder 26, 35; rape/sex 26, 35, 45–46, 150
Victoria, Queen 48, 81
Victorian era 4, 14, 48–52, 68, 90, 101, 116
Vidal, Gore 87
video-on-demand (VOD) 22, 28, 32
Video Recordings Act (1984) 70–71

violence 22–23, 30, 35, 40, 43, 48, 58, 67, 70, 72–73, 86, 116–19, 134, 137, 169; domestic 5, 77; in films 24–26, 71, 86, 124, 140; sexual 5, 12, 26, 29, 46, 65, 119, 171
virginity 46, 100; Virgin Mary 127

Walsh, Simon 26, 151–52; *see also* R. v. Walsh
Warner Brothers 136
The Weeknd 107, 173–74
West, Lindy 40, 41
West, Mae: *Sex* 133
WhatsApp 72, 173
white supremacy 24, 41
whitewashing 160
Whitney: Can I Be Me? see Houston, Whitney
Whittaker, Jodie 98
WHSmith 115–17
Wilde, Oscar 87
Williams-Haas, Mollena 24, 78; *The Toybag Guide to Playing with Taboo* 24
Winkleman, Claudia 162–163
Winterson, Jeanette 76, 86; *Why Be Happy When You Could Be Normal?* 86
Wire, Nicky 168
Wolfenden Committee 96, 144
Woman's Hour (UK) 31, 98, 107
women of color 44, 167
women's rights/liberation 8, 59, 83, 85, 138, 156
Woolf, Virginia: *Orlando* 85

xenophobia 7, 157

YouTube 40

www.ingramcontent.com/pod-product-compliance
Ingram Content Group UK Ltd.
Pitfield, Milton Keynes, MK11 3LW, UK
UKHW042012140426
5217IPUK00015B/1121